DISASTER GOVERNMENT:
NATIONAL EMERGENCIES, CONTINUITY OF GOVERNMENT & YOU

"The federal government warns you that in an emergency situation, you are going to have to fend for yourself."
P. 251

BRIAN TUOHY

ISBN: 0988901102
ISBN-13: 978-0-9889011-0-0

TABLE OF CONTENTS

ACKNOWLEDGMENTS

The first (and biggest) "thank you" must go to my wife Sarah whose love and support made this book possible. Without her understanding, I couldn't sit around night after night reading government files in order to turn them into this work.

I also thank my family and friends for always being there for me, no matter what. A special thanks to the Roundtable whose ideas likely seeped into this book whether I wanted them to or not.

Many others helped me along this path in making this book what it is, especially Michael Ravnitzky, Steven Aftergood, Bill Geerhart, John Pike, Phil Lapsley, Ian Punnett & all at Coast to Coast AM, Alex Jones, Dan Bidondi, Erskine, Richard Syrett, Jim Harold, and all the other authors, researchers, and radio show hosts who have come before me to help make this information available to those who seek it.

INTRODUCTION

Don't panic. Remain calm.

In a book discussing national emergencies and Continuity of Government (COG) programs, that's wise advice. It is very easy to become overwhelmed and lose one's sense of bearing when reading the facts contained within these pages. Part of what's dealt with is the absolute worst case scenarios imaginable: hurricanes, massive earthquakes, biological or chemical terrorist attacks, and all-out nuclear war. These are disasters, some certainly man-made, that truly could materialize on any day and at any time. If you're unlucky enough to be caught in harm's way, there is no place to hide.

Unless you're a high-ranking member of the federal government. If you happen to be one of those lucky few, then you can readily seek shelter. Fortifications exist deep underground or buried beneath mountains where you can not only wait out whatever disaster may have befallen, but can effectively lead the country from as well. That's what the concept of Continuity of Government is all about: the ability for America's leaders to continue our constitutional form of government no matter what occurs. The prevailing thought is that if our leaders are safe and sound, then they will be able to help the rest of us by more effectively managing the crisis as it occurs while better delegating authority in the resultant aftermath.

Of course, that assumes two things. One: that an entity as large as the federal government is competent enough to effectively organize and execute such emergency measures. Two: that we, the people, will still want the government around after a national emergency on the level of a nuclear war.

Which brings up the flip side of the Continuity of Government coin: the paranoia associated with it. It can be difficult to remain objective and not fall down the conspiracy theory rabbit hole when discussing this subject. As you will read, there are indeed laws, congressional acts and presidential executive orders that allow the government to do all the things you think the paranoid are only imagining. In times of national emergencies, the government—our United States federal government—can and likely will take control of all forms of communication, transportation and production, seize private property, and allow army troops to police American citizens by imposing martial law. This is not some delusion; it is a fact which comes straight out of documents written by our lawmakers.

As strange as it may seem, you should be all right with that. Well, to a degree. Everyone should have an emergency plan from the federal government down to each individual citizen. Whether it involves what to do if a fire breaks out, where to evacuate to when the next hurricane is looming, or even what one should store in the car should it break down in the middle of nowhere, emergency planning is not a bad thing. If the electricity went out in your home right now, do you know where the flashlight is? Do the batteries in it even work? Who do you call to report the problem? How can you call them? What's the number? Even a simple little scenario like a power outage can require knowledge that one may not have bothered to acquire prior to needing it. If one takes the time to anticipate these types of scenarios, when the moment does actually strike you'll be glad you were prepared. Such simple emergency planning should be a part of everyone's daily life. As much as one may not want to bother to think about worst case scenarios like fires, tornados, or even a terrorist attack, you should because they constantly happen.

Over the course of the past 60+ years, our government has attempted to do that very same sort of planning and preparing. Its biggest problem is that it doesn't need just one or two gallons of water should the pipes burst; it needs millions of gallons of water for entire cities or states should a flood sweep over the river banks. That is why the Federal Emergency Management Agency (FEMA) was created. The issue with FEMA is that it is not easy to accurately determine who needs what level of help on such a massive, multi-state scale when something like a hurricane strikes. Individuals will fall through the cracks. Not everyone can and will be helped. Fair or unfair, that is the reality. This is why the government implores people to be able to fend for themselves when a disaster strikes. One should not expect to completely rely on the authorities for immediate and comprehensive help, no matter the situation. Of course, like all things governmental, it could and should make this point much clearer to the general population.

While the United States has not felt a true threat to her borders since perhaps World War II, there has always loomed the possibility of attack. Should such an ambush arise, whether via terrorist action or another foreign nation, every citizen expects and perhaps demands an instant response from our government. Depending upon the circumstances surrounding such an assault, the federal government's response may include taking control of the airwaves to properly inform the nation or have army troops patrol the streets to maintain peace while keeping its citizens safe. These ideas are not too absurd as to be unrealistic. Such a heavy-handed response, given the proper situation, may be quite warranted and welcomed.

Where the fear and paranoia tends to creep in is in the fact that no one has clearly defined what a "national emergency" is despite being part of the federal government's lexicon for well over 100 years. It is an odd concept since rarely is there an emergency that truly touches every state in the nation. On some level, certain declared national emergencies would obviously affect us all even if in just a cursory way, like the events of 9/11 or Hurricane Katrina. But how about the civil war in Haiti that occurred in 1991? Did you realize that was a national emergency for the United States? Or what about the issues surrounding the democratic processes in Belarus? That, too, was declared a national emergency in the U.S. in 2006. The fact is the President of the United States can declare just about anything a "national emergency" through the use of executive orders. When and if such a declaration is made (which is invoked on a surprisingly frequent basis), then a whole slew of options opens up for the president. These range from the benign and rational all the way to running and hiding in an underground bunker while the army takes control of U.S. cities in the name of Continuity of Government. Attempts have been made to curb the freewheeling usage of national emergencies, but as always in the world of government and lawyers, there are massive loopholes to be taken advantage of. Until Congress steps up and strips the president of some of the power the White House awarded itself, the use of national emergencies will continue to be abused.

Though presidents of the past have greatly overstepped their constitutional bounds, *someone* has to be able to declare a national emergency and kick-start the process of dealing with and recovering from whatever that problem may be. Where should such a power lie? With Congress? By the time they are collected together, figure out what the issue is, and get to voting on it, it may be too late. Someone has to be able to act or react immediately in certain situations. That is why the office of the president took it upon itself to be the one. Someone equated the constitutional phrase "commander-in-chief" with "chief executive" and green-lighted the president to do what needs to be done in a self-proclaimed emergency. And again, that's not all bad.

What is bad is that most Continuity of Government operations are Top Secret. Some aspects of it are so secret that high-ranking members of the federal government don't know what the plans actually are—even though they are included in their implementation. Needless to say, this renders many of these best laid plans moot. On occasion, there is what's considered a national fire drill, where Continuity of Government is tested through FEMA and the recently created Department of Homeland Security

(DHS), but for various reasons not everyone is included who should be. So, when a true emergency breaks out, like that of 9/11, it's unsurprising to see so many government officials completely confused as to where they should go while not realizing what should be done or who's in command of what. Perhaps if the powers that be dropped the high level of secrecy surrounding the subject, everyone would have a better idea how to best act on the multi-billion dollar plans previously created.

Then again, this is the government we're talking about…

EXECUTIVE ORDERS AND THE LAW

"America is only a Presidential directive away from a civil security state of emergency."
- Northeastern University Professor Diana Reynolds

Before getting to the high weirdness of underground bunkers, martial law and other similarly controversial subjects, one must first realize where the concepts of presidential executive orders, national emergencies and Continuity of Government originated. Though it may not seem that way at first, these ideas are intertwined as different threads of the same fabric. It's difficult to pull one of the three away from the others and discuss it independently. Without a doubt, one thread would snag another and the created knot would have to be dealt with. So, the best place to start is with a cursory overview of American history in regards to national emergencies.

The Continental Congress and George Washington

The idea that a national emergency could occur arose prior to there even being a nation. The Continental Congress, before deciding that "When in the Course of human events it becomes necessary for one people to dissolve the political bands which have connected them with another…," passed a series of acts regarding a seemingly unavoidable emergency—the brewing Revolutionary War. Beginning in 1775 and continuing through the war until about 1781, the Continental Congress took it upon itself to operate on the emerging nation's behalf by exercising its believed authority to act during an emergency. Even though the war that granted the United States its independence was truly a national emergency affecting every citizen, when the Constitutional Convention began

11

in 1787, the concept of a "national emergency" was not broached. Hence, the men debating the "hows" and "whats" of the Constitution never gave any deep consideration to defining emergency powers. It's quite possible; however, that while emergency powers weren't delineated explicitly, they were granted implicitly in Article I, Section 8 of the Constitution where Congress has the power to "provide for the common Defense and general Welfare."

Take note that such a power, if granted, was given to Congress and not the president. This is not a concept to be understated. The Constitution, while never expressly giving power to anyone in particular to act in an emergency, seemed to lean in Congress's favor regarding such incidents. Remarkably, within five years of the passing of the Constitution, there was a clear example of Congress giving said emergency power to the president and *not* the president acting on his own.

In the middle of 1792, a sizable portion of the newly founded United States including residents of Virginia, Pennsylvania and both Carolinas began staging their own mini-revolution. Feeling the need to pay down the national debt resulting from the Revolutionary War, Secretary of the Treasury Alexander Hamilton convinced Congress to install a federal excise tax on distilled spirits. A large majority of the residents of those four states were making a living by producing such alcohol. They didn't take kindly to Hamilton's idea of taxing them, especially so soon after having suffered through a war which was waged partially over the excessive taxes England was imposing on the Colonies. Taking to arms to protect their believed rights, what's commonly known as the Whiskey Rebellion began.

Congress sensed that the tax levied on whiskey might cause some problems among the rabble. They quickly developed and passed legislation allowing for the raising of the militia—if need be—to suppress any resultant insurrections. As part of that statute, Congress required that a presidential proclamation be issued calling for the cessation of any such rebellion prior to the militia being unleashed on the common folk. In August 1794, President Washington did as Congress allowed. He issued an ultimatum ordering the distillers to stand down or else. Despite that action, the increasingly angry mob continued their grousing, eventually arming themselves to emphasize the point. Consequently, Washington raised a militia of roughly 13,000 men (about the size of the entire Colonial army during the Revolutionary War) and led them to put down the growing rebellion. Upon arriving in Pennsylvania, Washington and his troops couldn't find any armed, angry mob. Instead, they arrested about 20 protesters, tossed a few in prison, and fined the rest. So ended the Whiskey Rebellion.

What is most important to take from this footnote in history was the fact Congress gave the president the power to act in that emergency. Washington, by issuing his proclamation, responded to Congress that he was going to act and how he planned on performing that task. Washington didn't just call up the militia and lead them into Pennsylvania on his own. There was a direct cooperation between the executive and legislative branches of the government to address the emergency head on. The power and rights of both were clearly delineated. Unfortunately, it would be about the last time emergency powers were made this clear.

A scant two years after Washington put down the Whiskey Rebellion, he began to step outside the bounds of the executive branch as defined by the Constitution. In 1793, Washington issued a proclamation regarding the neutral stance the U.S. would take in the war raging in Europe between the French and pretty much the rest of the continent (Great Britain, Prussia, and the Netherlands to name but a few). Washington's proclamation read in part:

"I have therefore thought fit by these presents to declare the disposition of the United States to observe the conduct aforesaid towards those powers respectively; and to exhort and warn the citizens of the United States, carefully to avoid all acts and proceedings whatsoever, which may in any manner tend to contravene such disposition. And I do hereby also make known, that whosoever of the citizens of the United States shall render himself liable to punishment or forfeiture under the law of nations, by committing, aiding, or abetting hostilities against any of the said powers, or by carrying to any of them those articles, which are deemed contraband by the modern usage of nations, will not receive the protection of the United States against such punishment or forfeiture; and further, that I have given instructions to those officers, to whom it belongs, to cause prosecutions to be instituted against all persons, who shall, within the cognizance of the Courts of the United States, violate the law of nations, with respect to the powers at War, or any of them."

This proclamation was not intended as a direction for the U.S. government. It instructed private citizens to stay out of assisting either side of the war. The fear was that should a U.S. citizen acting as a war privateer enrage one side or the other, the rest of the country could be dragged into the conflict due to one individual's actions. Washington did not claim he had the power to do this from either the Constitution or some congressional mandate. His claim rose only from the "law of nations." While that was seen, even at that time, as overstepping the presidential role, Congress quickly caved in and enacted a law enforcing Washington's proclamation.

An extremely dangerous trend was started right then and there. Instead of Congress creating a law with the president signing (or vetoing) it into being as the Constitution requires, the exact opposite took place. Regardless of Washington's proclamation being a good idea or not, this was not—and still is not—a nation lorded over by the one man elected president. The Constitution was set up precisely to *not* have such a situation occur. Yet here Congress was, less than 10 years after the Constitution's signing, allowing the president to dictate to them how things were to be done.

Luckily for the nation in those formative years, that was by no means the norm. Washington's proclamation would today be known as a Presidential Executive Order (EO). It has been determined that from Washington's presidency through James

Buchanan's, only about 140 executive orders were issued in 72 years. In the meantime, Congress enacted various laws covering the response—be it military, economic or other—to national emergencies. Yet none of these emergency provisions were really put to the test until 1861. When Buchanan hightailed out of office after serving his four years, the man who replaced him would virtually govern the country via presidential orders based upon emergency conditions. Of course, he did have a bit of a civil war on his hands.

Abraham Lincoln and the Civil War

Abraham Lincoln was not the first president to have to contend with states wanting to secede from the United States. Upon renewing his oath of office for a second term in 1833, Andrew Jackson had to deal with South Carolina wanting out of the Union after about 50 years of being in it. Jackson managed to hold on to the state and keep the nation intact; however, by the time Lincoln was inaugurated on March 4, 1861, seven Southern states—Texas, Louisiana, Mississippi, Alabama, Georgia, Florida and that pesky South Carolina—had officially seceded from the United States. Not only that, but the Confederacy had already established a provisional government, ran an election, placed Jefferson Davis into their presidential office, and were in the process of raising an army. Lincoln was stepping into a maelstrom.

As the country became unglued, President Lincoln was virtually alone. On March 27, 1861, Congress adjourned "sine die" or "without day," meaning with the congressmen from the seven seceded Southern states unwilling to appear, Congress no longer had the quorum required by the Constitution in Article I, Section 5 to perform its tasks. By law, Congress must have a quorum—a majority of its elected members—to conduct business. With the South leaving the Union, a quorum was impossible. The only task available to Congress at the time was to set a date to reconvene, hopefully with its quorum intact. Yet Congress couldn't do even that since it had no idea when (or if) the representatives from those Southern states would return. (Some have suggested that since

Congress never set a date to reconvene on that original date of "sine die," Congress essentially dissolved and has never legally reconvened. It is an interesting concept considering what followed.)

On April 12, 1861, the Confederacy attacked the Union troops holding Fort Sumter in South Carolina, signaling the official start of the American Civil War. Not possessing a Congress to declare war, which was solely Congress's ability, Lincoln felt he had to do something to attempt to preserve the Union. So, on April 15, he issued what's known as Executive Order Number 1 which follows in its entirety:

"BY THE PRESIDENT OF THE UNITED STATES

"A PROCLAMATION.

"Whereas the laws of the United States have been for some time past, and now are opposed, and the execution thereof obstructed, in the States of South Carolina, Georgia, Alabama, Florida, Mississippi, Louisiana and Texas, by combinations too powerful to be suppressed by the ordinary course of judicial proceedings, or by the powers vested in the Marshals by law,

"Now therefore, I, Abraham Lincoln, President of the United States, in virtue of the power in me vested by the Constitution, and the laws, have thought fit to call forth, and hereby do call forth, the militia of the several States of the Union, to the aggregate number of seventy-five thousand, in order to suppress said combinations, and to cause the laws to be duly executed. The details, for this object, will be immediately communicated to the State authorities through the War Department.

"I appeal to all loyal citizens to favor, facilitate and aid this effort to maintain the honor, the integrity, and the existence of our National Union, and the perpetuity of popular government; and to redress wrongs already long enough endured.

"I deem it proper to say that the first service assigned to the forces hereby called forth will probably be to re-possess the forts, places, and property which have been seized from the Union; and in every event, the utmost care will be observed, consistently with the objects aforesaid, to avoid any devastation, any destruction of, or interference with, property, or any disturbance of peaceful citizens in any part of the country.

"And I hereby command the persons composing the combinations aforesaid to disperse, and retire peaceably to their respective abodes within twenty days from this date.

"Deeming that the present condition of public affairs presents an extraordinary occasion, I do hereby, in virtue of the power in me vested by the Constitution, convene both Houses of Congress. Senators and Representatives are therefore summoned to assemble at their respective chambers, at 12 o'clock, noon, on Thursday, the fourth day of July, next, then and there to consider and determine, such measures, as, in their wisdom, the public safety, and interest may seem to demand.

"In Witness Whereof I have hereunto set my hand, and caused the Seal of the United States to be affixed.

"Done at the city of Washington this fifteenth day of April in the year of our Lord One thousand, Eight hundred and Sixty One, and of the Independence the United States the Eighty fifth.

"ABRAHAM LINCOLN"

Apparently this wasn't the most popular move Lincoln could have made. On that same day, nearly immediately after Lincoln issued his order, Virginia, North Carolina, Tennessee and Arkansas also seceded from the Union to join the Confederacy. Those four states were not willing to kowtow to the new president and allow him to take control of their militias. Truly they cannot be blamed for doing so as Lincoln had no authority to engage in such an action.

Lincoln, correctly sensing that the country was spinning out of control, further overstepped his authority. On April 19, he ordered the blockade of ports in seven of the Southern secessionist states. He claimed to have the power to do this because (1) the seven states mentioned were in insurrection against the government, (2) the collection of revenue "can not be effectually executed therein conformably," and (3) for "the protection of the public peace and the lives and property of quiet and orderly citizens pursuing their lawful occupations." This was to continue, Lincoln proclaimed, until "Congress shall have assembled and deliberated" on the secession of states in which the ports were located. The next day, April 20, Lincoln ordered the building of 19 naval warships. This order also included Lincoln's direction to Secretary of the Treasury Salmon Portland Chase to dole out $2 million to certain private citizens for "requisitions" necessary for the military to provide defense and support for the government. This was in direct violation of Article I, Section 9 of the Constitution which states "No money shall be drawn from the Treasury, but in consequence of appropriation made by law." Since laws only originate in Congress, Lincoln should not have been able to force Chase's hand.

Lincoln was not nearly done. He quickly followed the April 20 decree with another order to add both Virginia and North Carolina to the list of states possessing ports in need of blockades. Then Lincoln again exceeded his constitutional authority on May 3, 1861 with his order to expand the military. Lincoln called for the regular army to be increased by 22,714 men, the navy by 18,000, and the raising of some 42,000 volunteers willing to serve three years. That clearly superseded Article I, Section 8 of the Constitution where only Congress was allowed "to raise and support armies" and "to provide and maintain a Navy." Lincoln, however, had little choice faced with this emergency in the form of the South's insurrection. He clearly did not feel the Southern states were within their rights to abandon the United States, and the only way to reconstruct the Union was through the use of force.

On July 4, Congress assembled as directed by Lincoln in Executive Order 1. Constitutionally, this was impossible. Congress did not have its quorum. If the Southern states were considered part of the country—even if in a state of rebellion as was believed—then for a quorum to exist, representatives from at least some of the 11 seceded Southern states would have needed to be present for Congress to conduct business. Yet, no congressman from any of the Southern states was in attendance. Technically, Congress could do nothing. If the Union considered a quorum to exist without any Southern congressmen appearing, they should have then recognized the Confederacy as an independent nation. This would have excluded all of the Southern states and their representatives from the nation and made a quorum an instant reality. Had Congress taken this step, immediately following should have been a formal declaration of war against the new nation of the Confederacy which would have been constitutionally necessary to engage the Southern states in battle. Lincoln, however, had previously refused to negotiate with envoys from the Confederacy on the grounds that theirs was not a legitimate government. Since the step to formalize the Confederacy was never taken and the Southern states were still considered legal U.S. territory, a congressional quorum never existed during the Civil War. Hence, Congress should have been rendered impotent to act in any way. The federal government should have therefore ceased to function, if not exist. Instead, Congress's acts during and immediately following the end of the Civil War effectively rendered the Constitution null and void.

If one wants to give Congress the benefit of the doubt and say that while the Southern states were in an open state of rebellion and should not have been allowed representation during that time, what Congress decided to do immediately after reconvening shouldn't make anyone much more proud. In a message written to Congress in July 1861, Lincoln wrote of his actions in Congress's absence, "These measures, *whether strictly legal or not*, were ventured upon under what appeared to be a popular and public necessity, trusting then, as now, that Congress would readily ratify them. It is believed that nothing has been done beyond the constitutional competency of Congress." In effect, Lincoln was stating he knew he had broken the law and violated the Constitution, but had Congress been around, it would have taken the same actions he did. Or so he presupposed, since when Lincoln issued his Executive Order 1, he gave Congress *three months* to come back to work, even in the face of a civil war. He could have called them back into session much sooner, but for his own reasons, did not.

Now, in July 1861, what remained of Congress was immediately put on the hot seat. They had a difficult choice to consider. They could jump on Lincoln's war bandwagon and go along with everything he had (unconstitutionally) done thus far, or else rescind all of Lincoln's previous orders. To do so would be tantamount to defeat. Having acted in a kingly fashion, Lincoln clearly had the war effort rolling. In calling his bluff, Congress would have put a halt to everything (even if only temporarily) and set back the Union's efforts to pull the country together. With their collective hand forced by Lincoln's earlier actions, Congress did exactly as Lincoln had predicted in his letter—they legalized everything Lincoln had ordered in their absence. In approving his orders retroactively, Congress basically green-lit the president—and any future president—to run amuck, especially in a time of presumed war.

Lincoln was not only able to hoodwink the legislative branch, but the judicial branch as well. Since Congress was gutless enough to allow Lincoln to do as he had pleased, the Supreme Court had little to no chance to challenge any of Lincoln's "laws." Not that they attempted to do so anyway. In fact, it wasn't until sometime after the end of the Civil War that the Supreme Court ruled it perfectly legal for Congress to ratify presidential orders after the fact, as long the belief existed that those presidential acts would have been "authorized" prior to the order being improperly enacted. So, as long as the president assumes Congress would have made his action into a law—had they been around to actually make a law—it's legal. Never mind how that seemed to circumvent the major ideas embedded in the Constitution.

Now fully vested in the war with the Confederacy, Lincoln remained content to let Congress act as the Constitution allowed. However, he wasn't finished in wielding his self-supposed executive power. On January 1, 1863, Lincoln issued his most famous—perhaps *the* most famous in American history—

proclamation. Known commonly as the Emancipation Proclamation, this single document without a doubt cemented Lincoln's legacy in American history. Truth be told, he didn't have the authority to institute what the proclamation demanded.

Most people believe the Emancipation Proclamation freed the slaves. This is not true. What Lincoln wrote in part was:

"That on the first day of January, in the year of our Lord one thousand eight hundred and sixty-three, all persons held as slaves within any State or designated part of a State, the people whereof shall then be in rebellion against the United States, shall be then, thenceforward, and forever free; and the Executive Government of the United States, including the military and naval authority thereof, will recognize and maintain the freedom of such persons, and will do no act or acts to repress such persons, or any of them, in any efforts they may make for their actual freedom."

His order did not affect the slaves in the crucial border states that clung to their status as members of the Union, nor did it free the slaves in the portions of the Southern states that were under Union control. Lincoln even went so far as to designate which states and counties he was referring to within the proclamation. His "freeing of the slaves" only affected those unfortunate souls who happened to be slaves where their owners were in rebellion against the United States, and no others.

Nonetheless, it is without a doubt that the Emancipation Proclamation altered the course of the Civil War. It turned the Union's struggle from a territorial one into a moral cause. (At the war's outbreak, Lincoln maintained that the South was in rebellion and their territories must be brought back in line with the U.S. government, not that the slaves needed to be freed). It helped the Union politically and even added numbers to their military as Lincoln, in the proclamation, ordered: "And I further declare and make known, that such persons of suitable condition, will be received into the armed service of the United States to garrison forts, positions, stations, and other places, and to man vessels of all sorts in said service." Lincoln wisely allowed these "freed" slaves to join the Union's side and help in the liberation of their brothers. By the end of the Civil War, nearly 200,000 black soldiers and sailors had served for the Union.

Here's the catch: Lincoln claimed authority to issue the Emancipation Proclamation based solely on his role as commander-in-chief. Needless to say, this doesn't exactly fit the title. As commander-in-chief, he could suppose command of the military, not slaves; even should they be residing in states effectively in armed rebellion. The only supporting theory that backed Lincoln's action was that as commander-in-chief he had the authority to seize any enemy property that was being used to wage war against the United States. Of course, as already noted, the U.S. wasn't "at war" because war was never officially declared, and the Southern states were still effectively part of the United States, albeit in a state of rebellion. If one granted Lincoln that ability via his own order, he would effectively been calling the slaves "property" and not seeing them as people. It is a rarely debated point, but was the truth nonetheless.

Unable to find a suitable loophole within the Constitution which allowed him to act as he wished, Lincoln simply forced one into existence. Congress or the Supreme Court never effectively challenged Lincoln on this. Because of their inability to question Lincoln's authority, a presidential precedent began which continues to this very day. The ability for a president, under his role as commander-in-chief, to act virtually in any way he chooses should a there be a state of war.

Stranger still, Lincoln did not even have to take this step. Congress had already done the job for him. On September 22, 1862, just after the Union's victory in the bloody battle at Antietam, Lincoln signed a lesser known, preliminary Emancipation Proclamation. In this document, he warned the South that he was planning on setting the slaves free and effectively gave the Confederacy 100 days to surrender (and had they, perhaps the slaves would not have been freed). Within this preliminary proclamation, Lincoln cited "an Act to suppress Insurrection, to punish Treason and Rebellion, to seize and confiscate property of rebels, and for other purposes" which Congress enacted on July 17, 1862. Section 9 of that congressional act read:

"And be it further enacted, That all slaves of persons who shall hereafter be engaged in rebellion against the government of the United States, or who shall in any way give aid or comfort thereto, escaping from such persons and taking refuge within the lines of the army; and all slaves captured from such persons or deserted by them and coming under the control of the government of the United States; and all slaves of such persons found on (or) being within any place occupied by rebel forces and afterwards occupied by the forces of the United States, shall be deemed captives of war, and shall be forever free of their servitude and not again held as slaves."

This was essentially (and nearly identical to) what Lincoln proclaimed in the final, official Emancipation Proclamation without ever citing Congress's previous act. It may also explain why Congress, and by extension, the Supreme Court never challenged Lincoln's claim that through his status as commander-in-chief he was able issue the Emancipation Proclamation. Congress had already granted him the go-ahead.

Following the cessation of the Civil War and Lincoln's subsequent assassination, all was still not well within Congress. Having won the war, Union congressmen were not about to let their compatriots from the South waltz right back into their former posts. When Congress reconvened in late 1865, the representatives from the Southern states were not allowed to be seated. The Union would not recognize the legitimacy of their states' governments. This harkens back to the argument of whether or not Congress during the Civil War ever possessed the necessary quorum to conduct business. Though the end of the Civil War spelled the defeat of the Confederacy, meaning the rebellious Southern states should have once again been seen as part of the nation, this was not the case. The United States was not yet united.

Possessing an opportunity to wield uncontrolled power, the

northern congressmen took over Congress. They passed a series of four acts, known as the Reconstruction Acts, in the year between March 1867-1868. In these four acts, the Southern states were forced to accept Congress's mandates prior to being accepted back into the Union and before reclaiming their seats in either House of Congress. This included that every state must write a new state Constitution which required the federal Congress's approval to pass, the states had to grant voting privileges to all men, and each state needed to pass the 14th Amendment to the Constitution (which in Section 3 barred any person having engaged in insurrection or rebellion against the United States the ability to serve in the federal government unless reinstated with a two-thirds vote from both Houses of Congress).

Their hands tied, every state capitulated with Congress's demands. Lincoln's successor, Andrew Johnson, vetoed all four acts. However, Congress—with virtually no internal dissention—overturned every one of Johnson's vetoes. Congress was in no mood to allow the new president to throw his weight around as Lincoln had done. Congress clamped down on the power of the presidency, virtually turning the post into a rubber stamping machine. From Johnson's administration through the turn of the century, virtually no presidential executive order or proclamation was issued. That state of affairs would not last.

The Roosevelts and War

A scant 12 years after Lincoln was killed, a man by the name of Rutherford B. Hayes stepped into the White House as the 19th President of the United States. Hayes was one of several "forgotten" presidents. As a testimonial to the excitement level during his reign, Hayes was one of only two presidents following Lincoln (with his immediate successor James Garfield being the other) to not issue a single presidential executive order. Sometime after his four years in office were served, an interview with Hayes appeared in the book *The Constitution of the United States, Its History, Application, and Construction* published in 1910 by David Watson. In it, Hayes was quoted: "The executive power is large because [it is]

Hayes

24

not defined in the Constitution. The real test has never come, because the Presidents have down to the present been conservative, or what might be called conscientious men, and have kept within limited range. And there is an unwritten law of usage that has come to regulate an average administration. But if a Napoleon ever became President, he could make the executive almost what he wished to make it. The war power of President Lincoln went to lengths which could scarcely be surpassed in despotic principle."

In September 1901, such a president stepped into office. Following the assassination of William McKinley by the anarchist Leon Czolgosz, Theodore Roosevelt became the 26th President of the United States. In no way did Roosevelt prescribe to Hayes's view of Lincoln. Just the opposite, Roosevelt considered Lincoln to be the greatest Republican president in history and felt he was truly the savoir of the Union. He believed in Lincoln so much as that it was Roosevelt who had Lincoln's likeness placed on the penny. Roosevelt, as president, was bound and determined to act in similar fashion as his hero.

It didn't take long for Roosevelt to fulfill that vow. Because of that, it can be argued Roosevelt was the nation's first "modern" president based upon his actions while in office. This consisted of doing as he pleased as he issued executive orders at a record pace. In Roosevelt's nearly eight years in office, he published 1,006 executive orders. All of those came without confronting any sort of national emergency on the scale Lincoln faced with the Civil War. This was approximately five times as many executive orders as had been issued by all of the presidents up to that point in American history. For their part, Congress did little to curtail Roosevelt's usage of the executive order as a means to legislate. Though a large majority of Roosevelt's orders were benign in the grand scheme of things, it did not mean that he was necessarily correct in issuing any of them.

Most of Roosevelt's justification for his actions came from his personal view of what a president should be able to accomplish. He considered the office of the president as a "steward" for the people. He felt that if the people required something and Congress wasn't able or even fast enough to act, then by golly, he would (and could) do it himself. In his autobiography, Roosevelt wrote that he "declined to adopt the view that what was imperatively necessary for the Nation could not be done by the President unless he could find some specific authorization to do it." It was that go-getter attitude of Roosevelt's that made him wildly popular among the people. It is also how the executive branch managed to tip the balance of power in its favor while gaining an excessive amount of control within the federal government.

To further detail Roosevelt's idea of the role of the president, allow him to speak for himself from his autobiography:

"My view was that every Executive officer...was a steward of the people bound actively and affirmatively to do all he could for the people and not to content himself with the negative merit of keeping his talents undamaged in a napkin...My belief was that it was not only [the President's] right but his duty to do any thing that the needs of the Nation demanded unless such action was forbidden by the Constitution or by the laws. Under this interpretation of executive power I did and caused to be done many things not previously done by the President and the heads of departments. I did not usurp power but I did greatly broaden the use of executive power. In other words, I acted for the common well being of all our people whenever and whatever measure was necessary, unless prevented by direct constitutional or legislative prohibition."

Take notice it was Roosevelt's own interpretation of executive power that allowed him to run roughshod through Washington during his time there. Because Congress never attempted to rope in Roosevelt, in retrospect he could see himself as having done the right thing. Never mind that he knowingly altered the office and role of the president ever afterwards.

Interestingly, Roosevelt's immediate successor was his Secretary of War, William Howard Taft. Despite being Roosevelt's personal choice for president prior to a public falling out which drove Roosevelt from the Republican Party, Taft held a completely opposite view of the president's assumed powers. In a series of lectures given at Columbia University just after leaving office, Taft said, "A President can exercise no power which cannot fairly and reasonably be traced to some specific grant of power." He added that for a presidential executive order to be acceptable "such specific grants must be either in the Federal Constitution, or in any act of Congress passed in pursuance thereof. There is no undefined residuum of power which he can exercise because it seems to him to be in the public interest." Taft wasn't completely against a president being able to act independently though, especially if an emergency arose. He summed up his lectures by saying, "Executive power is limited, so far as it is possible to limit such a power consistent with that discretion and promptness of action that are essential to preserve the interests of the public in times of emergency or legislative neglect or inaction."

Which of the two verbal combatants were correct? History would declare Roosevelt the clear victor. After all, it's his visage carved into Mount Rushmore and not Taft's. Future presidents also chose to emulate Roosevelt because he, with Congress's silent blessing, immensely freed the president to act independently from congressional oversight. Taft, despite his lecturing against a president's ability to abuse his power, issued nearly 700 executive orders in his four years in office. Taking that at face value, that's not showing the conservative restraint Taft preached during his political career. Much like Roosevelt before him, Taft's executive orders were not the type to alter the course of the nation. It would be his successor's orders that would severely change things.

Woodrow Wilson saw his job as president more closely aligned to the view previously held by Theodore Roosevelt. Wilson claimed at one point, "No one but the President seems to be expected…to look out for the general interests of the country." He embodied that idea by issuing a record 1,791 executive orders during his two terms in office. It was during his second term that

Wilson, much like Lincoln 50 years earlier, saw the outbreak of war as a chance to flex his presidential muscle.

With a promise of keeping the United States out of what would later be known as World War I (with the catchy campaign slogan of "He kept us out of the war"), Wilson narrowly won his reelection bid in 1916. In typical political fashion, Wilson would quickly renege on his campaign promise. Prior to even seeking that second term, Wilson had foreseen America's entry into the war as inevitable. Through his executive orders in 1915 and 1916, he had already begun to prepare the nation for war. Wilson never acted completely alone, however, in issuing those orders. Congress was consistently backing Wilson's decisions. Even when Wilson began establishing new federal agencies via executive orders—something no president had yet done—Congress subsequently approved of his moves. Born out of those were the likes of the Council of National Defense, the War Industries Board, the War Trade Board, the Food Administration, the Grain Administration, and the Committee on Public Information. Despite seemingly working together in their war preparation, the two sides would soon clash over a sticking point that Wilson would solve by acting independently.

Many people believe, incorrectly, that it was the German sinking of the steamship Lusitania in 1915 that brought America into World War I. In actuality, the ship was British, not American, although there were American lives lost on board. In the immediate aftermath, Wilson admonished the Germans and sought to mediate some sort of truce. While that failed, the incident led to Germany's vow to stop attacking passenger ships with their submarines. Germany's enemies seized upon this peace offering and began shipping supplies aboard similar ships which were now safe from attack. Enterprising (and perhaps greedy) American ship owners eager to aid the wartime effort often rented their ships to foreign countries for transporting war goods. In fact, so many American ships were being used for those ends that there eventually became a shortage of available ships within the U.S. for the country's own needs. By the beginning of 1917, Germany realized it could not continue to allow these ships through if it wanted to win the war, and once again began unrestricted submarine warfare against any and all maritime vessels. Due to that renewed aggression against U.S. ships (and the famous Zimmermann Telegram in which Germany sought Mexico's help should the U.S. enter the war) America cut its diplomatic ties with Germany. As a response to Germany's unwarranted attacks on U.S. ships, Wilson decided to arm merchant ships in an attempt to ward off further losses. Congress disagreed, and through a filibuster during discussion of the subsequent bill, Wilson's plan was defeated.

A young staffer of Wilson's, Assistant Secretary of the Navy Franklin D. Roosevelt, found a loophole. Roosevelt discovered a statute (which originally established the U.S. Shipping Board) under which Wilson could act and arm the ships without Congress's approval. One thing had to be done first—Wilson had to declare a "national emergency." For the first time in U.S. history, on February 5, 1917, a president officially declared a national emergency via an executive order. The order read in part:

"WHEREAS, Congress did by 'An Act to Establish a United States Shipping Board for the purpose of encouraging, developing, and creating a naval auxiliary and naval reserve and a merchant marine to meet the requirements of the commerce of the United States with its Territories and possessions and with foreign countries; to regulate carriers by water engaged in the foreign and interstate commerce of the United States; and for other purposes', approved September 7, 1916, provide that 'during any national emergency the existence of which is declared by proclamation of the President, no vessel registered or enrolled and licensed under the laws of the United States shall, without the approval of the board, be sold, leased, or chartered to any person not a citizen of the United States, or transferred to a foreign registry or flag';

"And whereas, many shipowners of the United States are permitting their ships to pass to alien registers and to foreign trades in which we do not participate, and from which they cannot be bought back to serve the needs of our water-borne commerce without the permission of governments of foreign nations;

"Now, therefore, I, WOODROW WILSON, President of the United States of America, acting under and by virtue of the authority conferred in me by said Act of Congress, do hereby declare and proclaim that I have found that there exists a national emergency arising from the insufficiency of maritime tonnage to carry the products of the farms, forests, mines and manufacturing industries of the United States, to their consumers abroad and within the United States, and I do hereby admonish all citizens of the United States and every person to abstain from every violation of the provisions of said Act of Congress, and I do hereby warn them that all violations of such provisions will be rigorously prosecuted, and I do hereby enjoin upon all officers of the United States, charged with the execution of the laws thereof, the utmost diligence in preventing violations of said Act, and this my proclamation issued thereunder, and in bringing to trial and punishment any offenders against the same."

In declaring a national emergency—some two months prior to Congress's official declaration of war against Germany on April 6, 1917—Wilson opened up a whole slew of stand-by statutory provisions, including Roosevelt's loophole, which would now be available for the president to enact. What is interesting to note was that Wilson's declaration was not based on his commander-in-chief status as most of Lincoln's actions were. No, Wilson claimed his authority directly from Congress. They had provided for him an open avenue in which to operate. Once he had grasped that emergency power, Wilson utilized it to the utmost. He gained almost total economic power for the course of the war and granted the War Industries Board powers over and above its predetermined limits. All of this, Wilson argued, was needed to effectively fight and win the war.

What was also needed to fight the "war to end all wars" were a few other questionable acts of Congress that Wilson pushed through. The first was the 1917 Trading with the Enemy Act. The purpose of the act was summed up in its first sentence: "An Act to define, regulate, and punish trading with the enemy, and for other purposes." The act defines an "enemy," however, as "any individual, partnership, or other body of individuals, of any nationality, resident within the territory (including that occupied by the military and naval forces) of any nation with which the United States is at war…" and war, even in the context of this act, must be one declared by Congress.

Also during this national emergency, Wilson ushered through Congress two bills—the Espionage Act of 1917 and the Sedition Act of 1918—which effectively suspended American citizens' First Amendment rights. Through these two acts, various civil liberties were taken away, justified by the excuse of "national emergency" (something we shall encounter repeatedly). For example, the U.S. Postal Service, citing the Espionage Act, refused to carry any materials that could be deemed critical of the war effort. As a result, some newspapers and magazines were no longer available to their customers through the mail. While Wilson wasn't in favor of censorship per se, he did believe that certain critical information should not be made readily available to the enemy during times of national emergency. Hence in the Sedition Act, which was essentially an amendment to the earlier Espionage Act, it became a crime to "utter, print, write, or publish any disloyal, profane…or abusive language" about the United States government. In other words, toe the government's line or else.

The good news was, once America and her allies had won the war, Wilson was willing to relinquish all of the powers given to him during that time. Not only was he willing, he actually asked Congress to repeal all of those emergency statues believed to have been needed to win the war. Congress was happy to oblige. On March 3, 1921, Wilson's last official day in office, Congress acted jointly in stripping away all of the wartime acts that had given Wilson his great powers. Both the Espionage Act and Sedition Acts were repealed, along with a slew of other seemingly necessary-at-the-time measures. One act, however, the 1917 Trading with the

Enemy Act, survived. It was this act that would play a significant role in the next national emergency (and several future emergencies).

The Great Depression

What's remembered as the Great Depression was indeed a national emergency. No state was left unaffected by its economic sting. Yet it took the newly elected Franklin D. Roosevelt to officially declare it as such. When Roosevelt was inaugurated on March 4, 1933, the depression already had its foot on the throat of the country. While announcing to his constituents that "the only thing we have to fear is fear itself," Roosevelt also indicated that he had a plan for confronting this economic crisis head-on. He just failed to mention that it wasn't constitutionally allowed. Roosevelt said during his inauguration:

"It is to be hoped that the normal balance of Executive and legislative authority may be wholly adequate to meet the unprecedented task before us. But it may be that an unprecedented demand and need for undelayed action may call for temporary departure from that normal balance of public procedure…But in the event that Congress shall fail to take one of these two courses, and in the event that the national emergency is still critical, I shall not evade the clear course of duty that will then confront me. I shall ask the Congress for the one remaining instrument to meet the crisis—broad executive power to wage a war against the emergency, as great as the power that would be given to me if we were in fact invaded by a foreign foe."

Despite claims within his speech that certain presidential actions "may" be required, Roosevelt and his cronies were ready to pounce the moment he took the oath of office.

The day after he was sworn in as president, March 5, Roosevelt ordered an extra session of Congress to meet on March 9. Just 24 hours after issuing that order, without discussing the matter with Congress, Roosevelt on March 6 declared a one week long "bank holiday," closing America's banks nationwide on his order alone. What follows is that order, known as Proclamation

2039, in its entirety:

"Whereas there have been heavy and unwarranted withdrawals of gold and currency from our banking institutions for the purpose of hoarding; and

"Whereas continuous and increasingly extensive speculative activity abroad in foreign exchange has resulted in severe drains on the Nation's stocks of gold; and

"Whereas those conditions have created a national emergency; and

"Whereas it is in the best interests of all bank depositors that a period of respite be provided with a view to preventing further hoarding of coin, bullion or currency or speculation in foreign exchange and permitting the application of appropriate measures to protect the interests of our people; and

"Whereas it is provided in Section 5 (b) of the Act of October 6, 1917 (40 Stat. L. 411), as amended, 'That the President may investigate, regulate, or prohibit, under such rules and regulations as he may prescribe, by means of licenses or otherwise, any transactions in foreign exchange and the export, hoarding, melting, or earmarkings of gold or silver coin or bullion or currency . . .'; and

"Whereas it is provided in Section 16 of the said Act 'That whoever shall willfully violate any of the provisions of this Act or of any license, rule, or regulation issued thereunder, and whoever shall willfully violate, neglect, or refuse to comply with any order of the President issued in compliance with the provisions of this Act, shall, upon conviction, be fined not more than $10,000, or, if a natural person, imprisoned for not more than ten years, or both…';

"Now, Therefore I, Franklin D. Roosevelt, President of the United States of America, in view of such national emergency and by virtue of the authority vested in me by said Act and in order to prevent the export, hoarding, or earmarking of gold or silver coin or bullion or currency, do hereby proclaim, order, direct and declare that from Monday, the Sixth day of March, to Thursday, the Ninth day of March, Nineteen Hundred and Thirty-three, both dates inclusive, there shall be maintained and observed by all banking institutions and all branches thereof located in the United States of America, including the territories and insular possessions, a bank holiday, and that during said period all banking transactions shall be suspended. During such holiday, excepting as hereinafter provided, no such banking institution or branch shall pay out, export, earmark, or permit the withdrawal or transfer in any manner or by any device whatsoever, of any gold or silver coin or bullion or currency or take any other action which might facilitate the hoarding thereof; nor shall any such banking institution or branch pay out deposits, make loans or discounts, deal in foreign exchange, transfer credits from the United States to any place abroad, or transact any other banking business whatsoever.

"During such holiday, the Secretary of the Treasury, with the approval of the President and under such regulations as he may prescribe, is authorized and empowered (a) to permit any or all of such banking institutions to perform any or all of the usual banking functions, (b) to direct, require or permit the issuance of clearing house certificates or other evidences of claims against assets of banking institutions, and (c) to authorize and direct the creation in such banking institutions of special trust accounts for the receipt of new deposits which shall be subject to withdrawal on demand without any restriction or limitation and shall be kept separately in cash or on deposit in Federal Reserve Banks or invested in obligations of the United States.

"As used in this order the term 'banking institutions' shall include all Federal Reserve Banks, national banking associations, banks, trust companies, savings banks, building and loan associations, credit unions, or other corporations, partnerships, associations or persons, engaged in the business of receiving deposits, making loans, discounting business paper, or transacting any other form of banking business."

Not 48 hours into his role as president, Roosevelt officially declared a national emergency, the first since America's involvement in World War I. As he had stated he would in his inaugural address, Roosevelt attacked the problem as if it were a foreign foe and the United States was at war (something future presidents would also do with national issues, like Ronald Reagan's famous "War on Drugs").

Even more amazing was how Roosevelt pulled off this feat. In a similar fashion to the way in which he helped Woodrow Wilson skirt around Congress in 1917, FDR took advantage of a loophole found in another, earlier congressional act. Shockingly, he cited the 1917 Trading with the Enemy Act as his source for proclaiming the bank holiday. The original act was a wartime measure meant to restrict U.S. citizens from dealing with its enemies. Deep within the Trading with the Enemy Act was an apparently useful subsection that read in part "the President may investigate, regulate, or prohibit, under such rules and regulations as he may prescribe, by means of licenses or otherwise, any transactions in foreign exchange and the export, hoarding, melting, or earmarkings of gold or silver coin or bullion or currency…." In his proclamation, FDR cited this passage as giving him the power to close the banks.

Clearly, FDR was wrong. The passage within the Act by no means granted him that power. He likely knew he was doing more than grasping at straws by citing the Trading with the Enemy Act within that proclamation, but once again, Congress—as well as the American public—did nothing to stop the abuse of power. And that was just the beginning of FDR's master plan.

Three days later, Congress was back in session as Roosevelt had ordered. Immediately, they were presented with the Emergency Banking Act. It first went to the House of Representatives, where only Speaker of the House Joseph W. Byrns had an actual printed copy of the act. No member of the House was able to read it. Byrns urged its passing, and after about 40 minutes worth of debate, a vote was requested. Because of the panic and sense of urgency to do *something* to halt the depression, it passed the House with few dissenting voices, even though no one really knew what was in the bill. They simply believed—or were led to believe—that this needed to pass to allow the president to do what was necessary, not just to re-open the banks, but solve the financial crisis at hand. Remarkably, under an identical set of circumstances in which no one was completely aware of the content of the bill, it passed the Senate on the very same day. By the end of that night, Roosevelt had signed the bill into law. In less than 24 hours, the Emergency Bank Act had been presented to Congress and signed into law. If that's not sickening enough, by passing the bill, part of which amended the Trading with the Enemy Act, Congress gave FDR—and any future president—the authority to use the act as a basis for further as-needed economic emergency actions.

That's not the end of the tale. One month later, on April 6, FDR released Executive Order 6102. It began:

"By virtue Of the authority vested in me by Section 5 (b) of the Act of October 6, 1917, as amended by Section 2 of the Act of March 9, 1933, entitled 'An Act to provide relief in the existing national emergency in banking, and for other purposes,' in which amendatory Act Congress declared that a serious emergency exists, I, Franklin D. Roosevelt, President of the United States of America, do declare that said national emergency still continues to exist and pursuant to said section do hereby prohibit the hoarding of gold coin, gold bullion, and gold certificates within the continental United States by individuals, partnerships, associations and corporations and hereby prescribe the following regulations for carrying out the purposes of this order…."

As FDR pointed out, the so-called bank holiday didn't put an end to the national emergency. It still existed. The next thing to try? How about seizing all of the gold in the nation, whether in private or corporate hands?

Though it claimed to "prohibit the hoarding of gold…within the continental United States," Executive Order 6102 effectively nationalized the ownership of all gold over and above the amount of $100. "Hoarding" was defined as "withdrawal and withholding" of gold from "the recognized and customary channels of trade." Yet no gold belonging to any foreign nation or foreign banks was included. All gold was to be exchanged at a branch of a Federal Reserve Bank (which are not actually part of the United States government, they are privately owned) by May 1, 1933. There was no choice in the matter. Failure to do so could lead to a $10,000 fine, 10 years in prison, or both. Owning gold within the United States was now a crime, and this was not a law passed by Congress. It was merely an order of the president which was based upon a self-declared national emergency, and assumed to be legal thanks to his previous use of the Trading with the Enemy Act which itself was a questionable motive to say the least. This action effectively took the nation off of the gold standard to which our paper money had been held against since the Coinage Act of 1792.

How the move of outlawing the owning of gold was supposed to help end the depression was never seen. Because no matter the rationale behind FDR's order (and many have cited the obvious sinister nature of the move to indicate more was going on than just the surface excuse of fighting to end the economic crunch), the Great Depression by no means ended then and there in the middle of 1933.

When Germany blitzkrieged into Poland on September 1, 1939, to initiate World War II, FDR seized the opportunity to further tighten his grasp on the reigns of the federal government. This took the form of Proclamation 2352:

"WHEREAS a proclamation issued by me on September 5, 1939, proclaimed the neutrality of the United States in the war now unhappily existing between certain nations; and

"WHEREAS this state of war imposes on the United States certain duties with respect to the proper observance, safeguarding, and enforcement of such neutrality, and the strengthening of the national defense within the limits of the peacetime authorizations; and

"WHEREAS measures required at this time call for the exercise of only a limited number of the powers granted in a national emergency:

"NOW, THEREFORE, I, FRANKLIN D. ROOSEVELT,

President of the United States of America, do proclaim that a national emergency exists in connection with and to the extent necessary for the proper observance, safeguarding, and enforcing of the neutrality of the United States and the strengthening of our national defense within the limits of peacetime authorizations. Specific directions and authorizations will be given from time to time for carrying out these two purposes."

FDR was in effect declaring a "limited" national emergency by which he claimed necessary only "a limited number of powers" which were normally only available during a full-fledged national emergency. Of course, there neither was nor is such an entity as a "limited national emergency," at least in a legal respect. The labeling of this as "limited" was to calm the public's fears that FDR was continuing on his own dictatorial ways. In truth, though, he was. A declared national emergency was just that, whether "limited" or not. With such a declaration, FDR now had his whole arsenal of commander-in-chief powers in hand. Note how at the end of the proclamation he forewarned Congress and by extension the rest of the country that "specific directions and authorizations will be given from time to time." In other words, when FDR felt he needed something done, he'd go ahead and do it. By his own proclamation, it would be legal for him to so.

If that weren't enough—and for Roosevelt, it wasn't—less than two years later as the war continued to rage in Europe, an apparently new threat faced the country. To fight it, a limited emergency wasn't enough. On May 27, 1941, a full five months prior to the Japanese bombing of Pearl Harbor, Roosevelt issued Proclamation 2487 declaring that the nation was now facing an "unlimited" national emergency. It read, in part:

"WHEREAS a succession of events makes plain that the objectives of the Axis belligerents in such war are not confined to those avowed at its commencement, but include overthrow throughout the world of existing democratic order, and a worldwide domination of peoples and economies through the destruction of all resistance on land and sea and in the air, AND

"WHEREAS indifference on the part of the United States to the increasing menace would be perilous, and common prudence requires that for the security of this Nation and of this hemisphere we should pass from peacetime authorizations of military strength to such a basis as will enable us to cope instantly and decisively with any attempt at hostile encirclement of this hemisphere, or the establishment of any base for aggression against it, as well as to repel the threat of predatory incursion by foreign agents into our territory and society,

"NOW, THEREFORE, I, FRANKLIN D. ROOSEVELT, President of the United States of America, do proclaim that an unlimited national emergency confronts this country, which requires that its military, naval, air, and civilian defenses be put on the basis of readiness to repel any and all acts or threats of aggression directed toward any part of the Western Hemisphere."

Amazingly in this declaration Roosevelt didn't give himself any further powers to fight the "unlimited" national emergency. This proclamation served primarily a warning to the nation—one that wasn't willing to enter the war—that the situation in Europe was worsening. Note that Roosevelt didn't want his citizens to prepare for an attack against just America (which would be logical), but the entire Western Hemisphere. America was supposed to repel an attack against South America? Cuba? Where did the Western Hemisphere begin and end? Who drew that map? Did it include the territory of Hawaii?

Though Roosevelt was the longest serving president, lasting 12 years in office, he issued more than twice as many executive orders as any president before or after him. Woodrow Wilson had previously held the record with nearly 1,800 orders, but FDR, facing national emergencies in the form of the Great Depression and World War II, issued an incredible 3,723 executive orders. He averaged one order for every 1.17 days served as president. Out of all those, perhaps his most famous was also the most controversial.

A Threat

While Executive Order 8983 established an investigation into the attack on Pearl Harbor which ultimately railroaded Pearl Harbor commanders Admiral Husband E. Kimmel and General Walter Short into taking the blame for the "surprise" attack, and while Executive Order 8985 established the Office of Censorship (talk about a straight forward title), it was in Executive Order 9066 that Roosevelt truly trampled upon the constitutional rights of thousands Americans. EO 9066 read in part:

"WHEREAS the successful prosecution of the war requires every possible protection against espionage and against sabotage to national-defense material, national-defense premises, and national-defense utilities as defined in section 4, Act of April 20, 1918, 40 Stat. 533, as amended by the act of November 30, 1940, 54 Stat. 1220, and the Act of August 21, 1941, 55 Stat. 655 (U. S. C., Title 50, Sec. 104):

"NOW, THEREFORE, by virtue of the authority vested in me as President of the United States, and Commander in Chief of the Army and Navy, I hereby authorize and direct the Secretary of War, and the Military Commanders whom he may from time to time designate, whenever he or any designated Commander deems such actions necessary or desirable, to prescribe military areas in such places and of such extent as he or the appropriate Military Commanders may determine, from which any or all persons may be excluded, and with such respect to which, the right of any person to enter, remain in, or leave shall be subject to whatever restrictions the Secretary of War or the appropriate Military Commander may impose in his discretion. The Secretary of War is hereby authorized to provide for residents of any such area who are excluded therefrom, such transportation, food, shelter, and other accommodations as may be necessary, in the judgement of the Secretary of War or the said Military Commander, and until other arrangements are made, to accomplish the purpose of this order. The designation of military areas in any region or locality shall supersede designations of prohibited and restricted areas by the Attorney General under the Proclamations of December 7 and 8, 1941, and shall supersede the responsibility and authority of the

Attorney General under the said Proclamations in respect of such prohibited and restricted areas.

"I hereby further authorize and direct the Secretary of War and the said Military Commanders to take such other steps as he or the appropriate Military Commander may deem advisable to enforce compliance with the restrictions applicable to each Military area hereinabove authorized to be designated, including the use of Federal troops and other Federal Agencies, with authority to accept assistance of state and local agencies."

Seemingly innocuous enough, isn't it? Yet with this order issued on February 19, 1942, FDR condemned some 110,000 U.S. citizens of Japanese descent into federally mandated "relocation" camps. How could that have possibly been allowed? It began with the illogical thought processes of one American General John L. DeWitt. General DeWitt was the commander of the Western Defense Command. Following the attack on Pearl Harbor, the West Coast of America was abuzz with thoughts of further Japanese attack or even a possible invasion. DeWitt, convinced that anyone who was of Japanese decent was still connected to or open for possible subversion by their homeland, felt any and all Japanese Americans needed to be closely monitored. Crazy as his reasoning was, General DeWitt was sure that since nothing had yet happened on the West Coast, something was certainly being concocted. In DeWitt's mind, silence equated with looming disaster. With the high concentration of Americans with Japanese ancestry located on the West Coast, sabotage was sure to occur. Where and when, DeWitt didn't know; yet he was certain it would come.

Somehow Roosevelt was convinced by the lunacy of General DeWitt's ideology. A little over two months after the attack at Pearl Harbor, FDR issued EO 9066. American citizens were removed from their homes, rounded up, and transported into camps where they were forced to live, under armed guard, for the duration of the war. Many of the Japanese-American citizens rounded up had roots that placed them well beyond being just first generation Americans, and most could not even speak Japanese. Still, they were deemed a threat to the nation. Remarkably, those Japanese-Americans were not alone. Because FDR had issued three proclamations (2525, 2526, and 2527) which had respectively designated Japanese, German, and Italian nationals as enemy aliens, Italian-American and German-American citizens were also interned in these camps. While rarely mentioned, upwards of 11,000 German-Americans were relocated under FDR's order.

This action, which eliminated the rights of American citizens as guaranteed in the Constitution and issued under the authority vested in the president as commander-in-chief, set a precedent that was to be used in later executive orders and Continuity of Government plans that potentially allow the federal government to establish martial law and round up other "dissenters" or "terrorists" as the president may see fit. While there were few dissenting voices calling for an end to the internment of those Japanese (and Italian and German) Americans, there were four lawsuits against FDR's EO 9066 that reached the Supreme Court. In every instance, the Supreme Court upheld FDR's action. In each ruling, the Supreme Court felt that during war or a national emergency, such "necessary" action was indeed constitutional.

What is forgotten about FDR's reign was that the entire 12-year long administration was run under a perpetual state of emergency. This gave him authorities (whether real or perceived) above and beyond the scope of what was allowable for most other presidents. Established within 48 hours of his taking office on March 6, 1933, that proclamation of national emergency would last not just through FDR's term (which ended with his death in 1945), nor just through to the end of World War II (officially in 1952), but *until forcefully ended by an act of Congress in 1976.*

Truman, Nixon, & Onward

Upon Franklin Roosevelt's death in April 1945, Vice President Harry Truman took control of the country and its current state of national emergency. As World War II drew to a close, Truman began to dismantle some of the mechanisms his predecessor had put in place; however, he took his sweet time in doing so.

Though the shooting aspect of World War II ended in 1945, Truman did not declare the end of hostilities until December 31, 1946. Officially the United States' war with Germany did not end until 1951 when Congress terminated the declared state of war with the country. It wasn't until the early part of 1952 that Congress did the same in regards to Japan. After both of those Congressional declarations, Truman, by his own proclamations, ended FDR's 1939 "limited" and 1941 "unlimited" states of national emergencies in April 1952. He did not touch FDR's original declaration of national emergency issued in 1933—that technically remained in effect, but most of FDR's other war- and emergency-related actions were ended or allowed expire as the war had finally come to a close.

Truman had learned a valuable lesson during his scant three month tenure as vice president under FDR: how to essentially make laws through presidential orders. Truman would dole out just over 900 executive orders during his seven-plus years in office. Several of his most controversial orders revolved around threatened or actual strikes in various labor sectors. Through his executive orders, which in most part were based on his assumed authority granted in various war acts such as the War Labor Dispute Acts, Truman seized control of mines, mills, refineries, railroads, and other manufacturing plants, all in attempts to mediate strikes and meddle with wages offered to the various unions involved. Of course, he had no right or power to do so, and the Supreme Court busted him on it.

In the case of *Youngstown Sheet & Tube v. Sawyer,* the Supreme Court found that Executive Order 10340 under which Truman took control of the steel mill in question was unconstitutional. In essence, the court determined that Truman did not have the power to do as he pleased via an executive order. The only way such an action was allowable and thus constitutional was for there to be a previous authority granted to him through either the Constitution or a congressional act. In this circumstance, the court determined that no statue could be identified that gave Truman the power to act as he had. To counter the court's findings, Truman and his council responded with the notion of his status as commander-in-chief and the ongoing national emergency as cited in Executive Order 10340. The court rejected the notion. They believed there were no inherent powers vested within the office of the president that arose simply out of the claim of "national emergency." In fact, the court believed that the authors of the Constitution foresaw such situations arising and intentionally left the president out of the mix to keep him from acting over and above the prescribed limits of his position.

If Truman eliminated FDR's previous national emergencies related to World War II, to what national emergency was he referring in Executive Order 10340? Surely it wasn't the ongoing emergency that was enacted in 1933 to declare FDR's "bank holiday?" Indeed it was not. Truman's national emergency was his self-proclaimed war with Korea. As stated in the Presidential Proclamation 2914, issued on December 16, 1950:

"WHEREAS recent events in Korea and elsewhere constitute a grave threat to the peace of the world and imperil the efforts of this country and those of the United Nations to prevent aggression and armed conflict; and

"WHEREAS world conquest by communist imperialism is the goal of the forces of aggression that have been loosed upon the world; and

"WHEREAS, if the goal of communist imperialism were to be achieved, the people of this country would no longer enjoy the full and rich life they have with God's help built for themselves and their children; they would no longer enjoy the blessings of the freedom of worshipping as they severally choose, the freedom of reading and listening to what they choose, the right of free speech including the right to criticize their Government, the right to choose those who conduct their Government, the right to engage freely in collective bargaining, the right to engage freely in their own business enterprises, and the many other freedoms and rights which are a part of our way of life; and

"WHEREAS the increasing menace of the forces of communist aggression requires that the national defense of the United States be strengthened as speedily as possible:

"Now, THEREFORE, I, HARRY S. TRUMAN, president of the United States of America, do proclaim the existence of a national emergency, which requires that the military, naval, air, and civilian defenses of this country be strengthened as speedily as possible to the end that we may be able to repel any and all threats against our national security and to fulfill our responsibilities in the efforts being made through the United Nations and otherwise to bring about lasting peace.

"I summon all citizens to make a united effort for the security and well-being of our beloved country and to place its needs foremost in thought and action that the full moral and material strength of the Nation may be readied for the dangers which threaten us.

"I summon our farmers, our workers in industry, and our businessmen to make a mighty production effort to meet the defense requirements of the Nation and to this end to eliminate all waste and inefficiency and to subordinate all lesser interests to the common good.

"I summon every person and every community to make, with a spirit of neighborliness, whatever sacrifices are necessary for the welfare of the Nation.

"I summon all State and local leaders and officials to cooperate fully with the military and civilian defense agencies of the United States in the national defense program.

"I summon all citizens to be loyal to the principles upon which our Nation is rounded, to keep faith with our friends and allies, and to be firm in our devotion to the peaceful purposes for which the United Nations was rounded.

"I am confident that we will meet the dangers that confront us with courage and determination, strong in the faith that we can thereby 'secure the Blessings of Liberty to ourselves and our Posterity'."

This proclamation, which justified America's military involvement in Korea under the guise of a "national emergency," was the standard to which nearly every subsequent military action the U.S. has taken was based (and note how Truman twice refers to the United Nations and their "peaceful purposes" as if that body and the United States are one). Congress never officially declared war—an act prescribed *only* to Congress in the Constitution—in what became known as the Korean War. In fact, Congress has never declared war on *any* country since World War II. Though the Supreme Court took Truman to task and declared his Executive Order 10340 unconstitutional in part because it was based on a false power assumed to derive from a proclaimed national emergency, the Court did not attack the national emergency—the resultant Korean War—itself. The Supreme Court was in effect saying:

Presidential seizing of a steel mill under a declared national emergency – illegal

Presidential declared national emergency starting war – legal

No matter one's personal views of the Korean War (just or unjust) one has to wonder exactly how this clear usurpation of power was allowed to take place. If the events taking place in Korea truly constituted a national emergency in the United States, then Congress should have taken over the reins and steered the country in the correct direction, even if it should have led to war. This wasn't the case. Congress did nothing. They did not declare war. They did not explicitly support the war effort. Nor did they even do the exact opposite and condemn Truman's actions. In its failure to act in any definitive way, Congress opened the door to Truman and every one of his successors to declare national emergencies and devise the response to them on a whim (even the War Powers Resolution which passed Congress in 1973 and was meant to curtail such action by the president has completely failed).

Perhaps even worse, when the armistice between North and South Korea was signed on July 27, 1953, Truman's national emergency regarding the situation wasn't formally ended. That emergency, much like FDR's declared emergency in 1933, continued to live on in a sort of limbo. Consequently, every president following Truman was able to continue to operate as if there were a national emergency in effect without having to declare their own, which was quite useful during the Cold War between the U.S. and its various communist enemies. It freed the president to act in response to "the ongoing national emergency" and continue to use the Trading with the Enemy Act in an "as needed" fashion. President Kennedy, as commander-in-chief, was able to send advisors/troops into Vietnam (which, amazingly, was *not* a national emergency) based directly on Truman's actions in response to the national emergency tied to Korea. Though Congress further approved the military action in Vietnam with the Southeast Asia Resolution (better known as the Gulf of Tonkin Resolution), truly by that point in time, President Lyndon Johnson didn't require it to continue to send troops into the on-going fray.

Congress didn't get their collective act together and attempt to solve this problem until President Richard Nixon's use of national emergency pushed them over the edge. Remarkably, this had nothing to do with the legendary Watergate scandal that would bring a premature end to his time in office. No, this was due to the national emergency declared as a result of a postal workers' strike. As per President Nixon in Proclamation 3972:

"WHEREAS certain employees of the Postal Service are engaged in an unlawful work stoppage which has prevented the delivery of the mails and the discharge of other postal functions in various parts of the United States; and

"WHEREAS as a result of such unlawful work stoppage the performance of critical governmental and private functions, such as the processing of men into the Armed Forces of the Untied States, the transmission of tax refunds and the receipt of tax collections, the transmission of Social Security and welfare payments, and the conduct of numerous and important commercial transactions, has wholly ceased or is seriously impeded; and

"WHEREAS the continuance of such work stoppage with its

attendant consequences will impair the ability of this nation to carry out its obligations abroad, and will cripple or halt the official and commercial intercourse which is essential to the conduct of its domestic business:

"NOW, THEREFORE, I, RICHARD NIXON, President of the United States of America, pursuant to the powers vested in me by the Constitution and laws of the United States and more particularly by the provisions of Section 673 of Title 10 of the United States Code, do hereby declare a state of national emergency, and direct the Secretary of Defense to take such action as he deems necessary to carry out the provisions of the said Section 673 in order that the laws of the United States pertaining to the Post Office Department may be executed in accordance with their terms."

To a degree, Nixon was correct. The stoppage of mail service was a national emergency, perhaps more so than Truman's declaration regarding Korea. At that time prior to the internet, email, electronic payments and other such modern conveniences, loss of a working mail system could have brought the nation to a standstill. In response to the work stoppage, Nixon's Executive Order 11519 called for members of the National Guard to reestablish the postal service nationwide. Consequently, the strike was soon settled.

Nixon wasn't yet finished declaring national emergencies. A little over a year after the postal strike, Nixon again proclaimed a national emergency on August 15, 1971. Proclamation 4074 read in part:

"WHEREAS, there has been a prolonged decline in the international monetary reserves of the United States, and our trade and international competitive position is seriously threatened and, as a result, our continued ability to assure our security could be impaired;

"WHEREAS, the balance of payments position of the United States requires the
imposition of a surcharge on dutiable imports;

"WHEREAS, pursuant to the authority vested in him by the Constitution and the statutes, including, but not limited to, the Tariff Act of 1930, as amended (hereinafter referred to as the "Tariff Act"), and the Trade Expansion Act of 1962, (Hereinafter referred to as "the TEA"), the President entered into, and proclaimed tariff rates under trade agreements with foreign countries;

"WHEREAS, under the Tariff Act, the TEA, and other provisions of law, the President may, at any time, modify or terminate, in whole or in part, and proclamation made under his authority:

"NOW, THEREFORE, I, RICHARD NIXON, President of the United States of America, acting under the authority vested in me by the Constitution and the statutes, including, but not limited to, the Tariff Act, and the TEA, respectively, do proclaim as follows:

"A. I hereby declare a national emergency during which I call upon the public and private sector to make the efforts necessary to strengthen the international economic position of the United States...."

Convinced there was an international monetary crisis, Nixon, as his presidential forerunners had done, decided to act without congressional approval. With this order he instituted various import controls in an attempt to thwart that growing "national emergency" and turn the tables in America's favor. Nixon's proclamation became the straw that finally broke the camel's back.

The National Emergencies Act

Led by Senators Frank Church of Idaho and Charles Mathias Jr. of Maryland, what ultimately resulted from the investigation into Nixon's national emergency declarations was *The Report of the Special Committee on the Termination of the National Emergency* issued by the 93rd Congress on November 19, 1973. To its own surprise, the Committee discovered that at the time of its formation the nation was under four separate, yet concurrent national emergencies— FDR's from 1933, Truman's from 1950, and both of Nixon's from

1970 and 1971. Because of this, the Committee discovered that: "These [national emergency] proclamations give force to 470 provisions of Federal law. These hundreds of statutes delegate to the President extraordinary powers, ordinarily exercised by the Congress, which affect the lives of American citizens in a host of all-encompassing manners. This vast range of powers, taken together, confer enough authority to rule the country without reference to normal Constitutional processes."

Apparently even members of Congress weren't too up-to-date with their own American and congressional history, but they were beginning to learn. The Committee eventually discovered: "A first and necessary step was to bring together the body of statutes, which have been passed by Congress, conferring extraordinary powers upon the Executive branch in times of national emergency. This has been a most difficult task. Nowhere in the Government, in either the Executive or Legislative branches, did there exist a complete catalog of all emergency statutes. Many were aware that there had been a delegation of an enormous amount of power but, of how much power, no one knew."

The committee wasn't about to let what proceeded it to continue. It wrote: "A majority of the people of the United States have lived all of their lives under emergency rule. For 40 years, freedoms and governmental procedures guaranteed by the Constitution have, in varying degrees, been abridged by laws brought into force by states of national emergency…It is a pattern showing that the Congress, through its own actions, transferred awesome magnitudes of power to the executive ostensibly to meet the problems of governing effectively in times of great crisis. Since 1933, Congress has passed or recodified over 470 significant statutes delegating to the President powers that had been the prerogative and responsibility of the Congress since the beginning of the Republic….Emergency powers laws are of such significance to civil liberties, to the operation of domestic and foreign commerce, and the general functioning of the U.S. Government, that, in microcosm, they reflect dominant trends in the political, economic, and judicial life in the United States....Congress has in most important respects, except for the final action of floor debate and the formal passage of bills, permitted the Executive branch to draft and in large measure to 'make the laws.'...Bills drafted in the Executive branch were sent to Congress by the President and, in the case of the most significant laws that ate on the books, were approved with only the most perfunctory committee review and virtually no consideration of their effect on civil liberties or the delicate structure of the U.S. Government of divided powers....**Because Congress and the public are unaware of the extent of emergency powers, there has never been any notable congressional or public objection made to this state of affairs. Nor have the courts imposed significant limitations.** [emphasis in original]"

The committee admitted to Congress's past failures to censor the president from taking those powers. It determined the basic reasoning behind why that had occurred, writing: "What these examples suggest and what the magnitude of emergency powers affirm is that most of these laws do not provide for congressional oversight or termination. There are two reasons which can be adduced as to why this is so. First, few, if any, foresaw that the temporary states of emergency declared in 1938, 1939, 1941, 1950, 1970, and 1971 would become what are now regarded collectively as virtually permanent states of emergency (the 1939 and 1941 emergencies were terminated in 1952). **Forty years can, in no way, be defined as a temporary emergency.** Second, the various administrations who drafted these laws for a variety of reasons were understandably not concerned about providing for congressional review, oversight, or termination of these delegated powers which gave the President enormous powers and flexibility to use those powers. [emphasis in original]"

What was the solution to this situation created originally by FDR's action back in 1933? The Committee determined two basic ideas. First was, "It is reasonable to have a body of laws in readiness to delegate to the President extraordinary powers to use in times of real national emergency." The second and more important decision was, "We may say that power to legislate for emergencies belongs in the hands of Congress, but only Congress itself can prevent power from slipping through its fingers." It was time for Congress to take back some of the power they had allowed the executive branch to consume when it failed to act in the past.

After the Committee ran its course and submitted its report, it was reestablished the following year in 1974 as the Special Committee on National Emergencies and Delegated Emergency Powers. What flowed out of that committee, based in large part on the findings of the previous committee, was the National Emergencies Act. While the passage of the act was bumped by the impeachment proceedings against President Nixon, and once he resigned, the nomination of Nelson Rockefeller as vice president to the new President Gerald Ford, the act eventually was signed into law by Ford on September 14, 1976.

The National Emergencies Act did a couple of important things. For one, it ended the four standing national emergencies that had been ongoing. It did not, however, end them instantaneously. Rather, it rendered all four ineffective. Because all four were based under the president's constitutional authority described in Article II, technically speaking, they could not be outright terminated. What happened instead was the statutory authorities those emergencies enacted were returned to a dormant state. That occurred via the first title of the National Emergencies Act which imposed a two year limit on all authorities issued under a national emergency. It was a roundabout way of doing it, but the job was finally completed.

Next, the act put a control on how national emergencies were proclaimed. The new declarations had to be made to Congress and subsequently published in the Federal Register. Not only that, but henceforth a president had to indicate under what authority he was claiming there to be a national emergency as well as what powers he planned on enacting to combat it. Though the idea here was to put a control upon what could be declared a national emergency and how the president could deal with it, in practice, this led to presidents becoming more vague and open ended in their wordings, allowing for much more wiggle room than was initially hoped.

Lastly, and perhaps most importantly, the act terminated any national emergency and the powers that would accompany it one year after its announcement. The only way for its continuance was to once again formally announce the national emergency as described above. Later, in 1985, an amendment was added to the act allowing Congress to end any national emergency through a joint resolution. Congress had seemingly taken back its control.

That was in theory. In practice, since the passing of the National Emergencies Act, the number of declared national emergencies *skyrocketed*. Between 1979 and 2012, more than 40 separate national emergencies have been declared. That's an average of more than one per year. Before you make up your mind on how ridiculous that is, what follows is a list of those emergencies by president and title:

Jimmy Cater

- **EO 12170** – 11/14/79 – Blocking Iranian Government Property
- **EO 12211** – 04/17/80 – Sanctions Against Iran

Ronald Reagan

- **EO 12444** – 10/14/83 – Continuation of Export Regulations
- **EO 12470** – 03/30/84 – Continuation of Export Regulations (this was a re-upping of EO 12444)
- **EO 12513** – 05/01/85 – Prohibiting Trade and Certain Other Transactions Involving Nicaragua
- **EO 12532** – 09/09/85 – Prohibiting Trade and Certain Other Transactions Involving South Africa
- **EO 12543** – 01/07/86 – Prohibiting Trade and Certain Transactions Involving Libya

- **EO 12635** – 04/08/88 – Prohibiting Certain Transactions with Respect to Panama

George H.W. Bush

- **EO 12722** – 08/02/90 – Blocking Iraqi Government Property and Prohibiting Transactions with Iraq
- **EO 12723** – 08/02/90 – Blocking Kuwaiti Government Property
- **EO 12724** – 08/09/90 - Blocking Iraqi Government Property and Prohibiting Transactions with Iraq
- **EO 12725** – 08/09/90 – Blocking Kuwaiti Government Property and Prohibiting Transactions with Kuwait (this was an update and rewriting of EO 12723 just seven days after the original)
- **EO 12730** – 09/30/90 – Continuation of Export Control Regulations
- **EO 12735** – 11/16/90 – Chemical and Biological Weapons Proliferation
- **EO 12775** – 10/04/91 – Prohibiting Certain Transactions with Respect to Haiti
- **EO 12808** – 05/30/92 – Blocking "Yugoslav Government" Property and Property of the Governments of Serbia and Montenegro

Bill Clinton

- **EO 12865** – 09/26/93 – Prohibiting Certain Transactions Involving UNITA
- **EO 12868** – 09/30/93 – Measures to Restrict the Participation by United States Persons in Weapons Proliferation Activities
- **EO 12923** – 06/30/94 – Continuation of Export Control Regulations (Clinton replaced Bush's previous EO 12730 with his own version here)
- **EO 12924** – 08/19/94 - Continuation of Export Control Regulations (Apparently not thrilled with the original wording of EO 12923, Clinton replaced that order with this updated version just 6 weeks later).

- **EO 12930** – 09/29/94 – Measures to Restrict the Participation by United States Persons in Weapons of Proliferation Activities (This was a continuation of Clinton's original EO 12868 as per the National Emergencies Act requirement of renewal after one year in existence).
- **EO 12934** – 10/25/94 – Blocking Property and Additional Measures with Respect to the Bosnian Serb-Controlled Areas of the Republic of Bosnia and Herzegovina
- **EO 12938** – 11/14/94 – Proliferation of Weapons of Mass Destruction (This was a substitution of Bush's original EO 12735 with a change in terminology from "chemical and biological weapons" to the more timely "weapons of mass destruction.")
- **EO 12947** – 01/23/95 – Prohibiting Transactions With Terrorists Who Threaten to Disrupt the Middle East Peace Process
- **EO 12957** – 03/15/95 – Prohibiting Certain Transactions With Respect to the Development of Iranian Petroleum Resources
- **EO 12978** – 10/21/95 – Blocking Assets and Prohibiting Transactions with Significant Narcotics Traffickers
- **Proclamation 6867** – 03/10/96 – Declaration of a National Emergency and Invocation of Emergency Authority Relating to the Regulation of the Anchorage and Movement of Vessels (This actually cites the 1917 Trading with the Enemy Act.)
- **EO 13047** – 05/22/97 – Prohibiting New Investment in Burma
- **EO 13067** – 11/03/97 – Blocking Sudanese Government Property and Prohibiting Transactions with Sudan
- **EO 13088** – 06/09/98 - Blocking Property of the Governments of the Federal Republic of Yugoslavia (Serbia and Montenegro), the Republic of Serbia, and the Republic of Montenegro, and Prohibiting New Investment in the Republic of Serbia in Response to the Situation in Kosovo
- **EO 13129** – 07/04/99 – Blocking Property and Prohibiting Transactions with the Taliban (This was the

first mention of both "Usama bin Ladin" and Al-Qaida in connection with a declared national emergency—a full two years prior to the attacks on 9/11).

- **EO 13159** – 06/21/00 – Blocking Property of the Government of the Russian Federation Relating to the Disposition of Highly Enriched Uranium Extracted From Nuclear Weapons (Clinton tied this in with his previous order and emergency declared in EO 12938 regarding weapons of mass destruction.)
- **EO 13194** – 01/18/01 – Prohibiting the Importation of Rough Diamonds from Sierra Leone (Clinton decided to throw this emergency out there just two days prior to leaving office.)

George W. Bush

- **EO 13219** – 06/26/01 – Blocking Property of Persons Who Threaten International Stabilization Efforts in the Western Balkins
- **EO 13222** – 08/17/01 – Continuation of Export Control Regulations (This "emergency" was issued by Clinton, Bush Sr., and Reagan, meaning it has lasted since 1983. Wasn't the National Emergencies Act supposed to put an end to that sort of practice?)
- **Proclamation 7463** – 09/14/01 – Declaration of National Emergency by Reason of Certain Terrorist Attacks (Oddly enough, this declaration came three days after 9/11 and did not trigger many of the emergency stand-by procedures available to a president.)
- **EO 13224** – 09/23/01 – Blocking Property and Prohibiting Transactions with Persons Who Commit, Threaten to Commit, or Support Terrorism
- **EO 13288** – 03/06/03 – Blocking Property of Persons Undermining Democratic Processes or Institutions in Zimbabwe
- **EO 13303** – 05/22/03 – Protecting the Development Fund for Iraq and Certain Other Property in Which Iraq Has an Interest

- **EO 13338** – 05/11/04 – Blocking Property of Certain Persons and Prohibiting the Export of Certain Goods to Syria
- **EO 13348** – 07/22/04 – Blocking Property of Certain Persons and Prohibiting the Importation of Certain Goods From Liberia
- **EO 13396** – 02/07/06 – Blocking Property of Certain Persons Contributing to the Conflict in Cote d'Ivoire
- **EO 13405** – 06/16/06 – Blocking Property of Certain Persons Undermining Democratic Processes or Institutions in Belarus
- **EO 13413** – 10/27/06 – Blocking Property of Certain Persons Contributing to the Conflict in the Democratic Republic of the Congo
- **EO 13441** – 08/01/07 – Blocking Property of Persons Undermining the Sovereignty of Lebanon or Its Democratic Processes and Institutions
- **EO 13448** – 10/18/07 – Blocking Property and Prohibiting Certain Transactions Related to Burma (This was a continuation of EO 13047 and EO 13310.)
- **EO 13460** – 02/13/08 – Blocking Property of Additional Persons in Connection with the National Emergency with Respect to Syria
- **EO 13464** – 04/30/08 – Blocking Property and Prohibiting Certain Transactions Related to Burma (This was a further expansion of EO 13448 which itself was an expansion of two other executive orders relating to our national emergency situation with Burma.)
- **EO 13466** – 06/26/08 – Continuing Certain Restrictions with Respect to North Korea and North Korean Nationals (This also cites the Trading with the Enemy Act).
- **EO 13469** – 07/25/08 - Blocking Property of Additional Persons Undermining Democratic Processes or Institutions in Zimbabwe (This was a continuation of EO 13288 and EO 13391.)

As of the end of 2008, this was the complete list of the national emergencies declared via presidential executive order since the passing of the National Emergencies Act. However, the latest trend has been to continue these declared national emergencies through the issuance of a Presidential Notice and not an actual executive order. As required by the National Emergencies Act, a president has to notify Congress of his intent to continue a national emergency prior to its one-year expiration. More often than not, this is now done through a formal notice if no changes are needed to the original executive order. In 2008 alone, President Bush issued the following notices, all of which continued the national emergencies previously declared through his own executive orders as listed above:

- 01/18/08 – Terrorists Disrupting Mid-East Peace Process
- 02/05/08 – Cote d'Ivoire
- 02/06/08 – Cuba
- 03/04/08 – Zimbabwe
- 05/07/08 – Syria
- 05/20/08 – Iraq
- 06/06/08 – Belarus
- 06/18/08 – Nuclear proliferation in Russian Federation
- 06/24/08 – Western Balkans
- 07/16/08 – The Liberian Regime of Charles Taylor
- 07/23/08 – Export Control Regulations
- 08/28/08 – The attacks of September 11, 2001
- 09/18/08 – Terrorism (or the threat of, to be precise)
- 10/16/08 – Significant narcotics traffickers centered in Colombia
- 10/22/08 – Democratic Republic of the Congo
- 10/30/08 – Sudan
- 11/10/08 – Iran
- 11/10/08 – Weapons of Mass Destruction

Just prior to leaving office in January 2009, Bush re-upped two of those emergencies. On January 15, Bush issued an official notice to the continuing emergencies in regards to "Terrorists Disrupting Mid-East Peace Process" and Cuba.

When Barack Obama became president, he did not break this trend. He issued notices continuing the national emergencies regarding the following:

- 02/04/09 – Cote d'Ivoire
- 03/03/09 – Zimbabwe
- 03/11/09 – Iran (which wasn't due to be re-issued until November)
- 05/07/09 – Syria
- 05/14/09 – Burma
- 05/19/09 – Stabilization of Iraq
- 06/12/09 – Belarus
- 06/18/09 – Nuclear Proliferation of Territories of the Russian Federation
- 06/22/09 – West Balkans
- 06/24/09 – North Korea
- 07/16/09 – Liberian Regime of Charles Taylor
- 08/13/09 – Export Control Regulations
- 09/10/09 – Terrorist attacks of September 11, 2001
- 09/21/09 – Persons who commit, threaten to commit, or support terrorism
- 10/16/09 – Significant narcotics traffickers centered in Colombia
- 10/20/09 – Democratic Republic of the Congo
- 10/27/09 – Sudan
- 11/06/09 – Weapons of Mass Destruction
- 11/12/09 – Iran (even those this had been re-upped in March)

Did this trend change throughout Obama's term in office? Not in the least. In fact, he added to the growing list:

- 1/20/10 – Terrorists who threaten the Middle East peace process
- 2/2/10 – Cote D'Ivoire
- 2/23/10 – Cuba
- 2/26/10 – Zimbabwe

- 3/10/10 – Iran
- 4/12/10 – Blocking Property of Certain Persons Contributing to the Conflict in Somalia (this is a new "emergency," based largely on the piracy problem there)
- 5/3/10 –Syria
- 5/12/10 – the "Stabilization of Iraq"
- 5/13/10 – Burma
- 6/8/10 – the Western Balkins
- 6/8/10 – Belarus
- 6/14/10 – North Korea
- 6/17/10 – Risk of Nuclear Proliferation in Russian Federation
- 7/19/10 – Former Liberian Regime of Charles Taylor
- 7/29/10 – Lebanon
- 8/12/10 – Export Control Regulations
- 8/30/10 – Blocking Property of Certain Persons with Respect to North Korea (an expansion on the original emergency in EO 13466)
- 9/10/10 – "Certain Terrorist Attacks" (this is ongoing since the original 9/11 attacks)
- 9/16/10 – Persons who Commit, or Threaten to Commit, or Support Terrorism
- 9/28/10 – Blocking Property of Certain Persons with Respect to Serious Human Rights Abuses by the Government of Iran and Taking Certain Other Actions (another new addition which was tacked onto the original EO 12957 issued in March 1995 that is still in effect)
- 10/14/10 – Narcotics Traffickers Centered in Columbia
- 10/22/10 – the Democratic Republic of the Congo
- 11/1/10 – Sudan
- 11/4/10 – Weapons of Mass Destruction
- 11/10/10 – Iran (yet again)

Every one of these "national emergencies" was continued in 2011 and 2012 with some verbiage tweaks or outright additions to the ever-expanding list. Despite the fact that between 2008 and

2012 the United States witnessed the burst of the "housing bubble," the collapse of several major financial institutions, the near or actual bankruptcy of the "Big Three" automakers, "Superstorm" Sandy, sharp increases in unemployment and a major downturn in the economy, none of this was considered to be an official national emergency. These situations affected almost every American citizen while the declared national emergencies listed above likely passed without notice. Where were the headlines informing the public of these national emergencies? Where were the reporters from CNN, FOX News, MSNBC, etc. standing on the White House lawn informing the nation of each breaking event? How can something that was declared a national emergency not be national news? It is an important question for citizens to ask because at the end of 2012 the United States was under *25 concurrent national emergencies.*

Amazingly, when these emergencies were declared, none were true in-need-of-action situations (arguably President Obama's Proclamation 8443 which declared the H1N1 influenza a national emergency in 2009 was such an instance; however, the subject of pandemic will be covered later). The reason all of these 25 current independent situations were turned into national emergencies were due to the *threat* of becoming something bigger. As admitted by all of the presidents from Carter onward in their own executive orders, those situations weren't truly emergencies, but looming threats of potential emergency. Most every one of the executive orders following the passage of the National Emergencies Act contains a variation of the phrase "this constitutes an unusual and extraordinary threat to the national security, foreign policy, and economy of the United States." Threat, not occurrence. In essence, an emergency declaration was enacted to stop said problem prior to it blowing up into a true national emergency. But is that how it should work? Would any of these situations, while perhaps tragic and horrific within their own countries of origin, have ever really become national emergencies within the United States? Would Americans standing on American soil be affected? Even in declaring these foreign events "emergencies," what has really been done to curb each situation? While each event is different, clearly the efforts the Bush administration put forth did little to stem the tide as President Obama had to extend 21 separate emergencies for another year as required by the National Emergencies Act. Then Obama had to extend all of these yet again, and again.

Truthfully these emergencies were not what they claimed to be. More often than not these declarations are just a way to dictate foreign policy outside of the normal realms of action. They act to restrict trade and access some enemy nations and terrorists have within this country. More than that, they have become a way for the president to act independently, and in many ways, outside of the constitutional bounds of his elected role. When President Truman originally declared a national emergency with regards to Korea, few Americans realized what that possibly could have meant. In a short time, they learned the horrid truth as the nation was plunged into an undeclared war. Nothing stands in the way to stop a similar situation from occurring. Today's national emergency with regards to Zimbabwe could easily become tomorrow's war within Zimbabwe's borders. In no way did the authors of the Constitution mean to allow the president's commander-in-chief role to become a method to push the country into war. That power lies solely with Congress. No executive order or national emergency should be able to pervert that.

What's worse, as the congressional committee that originally looked at the national emergency situation noted, when a national emergency is declared, a whole slew of extra-constitutional powers opens up to the president. The National Emergencies Act did nothing to curtail that fact outside of limiting the extent of said powers to one year after the emergency's declaration—that is, if that declaration was not extended. What powers, exactly, are available to a president during a national emergency? More than you'd believe possible in a so-called democracy...

(SOME) EMERGENCY POWERS

"Democracies don't prepare well for things that have never happened before."
- Richard C. Clarke, former White House counterterrorism chief

As the Committee on the Termination of the National Emergency led by Senators Church and Mathias pointed out, with the declaration of a national emergency nearly 500 provisions of federal law automatically open up and become available to a president. What can these provisions potentially allow a president to do? A whole hell of a lot as the committee quickly discovered. They wrote, "Under the powers delegated by these statutes, the President may: seize property; organize and control the means of production; seize commodities; assign military forces abroad; institute martial law; seize and control all transportation and communication; regulate the operation of private enterprise; restrict travel; and, in a plethora of particular ways, control the lives of all American citizens." This was not some paranoid conspiracy freak jabbering; it was the U.S. Senate talking. We better listen. Many of these provisions were not given by Congress to the president, but rather the president took them for himself via the use of executive orders. Whether a president ever has it within himself to use all of these provisions is the ultimate trillion dollar question because their use could very well mean the overthrow of our constitutional government.

Kennedy in Action

The idea that a national emergency could affect the performance of the federal government began to seep into the minds of the nation's leaders around the time of World War II.

Once the shooting aspect of the war came to a conclusion, government officials began to think back to the start of the war and wonder how they got caught with their collective pants down. While it doesn't seem possible, the government had no plans in place to deal with the sudden outbreak of a war or how to respond in the face of a national emergency. Clearly some sort of preparations needed to be considered for the future.

America's first post-war president, Harry Truman, took this notion and ran with it. He drafted Executive Order 10346 which was issued on April 17, 1952. It was directed to most of the departments of the federal government, reading in part:

"In furtherance of national planning for the utilization of the personnel, materials, facilities, and services of the Federal departments and agencies which will be required in the event of a civil-defense emergency, each Federal department and agency shall, in consultation with the Federal Civil Defense Administration, prepare plans for providing its personnel, materials, facilities, and services pursuant to the provisions of section 302 of the said Federal Civil Defense Act during the existence of a civil-defense emergency. The plans of each department and agency shall take into consideration the essential military requirements of the Department of Defense with respect to such department or agency."

What Truman had in mind was a joint effort combining the federal government and the military to form a civil defense program for the continuation of each and every governmental department. While he didn't specify what those plans should entail, he did recognize that contingency plans needed to be established. He left the details to the respective head of each department.

When President Kennedy took office nine years later in 1961, the Cold War was in full swing. The Soviet Union, and by extension any communist-leaning country, was America's sworn enemy. The U.S. had just come out of a war fighting the spread of communism in Korea and was already gearing up for a similar fight within Vietnam. Hanging over the head of every man, woman and child was the growing threat of a nuclear war. Such a horrific conflict was only possible between the two nuclear superpowers—the United States and the Soviet Union. Since these two countries were already fighting proxy wars via Third World countries, such a possibility was never too far out of the realm of possibility. Perhaps the closest the world ever came to this sort of tragedy was during John F. Kennedy's presidency, most specifically from mid-1961 through the end of 1962.

On January 1, 1959 Fidel Castro seized power in Cuba, overthrowing the pro-U.S. Cuban government in the process. By the end of 1960, Castro would publically align his country with the Soviet Union, thus placing a dreaded communist outpost just 90 miles off America's coast. Soon after that announcement, the U.S. government severed its diplomatic ties with Cuba. As tensions mounted between the U.S. and Cuba (and by extension, the Soviet Union), Kennedy did his best to maintain some control of the relations between them. Hoping to defuse the situation, in April 1961, Kennedy announced his pledge that America would not intervene militarily to overthrow Castro and his communist regime in Cuba. Just five days after Kennedy publicly gave his word to Castro, anti-Castro Cubans working alongside American CIA operatives attempted to do the exact opposite and invade Cuba. On April 17, 1961, the disastrous "Bay of Pigs" invasion took place.

How aware President Kennedy was of this plot is debatable; however, his refusal to assist in the operation led to its instant demise. Unwilling to renege on his promise less than a week after he had given it, Kennedy called off the invasion's Air Force support, leaving the anti-Castro Cubans and CIA operatives exposed on the Cuban beach. Without the air cover, Castro was able to wipe out the American-backed forces.

Two months later, Kennedy met with Soviet Premier Nikita Khrushchev in Vienna. The meeting was a disaster. Khrushchev attempted to bully Kennedy at every turn. He hammered Kennedy on Cuba, on the situation over the divided city of Berlin, and ultimately threatened Kennedy with outright war. Kennedy, unwilling to appear soft in front of the Russian leader, ended the meeting by basically agreeing to battle the Soviets if and when the time came. Shortly thereafter, the communists began construction on the Berlin Wall as the schism between both sides never seemed further apart.

War, whether conventional or of a nuclear sort, loomed on America's horizon. As militaries and weapons continued to modernize after the end of World War II, the world was faced with a new type of war. The battle lines were not going to be the sort where there was a clearly defined front line laced with trenches like there was in World War I. By the 1960s, both sides had bombers that could fly around the world and attack any city in any country at will. Nuclear missiles (at least the known technology in the American missiles) could easily launch from one country and strike another half way around the globe. Soldiers were no longer the primary targets. Civilians on both sides were in the line of fire no matter where they lived. The heads of state were not safe within their capital cities.

Realizing that potential, Kennedy acted to shore up America's infrastructure. He decided to take Truman's original civil defense notion and expand upon it. Rather than issue an order directed at the entire federal government as Truman had done, Kennedy addressed each department individually, tasking that department's head with specific ideas and plans. Through a series of 10 executive orders issued on February 16, 1962, Kennedy prepared the country to be able to react to the outbreak of nuclear war. What he may or may not have realized, however, was that these executive orders simply did not vanish when the Soviet threat slowly ebbed away after the Cuban Missile Crisis in October 1962. These orders stayed on the record and became available to any other president when faced with a national emergency, thanks to the open and sometimes ambiguous wording in each executive order. It was within these orders that our constitutional government appeared to be outright threatened in the name of preserving it.

The first in this series of orders was EO 10995 titled "Assigning Telecommunications Management Functions." For his authority in issuing this order, Kennedy cited the Communications Act of 1934. Within that (at that time, 30 year old) act, under Section 606, the powers granted to the president were listed. In short, the president was "authorized, if he finds it necessary for the national defense and security, to direct that such communications as in his judgment may be essential to the national defense and security shall have preference or priority with any carrier subject to this Act." It further added that "any carrier complying...shall be exempt for any and all provisions in existing law imposing civil or criminal penalties, obligations, or liabilities upon carriers by reason of giving preference or priority in compliance with such order or direction," and "upon proclamation by the President that there exists war or a threat of war or state of public peril or disaster or other national emergency, or in order to preserve the neutrality of the United States, the President may suspend or amend, for such time as he may see fit, the rules and regulations applicable to any or all stations within the jurisdiction of the United States...and may cause the closing of any station for radio communication and the removal therefrom of its apparatus and equipment, or he may authorize the use or control of any such station...by any department of the Government under such regulations as he may prescribe..." Any such incident leading to the usage of that act is now commonly known as a "606 emergency."

With EO 10995, Kennedy was re-affirming the powers granted to the president in the Communications Act of 1934. He assigned what was essentially the president's role to the newly created Director of Telecommunications Management "which position shall be held by one of the Assistant Directors of the Office of Emergency Planning" though everything was still "subject to the authority and control of the President." Two of the new Director of Telecommunications Management's directives were "(a) Full and efficient employment of telecommunications resources in carrying out national policies; (b) Development of telecommunications plans, policies, and programs under which full advantage of technological development will accrue to the Nation and the users of telecommunications; and which will satisfactorily serve the national security; sustain and contribute to the full development of world trade and commerce; strengthen the position and serve the best interests of the United States in negotiations with foreign nations; and permit maximum use of resources through better frequency management."

What EO 10995 did *not* state, at least explicitly, was that the president or government can seize control of all media communications during a national emergency. Of course, it did not need to say that as that authority was already granted to the president via the Communications Act of 1934. What EO 10995 did state was that a new post titled the Director of Telecommunications Management was being created which would be umbrellaed under the Office of Emergency Planning and that those directives will be the director's responsibility. Many of those duties revolved around telecommunications and national security, which by default, meant that if the right circumstances existed, the government could/would step in and take over. While that certainly does sound frightening on one level, in fact, such a thing can potentially be lifesaving.

Consider for a moment the Emergency Broadcast System (EBS) which in 1994 became known as the Emergency Alert System (EAS). Originally created by President Truman in 1951 as CONELRAD (Control of Electromagnetic Radiation), the idea was to create a warning system to alert the public in case of an attack (conventional or nuclear). CONELRAD worked through what was known as a Key Station System. Basic Key Stations were major radio and TV stations that would receive an emergency message through telephone lines from Air Defense Control Centers. These Basic Key Stations would then transfer the message to the Relay Key Stations for further broadcast. The original emergency broadcast consisted of the station shutting off for five seconds, returning to the air for five seconds, then shutting off for another five seconds followed by a 15 second warning tone. All television stations and FM radio stations would then silence themselves. Most AM radio stations would cease to transmit and the official warning for the situation would be broadcast on either AM 640 or 1240. The reason these two specific radio frequencies were chosen was not by accident. It was believed that incoming Russian bombers would use American TV and radio signals to hone in on major population centers. By switching off these stations and using just two frequencies, the Russians would be confused and unable to find their targets, or so the theory went.

In mid-1963, CONELRAD was replaced with the Emergency Broadcast System. The EBS and its current incarnation as the Emergency Alert System, which was incorporated into the Integrated Public Alert and Warning System (IPAWS) in 2006, are the best and easiest system with which to capture a large section of the population's attention. By April 2012 the familiar EAS warning tone and accompanying alert sirens were made available through cell phones thanks to the Federal Communications Commission's Commercial Mobile Alert System. This allowed phones to receive text message emergency information for both local and national emergencies directly from the government. The innovation has the potential to save countless lives. By combining the traditional sirens with modern text messaging, the population can be alerted to a variety of imminent situations ranging from a tornado on the ground to a major chemical spill to the outbreak of nuclear war, all of which is currently overseen by FEMA's National Warning System (NAWAS). This was exactly the intent of Section 606 of the Communications Act of 1934. While some may see darker uses for the act coupled with EO 10995, such as the ability for the government to take control of the airwaves and broadcast any message they may see fit (be it propaganda or not), the idea was to be able to keep the nation's limited communication lines open among government officials so that any disaster could be mitigated while the public was kept informed so as to remain safe. While the EAS has been activated thousands of times on a local level, since its inception, it has never been activated on a national scale (it was tested, however, for the first time on November 9, 2011). A separate designation called an Emergency Action Notification which can only originate with the president does exist if a nationwide alert needs to be transmitted.

While EO 10995 seemed innocuous enough, EO 10997, which was titled "Assigning Emergency Preparedness Functions to The Secretary of The Interior," began to show the possible extent of a government takeover during a national emergency. As the executive order stated, "The Secretary of the Interior…shall prepare national emergency plans and develop preparedness programs covering (1) electric power; (2) petroleum and gas; (3) solid fuels; and (4) minerals. These plans and programs shall be designed to provide a state of readiness in these resource areas with respect to all conditions of national emergency, including attack upon the United States." If the country was under attack, or suffering from some national emergency (and not the type relating to the Western Balkans, although technically, that does count), energy would become a high priority. As part of this order, the Secretary was to "develop systems for the emergency application of priorities and allocations to the production and distribution of assigned resources." Kennedy and his administration wisely foresaw that should the worse come to pass, someone would need to be in charge of fuel, energy, and its distribution. These problems and their solutions were left to the Secretary of the Interior.

As one delves deeper into EO 10997, the more the language changed and the more paranoid the reader could become. Under a section in the order titled "Claimancy," the Secretary was instructed to "prepare plans to claim materials, manpower, equipment, supplies and services needed in support of assigned responsibilities and other essential functions of the Department before the appropriate agency, and work with such agencies in developing programs to insure availability of such resources in an emergency." Note the key word "claim" in that sentence. The president was stating that if need be, we the government were going to take whatever we need when we need it because the country was in a state of national emergency. The Secretary was tasked with figuring out how best to do that, no matter whose toes were stepped on.

That was not all. Continued reading finds that the Secretary was to "[develop] plans and programs to insure the continuity of production in the event of an attack, and cooperate with the Department of Commerce in the identification and rating of essential facilities…[formulate] and [carry] out plans and programs for the stockpiling of strategic and critical materials, and survival items….Develop plans for the salvage of stocks and rehabilitation of producing facilities for assigned products after attack…development of economic stabilization policies…including rationing of power and fuel." The Secretary was to figure out ways to continue to produce those fuel types no matter the emergency (even nuclear war), stockpile it, salvage it if need be, and then determine the best way to stabilize the costs while rationing it among the population. That was no small task. It's Herculean, and depending on the circumstances, near impossible. Meanwhile, all of that production and pricing would be suddenly and completely removed from public hands and federalized. Where, exactly, was that mentioned in the Constitution? Was Kennedy suggesting that in times of war or national emergency, certain aspects—if not all aspects—of the Constitution were null and void? The immediate answer appeared to be "yes."

Don't for a second think that the government limited itself to this sort of behavior when dealing only with fuel sources. While fuel feeds the war machines, it's food that feeds the soldiers. Hence, in Executive Order 10998, the Secretary of Agriculture was essentially tasked with the same duties as the Secretary of the Interior. President Kennedy ordered the Secretary of Agriculture that he "shall prepare national emergency plans and develop preparedness programs covering: Food resources, farm equipment, fertilizer, and food resource facilities, as defined below; rural fire control; defense against biological warfare, chemical warfare, and radiological fallout pertaining to agricultural activities; and rural defense information and education." What followed from that were basically the same set of instructions that the Secretary of the Interior had pertaining to national emergencies and fuel, including: the ability to claim foods and food resources, management of food production and processing, salvage of food resources, stockpiling for survival purposes, price fixing, rationing, and in cooperation with the Department of Defense, facility protection.

President Kennedy did throw a couple of curve balls to the Secretary of Agriculture however. For one, there was that bit referring to defense against biological and chemical warfare and radiological fallout. Kennedy left that up to the Secretary to figure out for himself. The order stated, "Develop plans for a national program, direct Federal activities, and furnish technical guidance to State and local authorities concerning (1) diagnosis and strengthening of defensive barriers and control or eradication of diseases, pests, or chemicals introduced as agents of biological or chemical warfare against animals, crops or products thereof; (2) protective measures, treatment and handling of livestock, including poultry, agricultural commodities on farms or ranches, agricultural lands, forest lands, and water for agricultural purposes, any of which have been exposed to or affected by radiation." Without a doubt, someone had to be in charge of such scientific research. Contingency plans needed to be created. What Kennedy stuck into a couple of sentences, however, covered a vast array of knowledge and implementation. The ecology of the East Coast is nothing like the West Coast which is vastly different from everything that lies between the two. To think that Kennedy's Secretary of Agriculture, Orville Freeman, received this order in the midst of that chaotic time and was charged to figure out how to recover the nation's food sources and supplies should a nuclear war begin seems ridiculous.

While poor Orville had to be scratching his head over what to do in the name of Kennedy's order, imagine what some small farmer in the Midwest thought when he heard what followed. Kennedy instructed his Secretary to "conduct a rural defense information and education program to advise farmers that they will have a responsibility to produce food of the kind and quantity needed in an emergency and shall work with farmers and others in rural areas to reduce the vulnerability of hollies, crops, livestock, and forests, to either overt or covert attack." Which set up the following wild, yet frighteningly possible scenario: Nuclear war breaks out. You and your family manage to survive it holed up in the storm shelter on your Kansas farm. Your crops even withstand the attack and resultant fallout. When you emerge from the storm cellar, you find a government official waiting for you. He instructs you that your farm is now charged with producing food for not just your own survival or to sell at the market, but to help feed a starving nation. By the way, the president said it's okay if the government just goes ahead and takes your crops from you when they come in. Oh, and here's a gun in case any commies try to steal or wreck your crop. Remember; shoot just the commies coming to steal your crop, and not your friendly neighborhood government officials who are allowed to take them for the good of the nation. Thanks, and have a nice day.

The next executive order, EO 10999, put perhaps an even more enormous task into the hands of the Secretary of Commerce. Here, Kennedy authorized the Secretary to:

"Prepare national emergency plans and develop preparedness programs covering: (a) Development and coordination of over-all policies, plans, and procedures for the provision of a centralized control of all modes of transportation in an emergency for the movement of passenger and freight traffic of all types, and the determination of the proper apportionment and allocation of the total civil transportation capacity, or any portion thereof, to meet over-all essential civil and military needs.

"(b) Federal emergency operational responsibilities with respect to: highways, roads, streets, bridges, tunnels, and appurtenances; highway traffic regulation; allocation of air carrier aircraft for essential military and civilian operations; ships in coastal and intercoastal use and ocean shipping, ports and port facilities;

and the Saint Lawrence Seaway; except those elements of each normally operated or controlled by the Department of Defense."

In essence, through that order Kennedy gave the Secretary of Commerce the ability to take command of any means or mode of transportation—from major U.S. highways and seaports all the way down to your personal car or boat—for the government's usage during a national emergency. As it read in Section 2 of EO 10999:

"The Secretary shall develop long range programs designed to integrate the mobilization requirements for movement of all forms of commerce with all forms of national and international transportation systems including air, ground, water, and pipelines, in an emergency; more particularly he shall: (a) Obtain, assemble, analyze, and evaluate data on the requirements of all claimants for all types of civil transportation to meet the needs of the military and of the civil economy…[(c)] and develop policies, standards and procedures for emergency enforcement of controls through the use of means such as education, incentives, embargoes, permits, sanctions, clemency policies, etc."

That only made sense as it followed directly from the previous two executive orders claiming the government's rights to all the fuel, power, and food within the country. If the government felt the need to commandeer all of those supplies, then they obviously would need a clear pathway to ship those goods to areas and people in need. By laying claim to your car, the major roadways could be cleared for the immediate transportation of these supplies (or for the tanks to roll to the battle front in the event of an invasion). If the country's shipping fleet was somehow decimated as it was in World War I, your personal watercraft may be needed by the government for a variety of shipping reasons. So, too, may be your personal aircraft. This was why in EO 11003 Kennedy gave similar powers to the Administrator of the Federal Aviation Agency in regards to all things that fly, and in EO 11005 the Interstate Commerce Commission was granted authority over all other modes of transportation (most importantly the railroads) as well as all "public storage." Desperate times may indeed call for desperate measures. Should you have a say in the confiscation of your personal car, boat, plane, or storage space? Of course. In fact, the idea of governmental confiscation shouldn't even be part of the equation, but when designing contingency plans, the government often left no stone unturned.

Though the Commerce Commission was tasked in EO 11005 with the operational capacities of the roadways, including the monitoring for the potential contamination as well as planning to control "conflicts" and "bottle-necks," the Secretary of Commerce was given sole ownership of the nation's roadways in Section 6 of EO 10999. More specifically he was to: "Develop plans for a national program…for technical guidance to States and direction of Federal activities relating to highway traffic control problems which may be created during an emergency; and plans for barricading and/or marking streets and highways, leading into or out of restricted fallout areas, for the protection of the public by external containment of traffic through hazardous areas." As an addendum to that, the Secretary was to "prepare and issue currently, as well as in an emergency, forecasts and estimates of areas likely to be covered by fallout in event of attack and make this information available to the Federal, State, and local authorities for public dissemination."

Two ideas stand out from this section of EO 10999. One, Kennedy and the rest of the federal government were serious about the potential outbreak of a nuclear war. The readiness status of the military was set to DEFCON 2 by October 1962 (DEFCON is shorthand for Defense Condition and DEFCON 1 would signify a shooting war). Frighteningly enough, according to author Alan F. Philips, MD, by the end of 1962 there were 14 near accidental starts to a nuclear war with the Russians. As that fact and the other executive orders surrounding it show, preparations were being made to deal with a truly coast-to-coast national disaster. Kennedy put some of the nation's best minds to work on determining what the ultimate results would be from nuclear fallout and how to recuperate from its effects. All of those preparations, from

* September 1st 1962
in Iceland

controlling food and fuel to transportation, Kennedy felt needed to be done *now*.

Secondly, tied to the after-effects of a nuclear war, was the ability to evacuate people from the most devastated and radioactive areas. Luckily, that precaution was never needed. The planning that evolved from EO 10999, however, aids in the mass evacuations that are not uncommon in the United States today. Careful planning has gone into the evacuation routes that lace the southeastern U.S. for use during hurricane season, leading people away from the shoreline to safer inland destinations. Certainly, there are numerous snafus that go hand-in-hand with these mass exoduses when they are called, but the previously devised routes simplify the process. Should some chemical or nuclear disaster actually befall the country, it is nice to know that (at least at some point in time) someone devised an evacuation plan for all of the major metropolitan areas, hopefully streamlining that process and ultimately saving numerous lives. While it may sound ominous that the government can take your car if need be, the logical extension of such an order is that in the event of an emergency control of the roads and by extension your car may keep you from driving into a potentially life threatening situation of which you were never even aware.

Though the Secretary of Commerce may be plotting a way to abscond with your Segway in times of need, in Executive Order 11000 the Secretary of Labor was granted the ability to run away with you, your spouse, or the both of you and order you to work for the government at its discretion. In this order, Kennedy proclaimed: "The Secretary of Labor…shall prepare national emergency plans and develop preparedness programs covering civilian manpower mobilization, more effective utilization of limited manpower resources including specialized personnel, wage and salary stabilization, worker incentives and protection, manpower resources and requirements, skill development and training, research, labor-management relations, and critical occupations." Granted, that was only to take effect in the event of a true national emergency, one that eliminated a large section of the population and by extension the national workforce which would then require every citizen to chip in to do their part to revitalize the nation's domestic output. To some extent though, this order took on the feel of turning the nation's citizens into a slave labor force.

As read in Section 2, the Secretary was to:

"Develop plans and issue guidance designed to utilize to the maximum extent civilian manpower resources….Such plans shall include, but not necessarily be limited to: Recruitment, selection and referral, training, employment stabilization (including appeals procedures), proper utilization, and determination of the skill categories critical to meeting the labor requirements of defense and essential civilian activities….Procedures for translating survival and production urgencies into manpower priorities to be used as guides for allocating available workers….Develop plans and procedures for wage and salary stabilization and for the national and field organization necessary for the administration of such a program in an emergency, including investigation, compliance and appeals procedures; statistical studies of wages, salaries and prices for policy decisions and to assist operating stabilization agencies to carry out their functions….Develop plans and procedures for wage and salary compensation and death and disability compensation for authorized civil defense workers and, as appropriate, measures for unemployment payments, re-employment rights, and occupational safety, and other protection and incentives for the civilian labor force during an emergency….Develop… plans and procedures including organization plans for the maintenance of effective labor-management relations during a national emergency." Now, we were fighting *against* communism, right?

Many of the ideas tucked away in this order flew in the face of not just the American worker, but most of the basic ideals upon which America was founded. Within this order we are confronted with the notion that every American worker could have been displaced from his or her current occupation and forced to work in whatever field was deemed appropriate and necessary, for whatever wage the government felt was proper, and with a limited amount of benefits (if any). Oddly enough, the Secretary of Labor in conjunction with the Secretary of Commerce were to "develop and maintain a list of critical occupations...with lists of essential activities as developed by the Department of Commerce...[and] develop policies applicable to the deferment of registrants whose employment in occupations or activities is necessary to the maintenance of the national health, safety, or interest." Curiously, there was no mention of what those "critical occupations" or "essential activities" were. Saving the country, albeit one that was looking more and more like the enemy she was likely fighting, was deemed the priority.

The good news, however, was that when President Kennedy was laying the groundwork for a complete upheaval of the American way of life, he hadn't forgotten about the children. In Executive Order 11001, directed to the Secretary of Health, Education, and Welfare, Kennedy made sure that schools were to remain open, even if it meant the seeding of some propaganda into the daily curriculum. "'Education,' as used in this order, means the utilization of formal public and private school systems, from elementary through college, for the dissemination of instructional material guidance, and training in the protection of life and property from enemy attack." The Secretary was told to "develop and issue through appropriate channels instructional materials and provide suggestions and guidance to assist schools, colleges, and other educational agencies to incorporate emergency protective measures and long-range civil defense concepts into their programs. This involves assistance to various levels of education to develop an understanding of the role of the individual, family, and community for civil defense in the nuclear age, as well as the maintenance of relations with educators, national and State education associations, foundations, and other related organizations to foster mutual understanding and support of civil defense activities." This meant more than just the "duck and cover" instructions as seen in old black and white film footage where clean cut school children run and hide under their desks as a mushroom cloud forms outside the school's window. Long-range plans were to be included and children were to be taught to understand their role in civil defense.

Aside from corrupting the nation's youth through various mind altering methodologies, the Secretary had a few other tasks to which he needed to attend. This included:

"Prepare plans to assure the provision of usable public water supplies for essential community uses in an emergency. This shall include inventorying existing supplies, developing new sources, performing research, setting standards, and planning distribution….Develop and coordinate programs of radiation measurement and assessment….Develop and coordinate programs for the prevention, detection, and identification of human exposure to chemical and biological warfare agents….Prepare national plans for emergency operations of vocational rehabilitation and related agencies, and for measures and resources necessary to rehabilitate and make available for employment those disabled persons among the surviving population….Development of medical means for the prevention and care of casualties (including those from thermonuclear weapons, radiation exposure, and biological and chemical warfare, as well as from other weapons)…" and last, but not least, "Restore the physical and mental health conditions of the civilian population."

To tag along with the ideas in the other executive orders that immediately preceded it, EO 11001 paved the way for the government to take over all schools and health care facilities during a national emergency. Combined with it was the ability to "claim materials, manpower, equipment, supplies and services needed to carry out assigned responsibilities and other essential functions" as well as stockpile such necessities. As go the food and fuel, so too goes the medical supplies and your children.

If the government was going to put these plans into effect in a post-nuclear war environment, how would it be able to if it didn't know where you were? Into that void would step the faithful

Postmaster General. In Executive Order 11002, Kennedy tasked the Postmaster General to "assist in the development of a national emergency registration system." Part of this, of course, was for the safety of the nation's civilians. As the order stated, the Postmaster General was to "assist in planning a national program and developing technical guidance for States, and directing Post Office activities concerned with registering persons and families for the purpose of receiving and answering welfare inquiries, and reuniting families in civil defense emergencies." That could be a lifesaving measure. Essentially, it would be able to locate you and get emergency supplies—the proper amount thanks to the census designed by this program—to you and the others surviving in your home town. Perhaps even more importantly, at least to your mental well being, it could help you find your loved ones, or your loved ones find you after some sort of disaster. Who can argue with the need and want for that?

What was left unstated in this order was that the registration program was also designed to keep tabs on everyone, and to be able to locate whomever, for whatever reason, as needed. Don't want to work in that federally mandated job? Thanks to the Postmaster General, the government would be able to find you. Don't want to send your child to some new fangled government run school? The government would know little Johnny's missing and where to find him. Far-fetched? Perhaps, yet the order did lay the groundwork for such a system.

Piling on top of that notion was what is found in Executive Order 11004. The Housing and Home Finance Administrator "shall prepare national emergency plans and develop preparedness programs covering all aspects of lodging or housing and community facilities related thereto." This included: "Develop plans for the construction and management of new housing and the community facilities related thereto, when and where it is determined to be necessary with public funds through direct Federal action; or the construction of new housing through financial or credit assistance, in support of production programs…[and] plans for the selection, acquisition, development, and disposal of areas for civilian uses in new, expanded, restored, or relocated communities; and for the construction of housing for new or restored communities." Notice that "relocation" was included within that plan. Granted, should your home city be the target of a nuclear explosion, you may want to relocate on your own no matter the state of the housing market, but that was not how the order was worded. Under the heading "Population movement" it was written: "Participate in the preparation of plans for determining which areas are to be restored and in the development and coordination of plans for the movement of people on a temporary basis from areas to be abandoned to areas where housing is available or can be made available." There was no specification as to why certain "areas [are] to be abandoned." They just were. Such ambiguous wording allowed them to be abandoned at will. Couple that notion with the federal registration program as dictated in EO 11002 and what kind of power over the nation's populace did the government have?

Of course, that sort of almost dictatorial power wasn't (hopefully) planned in the writing of these orders. In further reading of EO 11004, the true nature of the president's order comes to the forefront. The main thrust was to set up some sort of system to help massive waves of people recover their homes or build new ones. This included: "develop plans for the emergency repair and restoration to use of damaged housing, for the construction and management of emergency housing units and the community facilities related thereto, and for the emergency conversion to dwelling use of non-residential structures with public funds through direct Federal action or through financial or credit assistance….Assist in the development of plans to encourage the construction of fallout shelters for both old and new housing in conformance to the national shelter policy…[and] the development of preparedness measures involving emergency financing, real estate credit, and rent stabilization." It would be hard to imagine what the repercussions would be from several major metropolitan areas becoming wastelands after a nuclear war. Where and how to house the survivors would be immediate questions in need of answers. In any sort of survival situation, shelter is a primary concern.

Not surprisingly, in thinking of potential wartime needs, the president thought not just of housing the civilians, but the military as well. Little did the population realize, but under the right circumstances, they would be the ones to shelter their own soldiers. Written into EO 11004 was the ability for billeting which is the civilian housing of the army. This was a practice not seen since the Civil War. Now with Kennedy's order, he was willing to bring it back into practice if the situation called. If the war was to be fought in America, among American neighborhoods, then perhaps it would be necessary for Americans to shelter their soldiers within the confines of their own homes as well. Whether you'd be open and willing to participate in such a program, well…that wouldn't be your decision to make.

On that fateful February day in 1962, President Kennedy outlined a plan through those 10 executive orders to allow the federal government to basically take over every aspect of modern American life in the event of war or a national emergency. Congress was not involved. They had no say. The Supreme Court wasn't asked to interpret these orders. They had no say. The people, the ones who would be the most directly impacted by these orders, had no say. Kennedy simply demanded it to be done. Once ordered, there was no turning back.

Even more frightening was considering the circumstances that surrounded Kennedy's presidency at the time, war was not a farfetched notion. How widespread and devastating such a war would be was unknown. Kennedy, attempting to predict the future, devised those executive orders to set his staff in motion to combat and counteract any and all contingencies. Would implementation of those plans overstep their constitutional bounds? Without a doubt. Would those knowingly extra-constitutional arrangements even be necessary? Who was to say? Perhaps should war have broken out, the government may not have needed to install such overreaching actions into their response to the crisis. Perhaps the national response would've fallen well short of suspending the Constitution. Perhaps it wouldn't have. Perhaps, given the proper situation, government control over certain aspects of society would've been greatly needed to survive such a war. Even if those measures did just accomplish their intended duty, who was to say how long those powers were to last? There was no built in cut-off date or time frame in any of those orders. The government could have retained those powers as long as they wished, as long as the "national emergency" lasted, which as we saw with FDR's original declaration, was well over 40 years. Did Kennedy and those who helped him draft those orders realize that?

A little over six months after Kennedy issued those 10 executive orders, he began to realize the overwhelming amount of information that was generated from them. As the various secretaries reported to the president on a multitude of subjects, the president was becoming more deeply embroiled in the Cuban situation which would reach its nadir in October 1962. To perhaps better focus his attention on Castro and less on the state of emergency preparedness within the nation, Kennedy issued Executive Order 11051 on September 27, 1962. Titled "Prescribing Responsibilities of the Office of Emergency Planning in the Executive Office of the President," this order created a new position—the Director of the Office of Emergency Planning. In essence, Kennedy was shirking the duty he originally took on in those previous 10 executive orders and dumped the associated responsibility onto this new position. This was not a cushy post. Working out of the executive office, the director, among other sundry tasks, had to:

"Maintain, with the participation and support of Federal agencies concerned, a national resources evaluation capability for predicting and monitoring the status of resources under all degrees of emergency, for identifying resource deficiencies and feasible production programs and for supplying resource evaluations at national and subordinate levels to support mobilization base planning, continuity of government, resource management and economic recovery...."

"Advise the President concerning the strategic relocation of industries, services, government and economic activities, the operations of which are essential to the nation's security. He shall coordinate the efforts of Federal agencies with respect to the application of the principle of geographic dispersal of certain industrial facilities, both government-and privately-owned, in the interest of national defense...."

"Advise and assist the President with respect to the need for stockpiling various items essential to the survival of the population, additional to food and medical supplies, and with respect to programs for the acquisition, storage, and maintenance of such stockpiles."

Some of these duties—such as the relocation of certain industries, services, etc. for strategic purposes—had previously been prescribed to various secretaries, but now were to be under the director's watchful eye. Adding to that, the director was given the reigns over the nation's telecommunications in accordance with Kennedy's EO 10995. Also, the director was to "[develop] in association with interested agencies, the emergency planning, including making recommendations to the President as to the appropriate roles of Federal agencies, in currently unassigned matters, such as, but not necessarily limited to, economic stabilization, economic warfare, emergency information, and wartime censorship...." Proving once again that when push came to shove, the government was going to pull out all the stops necessary to win.

Should the general havoc associated with the outbreak of war or a national emergency actually come to pass, the new director was the person to turn to with any needs or questions. He was effectively the quarterback running the nation's fire drill when the time came with some obvious exceptions left under the president's direct control. The director was to know it all—where the emergency stockpiles were, how they were to be distributed, where the proper authorities should be sent, etc. He would be allowed to implement the various plans and contingencies that grew out of Kennedy's 10 executive orders. Whether he had enough green lights at his disposal or not, we'll thankfully never know. A shooting war with Cuba or the Soviet Union never began.

Even as that threat level began to subside, Kennedy didn't leave the idea of emergency preparations on the back burner. He continued to secure the nation by issuing another set of executive orders that delegated emergency authorities to various secretaries and administrators that were overlooked, forgotten, or simply not considered during the initial go-around. On February 26, 1963, nearly a year to the date after the original 10 were issued, Kennedy published another group of nine executive orders. Numbered 11087 through 11095, these orders, when compared with the first 10, were rather benign. This is not to say that much of the wording and instructions read differently. Inside these nine orders were still the ideas and headings like "claimancy" and "stockpiling." What was different was that instead of granting authorities and powers that seem overreaching, these nine orders instruct the proper persons to begin devising some sort of emergency plans that cover their respective sphere of influence. There was less a sense of immediacy within the language of the latter set of orders and more of a general prodding to get that contingency planning in motion.

What follows is a list of these nine orders and to whom they were directed:

- EO 11087 – Emergency Preparedness Functions to the Secretary of State
- EO 11088 – Emergency Preparedness Functions to the Secretary of Treasury
- EO 11089 – Emergency Preparedness Functions to the Atomic Energy Commission
- EO 11090 – Emergency Preparedness Functions to the Civil Aeronautics Board

- EO 11091 – Emergency Preparedness Functions to the Civil Service Commission
- EO 11092 - Emergency Preparedness Functions to the Federal Communications Commission
- EO 11093 - Emergency Preparedness Functions to the Administrator of General Services
- EO 11094 – Emergency Preparedness Functions to the Board of Governors of the Federal Trade Reserve System, the Federal Home Loan Bank Board, the Farm Credit Administration, the Export-Import Bank of Washington, the Board of Directors of the Federal Deposit Insurance Corporation, the Securities and Exchange Commission, the Administrator of the Small Business Administration, the Administrator of Veterans Affairs
- EO 11095 – Emergency Preparedness Functions to the Board of Directors of the Tennessee Valley Authority, the Railroad Retirement Board, the Administrator of the National Aeronautics and Space Administration, the Federal Power Commission, the Director of the National Science Foundation

While it may seem odd that the likes of NASA or the Railroad Retirement Board needed to consider emergency preparation plans, posts with the stature of Secretary of State mandated such plans. Why some of these influential positions were ignored in Kennedy's first 10 executive orders on the subject isn't known. Perhaps it was because the original 10 dealt primarily with matters of national infrastructure, thus would be more immediately demanded of in a national emergency. With such an importance placed over matters of the economy today, it's surprising to find that the financial sector wasn't considered until the Secretary of Treasury was tapped in EO 11088 and major monetary players such as the Federal Reserve Trade System and the SEC until EO 11094. One would think that if one has control of the money, everything else would follow, but the monetary system wasn't addressed in that original set of orders; food, energy, and shelter were. Perhaps Kennedy did know what the nation's priorities would have been given a true emergency.

While the Cold War between the two superpowers that spurred all 19 of those orders continued unabated well into the 1980's, Kennedy's emergency preparations were never to be implemented. That doesn't mean they vanished. Certainly, as we've seen with the examples of the Emergency Alert System and mass evacuations, some of those emergency preparations have been utilized to the benefit of countless millions. Meanwhile the other plans—including the ones that may relocate you and your family while putting you to work doing what the government deems best—still sat on the books, ready to go "if need be." They were not forgotten.

Nixon's Turn

Much has been made in the conspiracy circles of President Richard Nixon's Executive Order 11490. Granted, Nixon had one of the more interesting terms of any recent president to sit in the White House, and that's prior to his near impeachment over the Watergate scandal. Even a cursory look at his time in office reveals that, among other national issues, he dealt with the officially undeclared war in Vietnam, opened up negotiations with communist China, and all the while had the underground hippie culture nipping at his heels, calling for his head. Volumes have been written by, and about, the man, but it's this one executive order that often riles up some people. Most likely it's because they never sat down and read it.

Many feel EO 11490 further set up a system within the federal government that would allow for the president to strip away American citizen's fundamental rights while granting himself dictatorial powers. In a sense, that was true. These same folks would further claim, however, that Nixon *intentionally* did this. That he granted himself these emergency powers because he was ready to create his own emergency and in effect seize control of the country. Some even postulate this executive order tied directly to the Watergate scandal and the impeachment proceedings that followed. Never mind the fact that the Watergate break-in occurred in 1972, and Nixon didn't resign under related suspicions until mid-1974, while EO 11490 was signed into being nearly five years earlier, in October 1969. Coincidentally (or not) the Nixon Administration had secretly placed U.S. nuclear forces on alert at this exact same moment in time. Amazingly, not even the Chairman of the Joint Chiefs of Staff was told why this was done, and to date no researcher has been able to discern exactly why this alert was issued. Did the one event begat the other? No one seems to know.

What Nixon's EO 11490 really did was rewrite Kennedy's previously issued 19 executive orders pertaining to national emergencies, making them null and void. Instead of separating his executive orders and directing them at their intended secretary or administrator, Nixon complied all of this information into one lengthy piece. As he wrote under "Purpose": "This order consolidates the assignment of emergency preparedness functions to various departments and agencies heretofore contained in the 21 Executive orders and 2 Defense Mobilization orders….Assignments have been adjusted to conform to changes in organization which have occurred subsequent to the issuance of those Executive orders and Defense Mobilization orders." This was an update more than anything else. Nixon did not completely destroy what Kennedy had created because his original ideas were seen as sensible and necessary. Nixon even retained the Kennedy-created Office of Emergency Preparedness and its post of director to oversee these plans. As America's place within the world continued to change, so too did the nation's emergency plans.

Nixon expanded on why this was necessary in the order's introduction: "Whereas our national security is dependent upon our ability to assure continuity of government, at every level, in any national emergency type situation that might conceivably confront the nation; and

"Whereas effective national preparedness planning to meet

such an emergency, including a massive nuclear attack, is essential to our national survival; and

"Whereas effective national preparedness planning requires the identification of functions that would have to be performed during such an emergency, the assignment of responsibility for developing plans for performing these functions, and the assignment of responsibility for developing the capability to implement those plans; and

"Whereas the Congress has directed the development of such national emergency preparedness plans and has provided funds for the accomplishment thereof; and   "Whereas   this   national emergency preparedness planning activity has been an established program of the United States Government for more than twenty years…."

Before delving into Nixon's reorganization of Kennedy's emergency plans, let us touch on an aspect of the government's emergency strategy that Nixon mentions in passing: Continuity of Government. This concept will be discussed in much greater detail later, but since Nixon touches upon it, some clarification is in order. Continuity of Government is simply the federal government's plans to keep itself operational during any and all national emergencies. The worry was should something (or some nation) cut off the government's operational head, the rest of the country would wither and die without it. While that is a debatable point, for those in power, there was no such debate. The government needed to continue to not just operate, but effectively manage and rule as it did prior to the outbreak of any such emergency.

In the world of Nixon's executive order, the concept of COG and emergency planning were tied closely together, if not one in the same. Whether the government could, as Nixon requested, "assure continuity of government, at every level, in any national emergency type situation that might conceivably confront the nation" was an entirely different question. The task at hand was to attempt to do so to the best of each of the federal government's departments' ability. What follows is a bit of Nixon's demands:

"(a) This order is concerned with the emergency national planning and preparedness functions of the several departments and agencies of the Federal Government which complement the military readiness planning responsibilities of the Department of Defense; together, these measures provide the basic foundation for our overall national preparedness posture, and are fundamental to our ability to survive.

"(b) The departments and agencies of the Federal Government are hereby severally charged with the duty of assuring the continuity of the Federal Government in any national emergency type situation that might confront the nation. To this end, each department and agency with essential functions, whether expressly identified in this order or not, shall develop such plans and take such actions, including but not limited to those specified in this order, as may be necessary to assure that it will be able to perform its essential functions, and continue as a viable part of the Federal Government, during any emergency that might conceivably occur. These include plans for maintaining the continuity of essential functions of the department or agency at the seat of government and elsewhere, through programs concerned with:

"(1) succession to office;

"(2) predelegation of emergency authority;

"(3) safekeeping of essential records;

"(4) emergency relocation sites supported by communications and required services;

"(5) emergency action steps;

"(6) alternate headquarters or command facilities; and

"(7) protection of Government resources, facilities, and personnel....

"(c) In addition to the activities indicated above, the heads of departments and agencies...of this order shall:

"(1) prepare national emergency plans, develop preparedness programs, and attain an appropriate state of readiness with respect to the functions assigned to them in this order for all conditions of national emergency;

"(2) give appropriate consideration to emergency preparedness factors in the conduct of the regular functions of their agencies, particularly those functions considered essential in time of emergency, and

"(3) be prepared to implement, in the event of an emergency, all appropriate plans developed under this order."

Does that read like the maniacal plan of an evil mastermind? Or does it sound downright rational? If one believes in truth, justice, and the American way, creating logical and sensible plans to not just save the government, but to save the government so it can in turn save American citizens makes perfect sense. It was perhaps within the realms of this plan's potential implementation where one can begin to see cracks in that patriotic façade. For even though Nixon's executive order replaced Kennedys' previous 19 orders, Kennedy's orders provided an excellent base upon which to build.

Interestingly, Nixon organized the bulk of EO 11490 not by some self ascribed priority or national importance, but rather by each secretary's position in the presidential line of succession. Hence, the first person tasked was the Secretary of State. Most of the Secretary's assignments seemed fitting for the post. He was instructed to:

"Provide to all other departments and agencies overall foreign policy direction, coordination, and supervision in the formulation and execution of those emergency preparedness activities which have foreign policy implications, affect foreign relations, or depend directly or indirectly, on the policies and capabilities of the Department of State. The Secretary of State shall develop policies, plans, and procedures for carrying out his responsibilities in the conduct of the foreign relations of the United States under conditions of national emergency, including, but not limited to

"(1) the formulation and implementation, in consultation with the Department of Defense and other appropriate agencies, and the negotiation of contingency and post-emergency plans with our allies and of the intergovernmental agreements and arrangements required by such plans;

"(2) formulation, negotiation, and execution of policy affecting the relationships of the United States with neutral States;

"(3) formulation and execution of political strategy toward hostile or enemy States, including the definition of war objectives and the political means for achieving those objectives;

"(4) maintenance of diplomatic and consular representation abroad;

"(5) reporting and advising on conditions overseas which bear upon the national emergency…"

That's pretty much the Secretary's job description, isn't it? Whether in a state of emergency or not, the Secretary of State meets with heads of state—be they allies, enemies, or neutral factions—on a regular basis. The idea was to have back-up plans available to keep those lines of communications open when and if real problems develop. That should mean more than just having the Kremlin's number on the secretary's cell phone.

There's a little more to the position than just meetings, however. The Secretary was also tasked with such duties as "(9) protection or evacuation of American citizens and nationals abroad and safeguarding their property; (10) protection and/or control of international organization and foreign diplomatic, consular, and other official personnel and property, or other assets, in the United States; (11) documentary control of persons seeking to enter or leave the United States; and (12) regulation and control of exports of items on the munitions list." This was potentially a much touchier subject. The secretary was charged with protecting Americans serving and living overseas as well as foreigners residing here in the U.S. That included domestic ambassadors spread out across the globe and the world's ambassadors stationed within our borders. Given the right set of circumstances, the secretary was either supposed to be able to extract our citizens from a foreign hot spot (like the evacuation of Saigon at the end of the Vietnam conflict) or potentially detain or expel foreign representatives residing within the United States. Not only that, but the secretary had overriding control over whether anyone could or could not enter or exit the United States. Want to leave the country because of the national emergency? Maybe you won't be allowed to go. Or were you outside the country when war broke out and you just want to return home? Maybe you'll be stuck where you are. All of these decisions were, and still are, ultimately the Secretary of State's call. These tasks are simply part of the job no matter the state of declared emergency.

The second secretary mentioned in EO 11490 was the Secretary of the Treasury who had a little extra put onto his emergency planning plate. He was to:

"Develop policies, plans and procedures for the performance of emergency functions with respect to

"(1) stabilization aspects of the monetary, credit, and financial system;

"(2) stabilization of the dollar in relation to foreign currencies;

"(3) collection of revenue;

"(4) regulation of financial institutions;

"(5) supervision of the Federal depository system;

"(6) direction of transactions in government securities;

"(7) tax and debt policies;

"(8) participation in bilateral and multilateral financial arrangements with foreign governments;

"(9) regulation of foreign assets in the United States and of foreign financial dealings (in consultation with the Secretaries of State and Commerce);

"(10) development of procedures for the manufacture and/or issuance and redemption of securities, stamps, coins, and currency;

"(11) development of systems for the issuance and payment of Treasury checks;

"(12) maintenance of the central government accounting and financial reporting system;

"(13) administration of customs laws, tax laws, and laws on control of alcohol, alcoholic beverages, tobacco, and firearms…"

Because when all hell breaks loose and nuclear bombs are falling, one should really be concerned with the collection of taxes on alcohol and tobacco.

In all seriousness, the job laid out before the Secretary of the Treasury was near impossible without completely trampling on both citizen's rights and the Constitution. Even then, the job may not have been remotely feasible. Think stabilization of the dollar is easy? Or the stabilization of any credit of financial system is completely possible? Just look at the circumstances that occurred in 2008-2009. When lenders collapsed the housing market and took with them several of the world's largest credit lenders, the stock market went haywire. Along with it, energy and fuel prices plummeted while the value of the dollar fluctuated wildly. Could the Secretary of the Treasury stop that and stabilize the situation even with the multi-trillion dollar bailout? Of course not as those incredibly intertwined market trends were out of the secretary's, or anyone's, complete control. Now consider a similar scenario, but caused and complicated by the outbreak of a war—which may become a worldwide nuclear war—or some other truly national emergency. Guess who would have control of the nation's money? The Secretary of the Treasury. Would anyone assigned such a post and facing a nationwide disaster really have the ability to stabilize the nation's wealth? The conditions that brought on the national emergency would be highly unpredictable and volatile. Any plans made ahead of time could be rendered instantly worthless. One would be better off with a stash of cash hidden away in a mattress than have it out in the Secretary of the Treasury's hands at that point.

While you might not suspect it, Nixon placed his own life in the Secretary of the Treasury's hands. The Secret Service was overseen by the Treasury Department at that time. When first incorporated after the conclusion of the Civil War, the Secret Service was charged with combating the counterfeit currency that flooded the country, hence it's placement under the Secretary of the Treasury's control. It wasn't until about 40 years later, after the assassination of President William McKinley, that the Secret

Service began full time protection the president. Congress didn't authorize the Secret Service to assume the responsibility of guarding the president officially until 1913. Ninety years later, the Department of Homeland Security swallowed the Secret Service, taking its authority away from the Treasury Department. When Nixon devised this executive order in 1969, his protection remained in the secretary's hands. Oddly enough, that wasn't the top duty on the secretary's list. It was listed as the 15th. Apparently the stabilization of the monetary, credit, and financial systems as well as the collection of alcohol, tobacco, and firearm taxes was more important than Nixon's own life.

Next in line in Nixon's executive order was someone that Kennedy completely ignored in his 19 emergency planning Executive Orders, the Secretary of Defense. Kennedy did issue Executive Order 10952 on July 20, 1961, in which he directed the Secretary of Defense to strengthen the nation's civil defense program. His order included developing: "(i) a fallout shelter program; (ii) a chemical, biological and radiological warfare defense program; (iii) all steps necessary to warn or alert Federal military and civilian authorities, State officials and the civilian population, (iv) all functions pertaining to communications, including a warning network, reporting on monitoring, instructions to shelters and communications between authorities, (v) emergency assistance to State and local governments in a postattack period, including water, debris, fire, health, traffic police and evacuation capabilities…." There was no mention of emergency preparedness. Nixon, however, did not keep the Secretary of Defense out of the loop.

One of the Secretary's commands was to "advise and assist the Office of Emergency Preparedness in the development and review of standards for the strategic location and physical security of industries, services, government, and other activities for which continuing operation is essential to national security, and exercise physical security cognizance over the facilities assigned to him for such purpose." Once again, as in Kennedy's orders, the idea of dispersing the nation's strategic reserves and production facilities was brought into play. With Nixon, though, this went beyond just manufacturing plants and fuel reserves to include the actual government itself. Hinting at COG plans not yet revealed this included not just alternate bases of operation, but evacuation plans and the protection of government officials by military officers.

Included within such alternate sites of government operations was the ability for those in power to communicate which each other no matter the situation. This is an essential element to all COG operations. Because of this need, the Secretary was directed to "advise on existing communications facilities and furnish military requirements for commercial communications facilities and services in planning for and in event of an emergency, including an attack on the United States." If the national contingency plan would spread out government officials at various locales across the nation, it's rather obvious at some point in time they would need to communicate with each other to coordinate a response. Interestingly, the Secretary was directed to work with private commercial interests to accomplish this. It wasn't a strict military or government project, but one to be collaborated upon with the likes of AT&T. Prior to cell phones and wi-fi networks, the government needed to use commercial telephone lines to transmit some of its most sensitive communications. In order to secure those essential briefings, it was necessary to reinforce the existing communication networks available not just to the government, but to the general public as well because they were often one in the same. Not that the common man would have had access to those lines in the event of an emergency, but it's nice to know that the infrastructure improvements helped us all.

In fact, the internet was a construct of the Cold War era. The Department of Defense (DOD) originally developed a precursor to the internet in order to maintain contact between its various bases of operation, including the government's top secret relocation sites. They began to realize in a nuclear war most traditional methods of communication would fail despite their best efforts. Yet continual communication would be a vital aspect for both retaliating and reorganizing in a post-nuclear war environment. Being able to exchange information electronically through fiber optic lines which were impermeable to the electro-magnetic pulses (EMPs) created by nuclear explosions would give the nation an advantage the enemy did not possess. It wasn't until decades later when the DOD had created a vast network of this infantile internet across the nation that the public was given access to those lines.

Interspersed within these mundane points of order to the Secretary of Defense were a couple of odd inclusions. For one, the Secretary was to "develop plans and procedure to carry out Department of Defense responsibilities stated in the National Censorship Agreement between the Department of Defense and the Office of Emergency Preparedness." There was a National Censorship Agreement? Yep. Actually, there was an Office of Censorship, too. E.J. Quindlen was the Assistant Director for Government Preparedness which was run out of the Office of Emergency Preparedness. In mid-1972, he testified before Congress on this very point, having been assigned that task as a direct result of EO 11490. As Quindlen stated to Congress:

"Upon my assumption of responsibility for this program in 1969, I moved to have its designation changed to the wartime information security program, as this term more appropriately describes the objectives of the program. When we discuss wartime information security, it is in a relatively narrow connotation and has nothing to do with the control of news at its source. We do not consider the term 'censorship' applicable to a situation where press and broadcast releases are covered by a code which is completely voluntary. The wartime information security program is the technical mechanism where international mail, telecommunications, and travelers can be controlled and where the domestic public media can cooperate in avoiding giving information to the enemy by adhering to a voluntary code which describes categories of information which could be of help to an enemy in prosecuting a war against this Nation."

That was a very truthful statement. The withholding of certain sensitive information from public dissemination may very well help save the country.

When one reads the original "Basic Plan for the Office of Censorship" though, what could be considered as "sensitive information" was rather open for interpretation. As the plan pointed out under the section heading "Definitions," it defined "Communication" as "The term 'communication' shall include any letter or book, plan, map, or other paper, picture, sound recording or other reproduction, telegram, cablegram, wireless message or conversation transmitted over wire, radio, television, optical or other electromagnetic system, and any message transmitted by any signaling device or any other means." To be clear, that was basically every form of communication with the exception of two people speaking face-to-face.

The next phrase defined was "rational censorship." That was "the control and examination of communications entering, leaving, transiting, or touching the borders of the United States and the voluntary withholding from publication by the domestic public media industries of military and other information which should not be released in the interest of the safety and defense of the United States and its allies." So, that, too, could basically be anything and everything, depending on who was doing the monitoring and the controlling. And they called that "rational."

Even so, it was not to be confused with "public media censorship" which was "the voluntary cooperation of the domestic press, publishing, broadcasting and motion picture industries in withholding from publication military and other information which should not be released in the interest of the safety and defense of the United States and its allies" or "telecommunications censorship" which was "within the scope of national censorship the control and examination of communications transmitted or received over the circuits of commercial communications companies classified by the Federal Communications Commission as 'common carriers' and not under the control, use, supervision or inspection of a Federal agency." What did that leave out then? Nothing. Nearly every form or variation of communication—as well as the message being sent—could fall under the umbrella of the Office of Censorship, no matter how Mr. Quindlen defended it. Given a national emergency, be it a war or not, letting such an ill-defined program loose could do more damage than good.

That was not all the Secretary of Defense had at his disposal thanks to Nixon. The final two bullet points Nixon included in EO 11490 were "(26) Develop with the Department of Transportation and Federal Communications Commission plans and programs for the control of air traffic, civil and military, during an emergency. (27) Develop with the Federal Communications Commission and the Office of Telecommunications Management (OEP) plans and programs for the emergency control of all devices capable of emitting electromagnetic radiation."

Clearly Number 26 harkened back to Kennedy's willingness to give control of your personal vehicle to the government in times of emergency. Although one wouldn't think that the Secretary of Defense needed the president's go-ahead to control military air traffic, with civilian air traffic, it would be a different story. As seen during the events of 9/11 when all civilian and commercial aircraft were ordered to clear the skies, that power actually came into play to the nation's benefit.

Turning to Number 27, a new wrinkle was added to what was in a sense a reiteration the Communications Act of 1934. This variation on the act now allowed the government to seize control of all communication devices—not just broadcasting stations—including personally owned TVs, radios, and phones (and if invented at the time, cell phones, personal computers, and iPods) since all such devices emit electromagnetic radiation. Don't want to bother initiating the Office of Censorship in some sensitive matter? Then just seize control of not only the broadcasting media, but every citizen's personal communication device as well. Then whatever message needed to be suppressed would be. Problem solved. Or so the thinking seemed to indicate.

A question may have risen in your mind by now asking, is all of this legal? Could the president, and by extension, the federal government actually do these things? Well, you wouldn't have been alone. For Nixon again tapped another cabinet member that Kennedy overlooked—the Attorney General. One of Nixon's primary concerns was the legality of all of this. In EO 11490, he put it on the Attorney General's shoulders to smooth out all potential legal issues. Nixon wrote:

"(2) Industry support. As appropriate, review the legal procedures developed by the Federal agencies concerned to be instituted if it becomes necessary for the Government to institute extraordinary measures with respect to vital production facilities, public facilities, communications systems, transportation systems, or other facility, system, or service essential to national survival.

"(3) Judicial and legislative liaison. In cooperation with the Office of Emergency Preparedness, maintain liaison with Federal courts and with the Congress so there will be mutual understanding of Federal emergency plans involving law enforcement and the exercise of legal powers during emergencies of various magnitudes.

"(4) Legal advice. Develop emergency plans for providing legal advice to the President, the Cabinet, and the heads of Executive departments and agencies wherever they may be located in an emergency, and provide emergency procedures for the review as to form and legality of Presidential proclamations, Executive orders, directives, regulations, and documents, and of other documents requiring approval by the President or by the Attorney General which may be issued by authorized officers after an armed attack."

In writing these orders to the Attorney General, Nixon didn't seem confident that the powers granted via those emergency measures were in fact legal or constitutional. When he instructed the Attorney General to "maintain liaison with Federal courts and with the Congress so there will be mutual understanding of Federal emergency plans involving law enforcement and the exercise of legal powers during emergencies," one gets the sense that Nixon was directing the Attorney General to get everyone working on the same page so there wouldn't be any problematic questions in some future time of crisis. Questions like, "Can the government legally do this?" Otherwise why would there be a need for a "mutual understanding" if everything was lawful? If the law stated that the president can do something during an emergency, then he should be allowed to when the time comes with no questions needed. It wasn't as if Nixon was asking the Attorney General to explain or clarify some of those issues for Congress or the courts, he was effectively saying, "Make sure they all know what I say I can do." That was the point. While Congress did provide the funds for emergency preparedness planning, it couldn't activate this executive order or the plans included within it, only the president could.

From this point forward, Nixon's EO 11490 reads much like Kennedy's previously discussed 19 orders. With the same basic instructions, responsibilities, and sometimes, extraordinary abilities granted to the Secretaries of Labor, Transportation, Commerce, etc. Occasionally an odd command cropped up within the remainder of the order, such as the development of plans to continue both Social Security and Medicare in a post-nuclear attack environment, the need for "rapid restoration and resumption of education at all levels after an attack," plans for "the acquisition, decentralization, and distribution of emergency supplies of currency," the weaponization of NASA, and the creation of "a nationwide system of post-attack registration of Federal employees to provide a means for locating and returning to duty those employees who become physically separated from their agencies after an enemy attack, and to provide for the maximum utilization of the skills of surviving employees."

Perhaps the most important duty out of all of those assigned in EO 11490 went to the General Services Administration (GSA). The GSA's normal agenda was control of all federal buildings and property, but Nixon ordered its workers to "develop emergency procedures for providing and making available, on a decentralized basis, a Federal Register of Presidential Proclamations and

Executive Orders, Federal administrative regulations, Federal emergency notices and actions, and Acts of Congress during a national emergency." In other words, create a system to let the people know what laws their federal government passed during a national emergency. Once it was safe to come out of hiding, it would be nice if the people could discover what was now legal or illegal and what new powers the president had awarded himself.

Nixon's EO 11490 would sit and languish on the record without an emergency situation occurring to test it. Aside from President Ford giving Nixon's order a minor tweaking in 1976 (most of Ford's additions or amendments were minor housekeeping issues, such as the change in name of the Office of Emergency Preparedness to the new Federal Preparedness Agency), this order would be the federal government's basic emergency guideline for nearly 20 years. All of that money spent, all of those plans created, and all of the public's concerns regarding its implementation would be for naught. It wouldn't be until Ronald Reagan had one foot out the door of the Oval Office that these plans would receive a much needed update.

Reagan (and Obama) Make it Simple

On November 18, 1988, just a scant few days after George H.W. Bush was elected to succeed him, Ronald Reagan issued three executive orders. One, EO 12658, established the President's Commission on Catastrophic Nuclear Accidents. Another, EO 12657, tasked the Federal Emergency Management Agency (FEMA) with preparing emergency plans surrounding commercial nuclear power plants. Lastly, in EO 12656, President Reagan decided it was high time someone updated Nixon's ideas as stated in EO 11490 just in case something like a nuclear war suddenly broke out.

Simply titled "Assignment of Emergency Preparedness Responsibilities," Reagan's EO 12656 officially rendered Nixon's previous emergency planning executive order moot. Nearly two decades had passed since EO 11490 and without a doubt the world had changed. So, too, had the make-up of the federal government.

New departments had replaced old (like FEMA taking over for the Office of Emergency Planning) and within all of those shake-ups, emergency planning had either been placed on the back burner or completely forgotten. Reagan was to remedy that situation.

What is perhaps the most interesting part of EO 12656 was the general blandness of the writing. It began with a nearly identical, word-for-word introduction as which accompanied Nixon's EO 11490. While it directed many of the same secretaries, administrations, and directors with the similar tasks as before, Reagan's EO 12656 did so with a limited vocabulary and a general vagueness not present in either Kennedy's or Nixon's orders. On the surface, it appeared to be benign. Gone were the outright demands and abilities to lay claim to personal vehicles or to the nation's farms or to force people into labor. Instead were notions of working together, compromise, and the nation's best interest. Despite this change in verbiage, Reagan's executive order is worth further investigation.

Once Reagan was finished copying forward Nixon's introduction and reasoning for issuing his version of the order, he wrote the order's preamble which read as follows: "Section   101. National Security Emergency Preparedness Policy. (a) The policy of the United States is to have sufficient capabilities at all levels of government to meet essential defense and civilian needs during any national security emergency. A national security emergency is any occurrence, including natural disaster, military attack, technological emergency, or other emergency, that seriously degrades or seriously threatens the national security of the United States. Policy for national security emergency preparedness shall be established by the President. Pursuant to the President's direction, the National Security Council shall be responsible for developing and administering such policy. All national security emergency preparedness activities shall be consistent with the Constitution and laws of the United States and with preservation of the constitutional government of the United States. (b) Effective national security emergency preparedness planning requires:

identification of functions that would have to be performed during such an emergency; development of plans for performing these functions; and development of the capability to execute those plans….This Order addresses national security emergency preparedness functions and activities. As used in this Order, preparedness functions and activities include, as appropriate, policies, plans, procedures, and readiness measures that enhance the ability of the United States Government to mobilize for, respond to, and recover from a national security emergency."

There were a couple of clear differences immediately noticeable between Reagan's order and what came before it. For one, Reagan didn't simply call these incidents "national emergencies" but rather "national security emergencies." A subtle, yet profound difference. An emergency is one thing, but something threatening "national security" is completely different. National security is the government's top priority. It is national security that keeps records on everything from the Kennedy assassination to some of the files requested for this very book and everything else in between still hidden from the public's view. You and your personal rights may be sacrificial, but national security never is. It is amazing how the addition of one simple word can alter both the definition of something as well as the immediate response to it.

Luckily for us, Reagan took the time to define what such a national security emergency might consist of, defining it in a roundabout way as something either natural or man-made that "seriously degrades or seriously threatens the national security of the United States." Though far from being specific, Reagan defined the term more specifically than any previous president. Kennedy and Nixon both left it simply to a "massive attack" or other emergency. Neither stated in a straightforward way how such an incident could and likely would affect national security. All of that was left to be assumed from what followed in each order. Reagan, while leaving a lot of wiggle room within his definition, made this perfectly clear. He even included the new category of a technological emergency, something neither Kennedy nor Nixon had to consider.

Another clear delineation Reagan made that his predecessors did not was the idea that not every so-called emergency was a truly national emergency. As he wrote, "This Order does not apply to those natural disasters, technological emergencies, or other emergencies, the alleviation of which is normally the responsibility of individuals, the private sector, volunteer organizations, State and local governments, and Federal departments and agencies unless such situations also constitute a national security emergency." Reagan drew a line in the sand, saying certain disasters were not the federal government's responsibility unless, of course, national security was threatened.

Within this order Reagan took a bit of a step back, leaving disaster recovery operations to the likes of the individual states and their localized governments or entities such as the Red Cross. This is how it should be. While FEMA has been taken to task for its seeming failures in response to natural disasters such as Hurricane Katrina, as Reagan pointed out in this order, it was not the federal government's duty to respond. Since the government seems to have reached into nearly every nook and cranny of our daily lives, many feel the government should be there to protect us in an emergency. Yet this is not the case. It was never a constitutional decree, nor is it a rational demand of our federal government. In a massive disaster, no one—not the federal government, local governments, or private institutions—can effectively respond to meet all of the needs of those crying out for help. It is a sad but undeniably true fact. Reagan, perhaps seeing into the future, took a stand here in saying the federal government's duty was to respond only to emergencies that threaten national security. While that definition remains open to debate, it was clear an event such as a blackout or a tornado or even a massive earthquake, while potentially disastrous for those directly affected, does not necessarily threaten us all or the nation's security.

The argument that naturally follows then is if a disaster on par with Hurricane Katrina was not a national emergency, how can the situation in countries like Belarus or Zimbabwe be? Hurricane Katrina affected millions of Americans. It was national news for months. Millions donated time and money to the recovery which took years to complete. Meanwhile, the political nightmares in those foreign countries, while equally horrible to those living there, do not affect Americans. There is scant news coverage. Donations are limited, sporadic, or nonexistent. Yet the latter has been officially labeled a national emergency and the former never was. Why? It all harkens back to Reagan's EO 12656 and the notion of national security. The political situations within those far away nations could potentially have ramifications that might ultimately plunge America into war, therefore national security is deemed to be at stake. With a disaster even as massive as Hurricane Katrina, national security was never felt to be threatened. Important resources such as the oil rigs in the Gulf of Mexico were affected, and indeed people's lives—American lives—were lost, yet the nation as a whole was inherently protected. It may be a harsh division between ideas, yet the logic behind it is sound. If the federal government was forced to respond to every natural disaster (be it labeled a national emergency or not) a slippery slope would form that could ultimately lead to the federal government being forced to respond to everything down to a house fire. The argument would always be available that "if the government helped them for that, then it should help me for this." This was why such a designation was a necessity.

The determination of whether or not an emergency threatened national security was placed in the hands of the National Security Council (NSC). Interestingly, while the NSC had been in existence since 1947, it was never assigned such a duty until Reagan's order. The NSC's primary directive has always been to consider the nation's foreign policy as well as national security matters. Since Reagan changed the idea of national emergencies into national security emergencies, it only followed that the NSC would add this onto its plate for consideration. Perhaps this was the best home for it all along since the NSC is comprised mainly of the same secretaries that had previously been tasked with emergency planning in both Kennedy's and Nixon's orders, including the Secretaries of State, Treasury, and Defense. By making emergencies a NSC issue, other VIPs such as the vice president, the Chairman of the Joint Chiefs of Staff, and the Director of National Intelligence were now added to the mix. While logical on one end of the spectrum, this move created a strange composition of bedfellows to prepare the nation's contingency plans. Why? Certain members of the NSC, including the vice president, members of the Joint Chiefs and the intelligence community, were never directly tasked with any specific planning functions in Reagan's executive order. Meanwhile, someone who would seem like a major contributor in all of this, the Director of FEMA, was relegated to "serve as an advisor to the National Security Council on issues of national security emergency preparedness, including mobilization preparedness, civil defense, continuity of government, technological disasters, and other issues, as appropriate."

In the remainder of Reagan's reworking, two things primarily stand out: the language and the expectations. The first was more open-ended, soft and vague, and the second was, well…lowered. The very first provision in Reagan's EO read: "The head of each Federal department and agency, as appropriate, shall: (1) Be prepared to respond adequately to all national security emergencies, including those that are international in scope, and those that may occur within any region of the Nation." Adequately? That's the best Reagan was demanding of his staff? An adequate response to a national security emergency? No president before Reagan dared to use such weak language. Now, taking the perspective of a realist, perhaps an adequate response wouldn't be all bad. Maybe, after having served nearly two full terms as president by the time this order was issued, Reagan realized that adequate was the best one could hope for coming from something as large and mismanaged as the federal government. It would still be better than nothing, right?

If that weren't enough, Reagan's next demand was, "(2) Consider national security emergency preparedness factors in the conduct of his or her regular functions, particularly those functions essential in time of emergency." Don't necessarily make any plans, simply consider them. Wasn't that language getting just a little too touchy-feely? Where were the bold commands that should come rumbling down from the president like an avalanche? Instead, the nation was supposed to feel comforted with considered plans that would ultimately be deemed adequate. Just what one would want in an emergency.

The general softness of the ever-growing politically correct language permeates the entire document. There was a good reason why. After over 40 years of working and reworking emergency plans and responses without ever even activating one of them, the whole notion had to feel a little like the boy who cried wolf. This shouldn't have let anyone off the proverbial hook. As the Cold War was nearing an end, perhaps the feeling running through the White House was that we, as a nation, could finally relax a little bit. With that feeling of safety came complacency. Why work so hard on such plans if they were never going to be used? Of course, that's exactly why everyone should make such back-up plans— because you never know when or why you may need them. Reagan took both notions to heart. Yes, the nation obviously needed emergency preparedness plans, yet the creation of such weren't as immediately necessary as they were when Kennedy was embroiled in the Cuban situation.

As Reagan assigned these duties in his executive order, it appeared as if each secretary didn't have to buckle down and concern himself so much with planning contingencies. While most positions were individually recognized and tasked, their duties were split into "Lead Responsibilities" and "Support Responsibilities." Many assignments that may have been individual responsibilities or required some sort of communication with the Department of Defense in past were now often shared between various non-military departments depending on the task at hand. While the

Department of Defense was kept in the mix, even those shared duties were to be overseen by the NSC, the Director of FEMA, or both. It was as if the federal government was to come together, and if you'd believe it, act as one.

While some things clearly had changed with Reagan's Order, others did not. For example, consider the following:

Directed at the Secretary of Labor, Kennedy's E.O. 11000 read in part: "The Secretary of Labor (hereinafter referred to as the Secretary) shall prepare national emergency plans and develop preparedness programs covering civilian manpower mobilization, more effective utilization of limited manpower resources including specialized personnel, wage and salary stabilization, worker incentives and protection, manpower resources and requirements, skill development and training, research, labor-management relations, and critical occupations...." He was also to:

"Develop plans and issue guidance designed to utilize to the maximum extent civilian manpower resources...Such plans shall include, but not necessarily be limited to: Recruitment, selection and referral, training, employment stabilization (including appeals procedures), proper utilization, and determination of the skill categories critical to meeting the labor requirements of defense and essential civilian activities...Procedures for translating survival and production urgencies into manpower priorities to be used as guides for allocating available workers...Develop plans and procedures for wage and salary stabilization and for the national and field organization necessary for the administration of such a program in an emergency, including investigation, compliance and appeals procedures; statistical studies of wages, salaries and prices for policy decisions and to assist operating stabilization agencies to carry out their functions...Develop plans and procedures for wage and salary compensation and death and disability compensation for authorized civil defense workers and, as appropriate, measures for unemployment payments, re-employment rights, and occupational safety, and other protection and incentives for the civilian labor force during an emergency...develop...plans and procedures including organization plans for the maintenance of effective labor-management relations during a national emergency...." Kennedy's Order here to the Secretary of Labor was intense and not limited to what was printed above. It was long winded, overbearing, and overwrought, even considering the atmosphere in which it was written.

In Reagan's re-engineered version, it read under the Secretary of Labor's "Lead Responsibilities":

"The Secretary of Labor shall: (1) Develop plans and issue guidance to ensure effective use of civilian workforce resources during national security emergencies. Such plans shall include, but not necessarily be limited to: (a) Priorities and allocations, recruitment, referral, training, employment stabilization including appeals procedures, use assessment, and determination of critical skill categories; and (b) Programs for increasing the availability of critical workforce skills and occupations; (2) In consultation with the Secretary of the Treasury, develop plans and procedures for wage, salary, and benefit costs stabilization during national security emergencies; (3) Develop plans and procedures for protecting and providing incentives for the civilian labor force during national security emergencies; (4) In consultation with other appropriate government agencies and private entities, develop plans and procedures for effective labor-management relations during national security emergencies."

Under "Support Responsibilities" it continued: "(1) Support planning by the Secretary of Defense and the private sector for the provision of human resources to critical defense industries during national security emergencies; (2) Support planning by the Secretary of Defense and the Director of Selective Service for the institution of conscription in national security emergencies."

For Reagan, that was the complete direction for the Secretary of Labor. It was streamlined and to the point. Yet it still retained the potency Kennedy's order possessed. Reagan still had the ability to force anyone to work where needed in what was now called a "national security emergency," but he didn't need so many directives to convey that notion.

While lengthy in overall scope, Reagan's order was rather short and sweet in terms of wording. It was a new envisioning of the nation's emergency policy, yet not all of the scary parts were stripped from it. Where Nixon had asked the Attorney General to talk to Congress and the courts so there was a "mutual understanding" when it came to emergency actions, Reagan now changed that request to the Attorney General to "provide information and assistance to the Federal Judicial branch and the Federal Legislative branch concerning law enforcement, continuity of government, and the exercise of legal authority during national security emergencies." Slightly different wording, yet it retained the same underlying theme. Reagan, like Nixon, was instructing the Attorney General to clarify these issues for the benefit of all involved. If they were all working within the same basic framework, was this step even necessary? Shouldn't everything have been already squared away?

Reagan's order continued to make similar alterations to each secretary's duties throughout its course. While such startling headings such as "Claimancy" and "Stockpiling" had been eliminated, those notions were not forgotten. They became enveloped in softer verbiage and more open interpretations than ever before. Perhaps by that point in history, those ideas were just givens and didn't need to be laid out so shockingly bare. It had been made clear that in a time of a national security emergency the government could and would lay claim to whatever was needed and deemed essential for powering the country through the crisis.

Up until 2012, Reagan's EO 12656 stood as the basis for the nation's emergency planning considerations. It was amended on just three occasions. The first was by President Clinton on February 9, 1998 in his Executive Order 13074. Clinton added simply one line to the Lead Responsibilities of the Secretary of Defense: "Subject to the direction of the President, and pursuant to procedures to be developed jointly by the Secretary of Defense and the Secretary of State, be responsible for the deployment and use of military forces for the protection of United States citizens and nationals and, in connection therewith, designated other persons or categories of persons, in support of their evacuation from threatened areas overseas."

Prior to this minor addition, President Clinton did address the nation's emergency needs in an executive order of his own. Clinton's EO 12919, titled "National Defense Industrial Resources Preparedness" and issued on June 3, 1994, touched on several subjects that Reagan's order had seemingly covered. The first "General Function" of Clinton's order stated it was to "identify requirements for the full spectrum of national security emergencies, including military, industrial, and essential civilian demand...." The order went on to detail the ways and means the nation should prepare its industries for any potential national emergency (Clinton did not consistently use Reagan's "national security emergency" terminology). EO 12919 tasked many of the usual suspects (Secretary of Commerce, Labor, Defense, etc.) with many of the same preparedness ideals including stockpiling of strategic materials, the guaranteeing of loans for production purposes, "the supply of workers for purposes of national defense," and "direction, control, and coordination of civil transportation." It also included the new idea of monitoring the foreign acquisition of American companies that may provide critical resources and their means of production which have been deemed essential for the country's preparedness. Interestingly, only that final detail pertaining to the foreign acquisition of companies was revoked (by Bush's Executive Order 13456 issued in January 2008), the remainder is still effective to date.

The other two amendments to Reagan's EO 12656 came from President George W. Bush. These derived directly from the creation of the Department of Homeland Security (DHS). The first was EO 13228 which established the DHS itself in October, 2001. In its creation, the DHS absorbed FEMA as one of its branches and was placed in charge of all Continuity of Government operations. It also created the Homeland Security Council (HSC) which was basically another version of the National Security Council, including many of the same members. Hence, President Bush wedged both the DHS and the HSC into the wording of Reagan's EO 12656. Bush's second related order, EO 13286, came in February 2003 and was an amendment to the original order that created the DHS. This order was a piece of legislative housekeeping more than anything. It did, however, include one interesting change to Reagan's EO 12656. In section 201 of Reagan's order, Bush changed the wording of the directive aimed at every secretary from the original "consult and coordinate with the Director of the Federal Emergency Management Agency to ensure that those activities and plans are consistent with current National Security Council guidelines and policies" to "consult and coordinate with the Secretary of Homeland Security to ensure that those activities and plans are consistent with current Presidential guidelines and policies." The main switch was not the change from the Director of FEMA to the Secretary of the DHS, but rather the elimination of the NSC's policies to ones that were strictly the president's. How often the president—any president—acts outside the recommendations of the NSC, few could say. Bush apparently thought that making this switch in the language was necessary.

In March 2012, President Obama made headlines with Executive Order 13603, titled "National Defense Resources Preparedness." These news stories were focused mainly on the "shocking" revelation regarding Obama's ability to declare martial law which was tucked into the document (which, as we've seen, is nothing new); however, the real thrust of this new executive order was not so much on national emergencies as it was on general national defense. As Obama wrote, "The United States must have an industrial and technological base capable of meeting national defense requirements and capable of contributing to the technological superiority of its national defense equipment in peacetime and in times of national emergency. The domestic industrial and technological base is the foundation for national defense preparedness. The authorities provided in the Act shall be used to strengthen this base and to ensure it is capable of responding to the national defense needs of the United States."

The main people tasked with implementing this new version of preparedness was the Secretary of Homeland Security and a newly established Defense Production Act Committee. This 17-member committee didn't stray far from the usual suspects that make up the NSC. It merely added a few other, often overlooked entities including the likes of the Secretary of the Interior, Agriculture, Health & Human Services, and for some reason, the Administrator of NASA. The first "General Function" this group was to serve was to "identify requirements for the full spectrum of emergencies, including essential military and civilian demand."

To achieve its goals, Obama's EO 13603 was even more straightforward than Reagan's. Instead of directing a paragraph (or more) toward each Secretary, EO 13603 gave "Priorities and Allocations," for example, to the Secretary of Energy "with respect to all forms of energy." That was it. One sentence. Done. Of course, Obama's order was not rescinding or replacing Reagan's; it was updating Clinton's similarly themed EO 12919. Hence, Reagan's 25+ year old order is still the benchmark for our nation's emergency plans.

The Bushes Enact

What was dubbed the Gulf War or the Persian Gulf War was not, in fact, a war. It was not declared as such by Congress and was not solely a U.S military action. Rather, it was an attack on Iraq and its troops via a United Nations resolution. The United States just happened to be a (the?) key motivator in the international situation. Nonetheless, President George H.W. Bush saw this military action as a good time to enact some of those emergency orders and authorizations that had been sitting idly by on the books. Of course, in order to do so, there had to be an official national emergency.

On August 2, 1990, Iraqi leader Saddam Hussein ordered his forces into Kuwait to reclaim the territory he felt was rightfully Iraq's. What Hussein either didn't realize or perhaps expect was that most of the rest of the world wouldn't agree with his claim. On that same August day, as Iraqi troops were storming across the border between the two nations, President Bush issued two executive orders—EO 12722 and 12723. Each order declared a separate national emergency with respect to the situations in Iraq and Kuwait. In declaring these emergencies, Bush acted to block Iraqi and Kuwaiti governmental property as well as prohibit any transactions with regards to Iraq. Both orders were short and straightforward. They were also remarkably short lived. Just seven days later, Bush revoked both orders and replaced them with new versions in EO 12724 and 12725. The new editions of each order cited not just U.S. law as a justification for its issuance, but now included the United Nations since the August 6, 1990 passage of United Nations Security Council Resolution Number 661 which was directed at the growing situation in Kuwait.

Bush was able to block both countries' property thanks to the International Emergency Economic Powers Act (IEEPA). For all intents and purposes, the IEEPA is the 1917 Trading with the Enemies Act modernized to cover national emergencies. Since Bush's use of it in 1990, the IEEPA has been perhaps the most cited act used in the president's arsenal to combat these foreign-born national emergencies.

While a simple border dispute occurring halfway around the world from the United States didn't seem like a national emergency when it began, President Bush was ready and willing to make it one. As Saddam Hussein continued to ignore the sanctions against Iraq and mandates to pull his forces from Kuwait, the United States prepared to enforce the world's demands. Bush issued six executive orders pertaining to the Iraq-Kuwait situation in the remainder of 1990. Four of these orders–EO 12727, 12728, 12733, and 12734—dealt with the nation's military build-up for what seemed to be an inevitable conflict. These stemmed directly from Bush's commander-in-chief powers. Another of the orders, EO 12738, simply amended a previous order regarding foreign assistance and arms controls. The final order in this series, EO

12735, created a third national emergency.

Not content to exist under the two already on-going emergencies, Bush created another based on the proliferation of chemical and biological weapons. This, of course, was to contend with and control these types of weapons the U.S. assumed the Iraqis possessed (since the U.S. Government had sold the Iraqis similar weapons in their war against the Iranians just a few years prior). The belief was the Iraqis were ready to use these weapon-types against our troops. Interestingly, Bush's order does not specifically name Iraq, or any country for that matter, in regards to these horrific instruments of war.

Bush was just warming up. Nine days prior to the January 17, 1991 deadline set by the United Nations for Iraq to pull its troops from Kuwait, Bush signed EO 12742. Titled "National Security Industrial Responsiveness," Bush was primed and ready to lead the nation into war. The order's stated purpose was: "The United States must have the capability to rapidly mobilize its resources in the interest of national security. Therefore, to achieve prompt delivery of articles, products, and materials to meet national security requirements, the Government may place orders and require priority performance of these orders." What followed were commands for the prompt delivery of the necessary war-making materials. When one reads it with the knowledge of the vast array of emergency planning executive orders that preceded it, EO 12742 seemed frightfully close to those demands of claimancy made in Kennedy's and Nixon's orders. It read:

"(a) Subject to paragraph (b) of this section, the authorities vested in the President, under with respect to the placing of orders for prompt delivery of articles or materials…are hereby delegated to: (1) The Secretary of Agriculture with respect to all food resources; (2) the Secretary of Energy with respect to all forms of energy; (3) the Secretary of Transportation with respect to all forms of civil transportation; and (4) the Secretary of Commerce with respect to all other articles and materials, including construction materials.

"(b) The authorities delegated by paragraph (a) of this section shall be exercised only after: (1) a determination by the Secretary of Defense that prompt delivery of the articles or materials for the exclusive use of the armed forces of the United States is in the interest of national security, or (2) a determination by the Secretary of Energy that the prompt delivery of the articles or materials for the Department of Energy's atomic energy programs is in the interest of national security."

Obviously, if—or what was more likely in that case, when—the U.S. was to enter into an undeclared war with Iraq, we would want our military to be fully supplied and ready to attack. That was what this order intended to accomplish. The secretaries were not to lay claim to these materials, just order and rapidly organize them with regards to the Department of Defense. Yet it seemed that executive order was beginning to grease the wheels for the government to step in and claim those materials, depending how the yet-to-be-waged war developed. This might have been especially true when one considers the odd request made within the order under "Implementation": "All departments and agencies delegated authority under this order are hereby directed to amend their rules and regulations as necessary to reflect the new authorities delegated herein that are to be relied upon to carry out their functions." Why would every government department and agency need to "amend their rules and regulations" just to make a few orders for war-making supplies? Sure, there might be a need to re-prioritize some things to make those materials the number one issue at hand, but did the rules need to be rewritten? How far was Bush willing to go?

Thankfully, the citizens of the United States would never know the answer since the U.S.-led response to the Iraqi invasion was over in less than four months. While Bush possessed the opportunity to unleash any or all of the emergency powers past presidents had awarded him, he never did. Perhaps he didn't have the chance. Or, more likely, he never even contemplated doing so since the national emergency with regards to Iraq was not rescinded once the fighting stopped. It was allowed to run its natural course and fade away after a year had passed. In that brief time of an actual shooting conflict, Bush squeezed in only four more executive orders. All were related to the military action, none of which had any significance on the American people.

Ten years later, Bush's son, the newly elected President George W. Bush, faced a national emergency unlike any that had come before it. With the terrorist attacks of September 11, 2001, the citizens of the United States faced an actual national emergency that occurred within the borders of their country. What came out of the federal government that day was a rather haphazard response.

Bush did not officially recognize the acts of 9/11 as a national emergency until three days later. On September 14, 2001, Bush issued Proclamation 7463 which read:

"A national emergency exists by reason of the terrorist attacks at the World Trade Center, New York, New York, and the Pentagon, and the continuing and immediate threat of further attacks on the United States. Now, Therefore, I, George W. Bush, President of the United States of America, by virtue of the authority vested in me as President by the Constitution and the laws of the United States, I hereby declare that the national emergency has existed since September 11, 2001, and, pursuant to the National Emergencies Act (50 U.S.C. 1601 et seq.), I intend to utilize the following statutes: sections 123, 123a, 527, 2201(c), 12006, and 12302 of title 10, United States Code, and sections 331, 359, and 367 of title 14, United States Code."

One would think if George H.W. Bush could issue two executive orders, both of which declared national emergencies in response to Iraq's invading of Kuwait on the very day it occurred, then George W. Bush could have done the same on 9/11. Let's face it; by September 14 when Bush finally did make his declaration, the actual emergency was over. Even more remarkable was by that late date, he had already issued two other proclamations directly related to 9/11. The first, Proclamation

7461 issued on 9/11 itself, honored those that died that day and ordered the nation's flags be flown at half staff until the September 16. The other, Proclamation 7462 issued on September 13 (which actually uses Bush's famous term "evildoers" in its text), declared that the following day—September 14—would be a national day of prayer and mourning.

Aside from Bush's belated response to 9/11, the actual measures he employed to combat the resultant national emergency were quite tame. While many in the conspiracy theory realms as well as some in the mainstream media believed Bush opened the door to such provisions as total media censorship and an ever-escalating march on the path to martial law, he did no such thing. Of course, should he have wanted to take such actions, he very well could have thanks to the presidential emergency preparedness orders that preceded him. That was not the reality of the situation in September 2001, however. As plainly noted in his proclamation which stuck to the letter of the National Emergencies Act, Bush listed exactly the statues he was going to put into effect as a result of the now declared emergency. What were those statues? Let's have a look, taking the last few first.

Title 14 of the United States Code is concerned with the United States Coast Guard (USCG). The three sections of 14 U.S.C. Bush enacted—331, 359, and 367—affected the recruitment and composition of that unit. It allowed Bush to order retired enlisted and regular members of the USCG back to active duty. It also allowed the Secretary of Transportation to retain enlisted members of the USCG beyond their terms of service if need be. The USCG is one of the main components in protecting the nation's borders. Holding all active members in service as well as bringing back certain experienced veterans could instantly bolster the USCG's ranks in hopes of elevating the nation's protective capabilities. In light of the 9/11 attacks, that response makes perfect sense.

The other provisions Bush enacted dealt with Title 10 of the United States Code. Title 10 pertains to the armed forces and general military law. So, by citing sections of Title 10 including 10 U.S.C. 123, 527, 12006, and 12302 as stated in his proclamation, Bush was using his commander-in-chief powers to bolster the military for the response to the 9/11 attacks. All four of those sections authorize the president, in times of war or national emergency, to do such things as suspend promotions or retirement from the armed forces, control the distribution of commissioned officers on active duty, and call members of the Ready Reserve to active duty. Notice there's no extraordinary demands such as the implementation of martial law here. These are simply actions similar to the ones Bush performed with regards to the Coast Guard—rational and measured responses.

Sections 123(a) and 2201(c) of 10 U.S.C. are concerned with the budgetary ways and means of the military. This was where we taxpayers ought to have paid a little more attention. 10 U.S.C. 123(a) states:

"(a) During War or National Emergency. - If at the end of any fiscal year there is in effect a war or national emergency, the President may waive any statutory end strength with respect to that fiscal year. Any such waiver may be issued only for a statutory end strength that is prescribed by law before the waiver is issued.

"(b) Upon the termination of a war or national emergency with respect to which the President has exercised the authority provided by subsection (a), the President may defer the effectiveness of any statutory end strength with respect to the fiscal year during which the termination occurs. Any such deferral may not extend beyond the last day of the sixth month beginning after the date of such termination.

"(c) Statutory End Strength. - In this section, the term "statutory end strength" means any end-strength limitation with respect to a fiscal year that is prescribed by law for any military or civilian component of the armed forces or of the Department of Defense."

So, if a president can defer any "end strength" limitation on his spending during such national emergency until that emergency ends, then the president effectively can spend the taxpayers' money over and above any budgetary constraints. This would be allowed to last until the termination of said national emergency. In the case of 9/11 and the resultant military operations in both Iraq and Afghanistan, these national emergencies are still on-going, 10+ years after their start. So, President Bush and even President Obama has had a blank check available to cover any and all costs associated with these military actions related to the declared national emergencies. As long as the national emergencies involved continue to be reinstated after their one year limit, that unchecked spending could go over forever.

Backing up this notion was Chapter 34 of 50 U.S.C. which pertains to the "Accounting and Reporting Requirements of [the] President." This details, however briefly, how the president was supposed to report to Congress all of the expenditures that accumulated during a national emergency. Section C of Chapter 34 reads: "When the President declares a national emergency or Congress declares war, the President shall transmit to Congress, within ninety days after the end of each six-month period after such declaration, a report on the total expenditures incurred by the United States Government during such six-month period which are directly attributable to the exercise of powers and authorities conferred by such declaration. Not later than ninety days after the termination of each such emergency or war, the President shall transmit a final report on all such expenditures." Notice this does not say the president was to report these expenditures to Congress for their approval. There was no apparent budgeting for that. The president was just to keep Congress aware of how much money was being sucked up by said national emergency. This runs contradictory to the Constitution which clearly states that Congress was in charge of distributing the nation's funds. But, oh well, there's a national emergency to attend to. As for that "final report" to follow the cessation of whatever national emergency was at hand, how long should Congress hold their collective breath for it when, as has been noted before, these national emergencies never actually end?

The other section of 10 U.S.C. that allowed the president to spend over and above his apparent means was the aforementioned 10 U.S.C. 2201(c). This reads: "Exemption From Apportionment Requirement. If the President determines such action to be necessary in the interest of national defense, the President may exempt from the provisions of section 1512 of title 31 appropriations, funds, and contract authorizations available for military functions of the Department of Defense." In plain English, this allows the president to increase the number of members of the armed services on active duty above and beyond the number for which funds have been previously provided to the Department of Defense.

Both of these provisions seem logical on one hand and preposterous on the other. On the logical side, if there was a national emergency of extended length it makes sense to allow the president to bolster the military to provide for the common defense of the country no matter the constraints of the federal budget. There may come a time when immediate action is needed, and it is much easier to get one president to act rather than wait for the machination of the entire federal government to churn out a result. Yet by allowing the president that ability, Congress effectively gave up its constitutional powers. According to the Constitution, only Congress has the power to raise and support an army. If in 10 U.S.C. 2201(c), the president can increase the size of the armed forces by his own power alone with no regards to the money Congress provided for such actions, then what power does Congress still possess in those regards? If the president is also able to spend freely because such money was necessary to combat the declared national emergency—a national emergency that was the president's own call, and one which he continued to renew ad nauseum—then Congress again has completely lost its constitutional ability to control the nation's funds and appropriations. Of course, Congress could rescind the president's national emergency through a joint resolution, ending such reckless spending and regaining some of its authority in the process, yet such an incident has never occurred in the nation's history.

Nine days after Proclamation 7463, Bush issued Executive Order 13224. Using the same International Emergency Economic Powers Act that his father had used against Iraq and Kuwait in 1990, Bush now directed the IEEPA against not a known state or country, but against "terrorists" and anyone who acted in concert with them. During his presidency, President Clinton had used the IEEPA in a similar fashion, directing it against anyone who threatened the Middle East peace process (worked well, didn't it?). Now Bush was doing essentially the same thing, against the same people, for the same reason, and with the same non-existent results. The IEEPA allowed for this vague implementation because it could be directed against any foreign country or national thereof.

Following its publication, the Department of Treasury routinely issued annexes to EO 13224 that named the names of the terrorists to be sanctioned by the IEEPA. The first annex was made almost immediately on October 12, 2001. The last annex available was made on July 17, 2008. On these annexes are lists of "Specifically Designated Global Terrorist Entities" or SDGTs. How many names are listed? Thousands. Without providing a direct count, one should acquire a general idea of how many SDGTs are named in the annexes just by seeing its length. The annexes exceeded 115 pages of names of individuals and institutions (with their aliases). On over 90 of those pages, the names are in a 10-point font, single spaced, and listed in two columns per page.

Two months after issuing EO 13224, Bush brought forth Executive Order 13235. It tapped into the president's emergency powers as granted by Title 10 of the United States Code, specifically section 2808, which read in part:

"(a) In the event of a declaration of war or the declaration by the President of a national emergency in accordance with the National Emergencies Act (50 U.S.C. 1601 et seq.) that requires use of the armed forces, the Secretary of Defense, without regard to any other provision of law, may undertake military construction projects, and may authorize the Secretaries of the military departments to undertake military construction projects, not otherwise authorized by law that are necessary to support such use of the armed forces. Such projects may be undertaken only within the total amount of funds that have been appropriated for military construction, including funds appropriated for family housing, that have not been obligated."

Nowhere does it state what those "construction projects" can or cannot be. In essence, they could be anything—and I mean *anything*—deemed militarily useful since they could be "not otherwise authorized by law." If that makes you feel a bit squeamish, it was refreshing to note that those construction projects must take place within the military's construction budget, however high that may have been, and even if it meant displacing a few (or a few thousand) military families.

Once President Bush led the country into another undeclared war against Iraq that was conveniently tied to the attacks of 9/11, he only issued two more executive orders that flexed his emergency powers muscle. Neither was noteworthy. The first was EO 13303 issued on May 22, 2003. Once again, a national emergency was declared in regards to Iraq and once again the IEEPA was enacted to combat it. The other was EO 13321 issued in December 2003. Citing 10 U.S.C. as its basis, this allowed Bush (or the Secretary of Defense) to appoint any qualified persons to any officer grade in the armed forces. That was it. Could Bush have taken his powers further? Yes. How so? For example, he could've ordered the round up of all the aliens over the age of 14 and quarantined them much like FDR did to the Japanese Americans during World War II.

Section 21 of Chapter 3 of Title 50 U.S.C. is titled "Alien Enemies—Restraint, Regulation, and Removal." If that doesn't sum up what's possibly in store for those unfortunate souls, then perhaps the wording of the actual section will. Section 21 reads:

"Whenever there is a declared war between the United States and any foreign nation or government, or any invasion or predatory incursion is perpetrated, attempted or threatened against the territory of the United States by any foreign nation or government, and the President makes public proclamation of the event, all natives, citizens, denizens, or subjects of the hostile nation or government, being of the age of fourteen years and upward, who shall be within the United States and not actually naturalized, shall be liable to be apprehended, restrained, secured, and removed as alien enemies. The President is authorized in any such event, by his proclamation thereof, or other public act, to direct the conduct to be observed on the part of the United States, toward the aliens who become so liable; the manner and degree of the restraint to which they shall be subject and in what cases, and upon what security their residence shall be permitted, and to provide for the removal of those who, not being permitted to reside within the United States, refuse or neglect to depart therefrom; and to establish any other regulations which are found necessary in the premises and for the public safety."

This states in no uncertain terms that if the president calls for it, any non-naturalized citizen of a questionable foreign nation can and will be detained and potentially deported for the safety and security of the nation at large. How was this legal, you ask? Easy—these aren't actual American citizens we're talking about. They are foreigners. The United States government can do whatever it pleases when dealing with foreigners, especially if they've been deemed "hostile."

For all the fear of oppression that potentially stems from this looming law, remember, America is going on over three decades of living in a war-like state when dealing with such Middle Eastern countries as Iran and Iraq. This law has remained tucked away on the books. No president has enacted it, even though any of them could have. In fact, in light of the "war on terror," it's rather surprising it *hasn't* been enacted. As clearly stated in Section 21, America doesn't have to be in a declared war with any particular country, there simply has to be a declared "threat." If the creation of the Department of Homeland Security, its sub-agency the

Transportation Security Administration (TSA), and the colored coded "terror threat levels" attached to both agencies doesn't signal such a state or constitute enough of a breach of national security to allow the president to make a declaration against certain foreign countries and their "denizens" to allow for their round-up and deportation, what will? Yet while conspiracy theorists and their ilk raged over the diminishing rights of Americans under President Bush since 9/11, here was a chance for Bush to actually implement a crack down on such rights—albeit against foreigners and not U.S. citizens—and he never did it. So maybe things aren't as horrific as some would make them out to be.

Then again, maybe they are.

There are executive orders, Presidential Decision Directives (PDD), National Security Presidential Directives (NPSD) and other similar top level papers that have been issued that haven't been discussed here—because it is not possible to do so. These emergency plans and executive actions remain Top Secret and available only to those with the highest security clearances. Many of these documents have been known to be officially issued, since their cataloging numbers have been used, however, even the *title* of these documents remains classified. What should make you a little uneasy as you ponder this fact is that even Congress doesn't know what these documents consist of and some, like executive orders, are in effect *laws*.

In May of 1997, five-term Senator Jesse Helms (R-NC) made a statement before the Senate Committee on Governmental Affairs on Government Secrecy. He stated, "Secrecy all too often then becomes a political tool used by Executive Branch agencies to shield information which may be politically sensitive or policies which may be unpopular with the American public. Worse yet, information may be classified to hide from public view illegal or unethical activity. On numerous occasions I, and other Members of Congress, have found the Executive Branch to be reluctant to share certain information, the nature of which is not truly a 'national secret,' but which would be potentially politically embarrassing to officials in the Executive Branch or which would make known an illegal or indefensible policy."

The main question is: to what extent can a president act secretly? What could the president do without the general public or even Congress discovering?

Ever hear of the National Security Agency (NSA)? The NSA is the home of America's secretive intelligence branch focused primarily on code breaking and cryptography. It is believed that the NSA intercepts every form of communication throughout the entire world—phone, cell phone, email, radio, etc. It can target certain key words and phrases, and will sort through hundreds of millions of communications to find them. If one of these terms crop up, the NSA will pull said communication, analyze it, and if need be, continue to monitor that individual (and with whom he was communicating) for further surveillance. Usually discreet and unrecognized, the NSA recently made headlines by being the main culprit involved in the illegal wiretapping of U.S. citizens (as authorized, secretly, by President Bush's White House). The NSA was created by President Truman in 1952; however, the existence of the NSA was classified for over two decades. Though the agency spent billions of dollars during that time, it was not directly funded by Congress because it didn't officially exist. Instead, the NSA's funding was routed through other various agencies to keep its secret intact. This was an entire branch of the intelligence community, backed by hundreds of millions of dollars, and yet officially, there was no NSA.

In 1995, it became public that an agency known as the National Reconnaissance Office (NRO) existed. The NRO was created, much like the NSA, not by Congress but by President Eisenhower in 1960. The NRO's primary mission was overseeing the nation's network of spy satellites. Today the NRO's job has expanded to include "the research, development, acquisition, launch and operation of overhead reconnaissance systems and other missions as directed to solve intelligence problems" according to its 2008 congressional budget, which was publicly released, albeit in a redacted form. Remarkably, the NRO's existence—including its very name—remained classified for nearly *35 years*. Also like its brethren agency the NSA, the billions of dollars allocated for the NRO during that classified time were not distributed directly to the agency because it officially did not exist.

It is extremely likely that other shadowy government agencies exist that 99.9% of the American populace don't know about. Even federal government oversight committees likely don't realize these secret agencies have been created, are currently at work, and spending tax dollars by the boatloads. How much money is going to these agencies and what work they are engaged in remains on a "need to know" basis.

News stories occasionally highlight similar discoveries that shock even congressmen. In 2008, a memorandum written by John Yoo of the U.S. Justice Department surfaced. Written over a nine month span in 2003, the memo detailed the law the Bush administration was following in regards to the torture of suspected terrorists. As Senator Russ Feingold (D-WI) wrote in the *Los Angeles Times* in 2008 regarding the situation, the law Yoo was referring to "was essentially a declaration that the administration could ignore the laws passed by Congress." Circulated in secret, Yoo's memo was classified even though it didn't pass any standard test allowing for such classification. Feingold wrote, "The memos on torture policy that have been released or leaked hint at a much bigger body of law about which we know virtually nothing. The Yoo memo was filled with references to other Justice Department memos that have yet to see the light of day, on subjects including the government's ability to detain U.S. citizens without congressional authorization and the government's ability to bypass the 4th Amendment in domestic military operations."

Pressing further, as reported by Projected Censored and elsewhere, it has been discovered that a president's executive orders can be changed secretly without anyone's knowledge. How can an executive order, which is in effect a law, be changed without issuing a statement declaring so? Simple. Just don't follow it.

This insane notion was brought to the public's knowledge by Senator Sheldon Whitehouse (D-RI) late in 2007. Senator Whitehouse, in researching the Protect America Act, ran across documents from the Office of Legal Counsel (OLC), an arm of the Justice Department. These documents plainly stated three ideas: (1.) The President was not limited by an executive order, even if he was the issuer of said order. There was no requirement for the president to issue a new order if he intends on departing from the intent of the original one. (2.) Thanks to Article II of the Constitution, the president can himself determine what a lawful exercise of his own power was. (3.) The Justice Department was bound to the president's determinations. As Senator Whitehouse said to the rest of the Senate: "These three Bush administration legal propositions boil down to this: one, 'I don't have to follow my own rules, and I don't have to tell you when I'm breaking them;' two, 'I get to determine what my own powers are;' and three, 'The Department of Justice doesn't tell me what the law is, I tell the Department of Justice what the law is.'"

From those revelations, Senators Whitehouse and Feingold introduced the Executive Order Integrity Act of 2008. The main thrust of the act was to "prevent secret changes to published Executive Orders by requiring the President to place a notice in the Federal Register when he has modified or revoked a published Order." As Senator Feingold stated to Congress when the act was introduced, "The principle behind this bill is straightforward. It is a basic tenet of democracy that the people have a right to know the law. Indeed, the notion of 'secret law' has been described in court opinions and law treatises as 'repugnant' and 'an abomination.' That is why the laws passed by Congress have historically been matters of public record." While that act should have been a no-brainer for Congress to pass, it did not survive the 110th Congress.

It may be quite imperative that Congress act on such matters sooner rather than later. In the February 2, 2009 issue of *Newsweek* magazine, the article "A Loophole in the Rules" by Mark Hosenball revealed that the newly elected President Obama and his staff were looking to act as cavalier as the previous Bush administration did. Hosenball wrote:

"A day before Obama signed executive orders closing Guantanamo Bay and banning torture, the White House's top lawyer privately indicated to Congress that the new president reserved the right to ignore his own (and any other president's) executive orders. In a closed-door appearance before the Senate intelligence committee, White House counsel Gregory Craig was asked whether the president was required by law to follow executive orders. According to people familiar with his remarks, who asked for anonymity when discussing a private meeting, Craig answered that the administration did not believe he was. The implication: in a national-security crisis, Obama could deviate from his own rules." Apparently the more things change; the more they stay the same when it comes to the president's response to an emergency.

If the secretive changes to the law and the powers available to the president in an emergency situation bother you, one has two choices in the matter: Either become involved and attempt to change that governmental attitude, or silently sit back and enjoy the ride. If you wait too long to counter these governmental abuses, there will come a time when the forces that lord over us all will be in places and positions that no one—not you, not the invaders, not the scores of nuclear bombs—can reach.

FIRST RESPONDERS

"I have been asked whether in the years to come it will be possible to kill forty million American people in the twenty largest American towns by the use of atomic bombs in a single night. And I'm afraid that the answer to that question is yes."
- Dr. J. Robert Oppenheimer, "father" of the atomic bomb, circa 1945

Few Americans have a healthy enough fear of nuclear weapons. Most have forgotten or in some cases never learned just how destructive they would be if unleashed upon the world. The atomic bomb was created in the utmost secrecy, even though thousands of people worked on various aspects of the compartmentalized project. Though President Franklin Roosevelt was well aware of its creation, his vice president, Harry Truman, didn't learn about its existence until Roosevelt died and Truman stepped into the presidency. The first A-bomb was detonated in the New Mexico desert at the Trinity Site in 1945. While bets were made by the scientists responsible for its creation as to whether it would even work (or, in some of their circles, whether it would ignite the Earth's atmosphere and kill us all), when it did explode, it sent up the now familiar mushroom cloud and scorched some barren desert land. No one was killed and no one was directly irradiated by the resultant fallout. In fact, this historic location and the original crater created by the blast can be visited today. It is an eerie experience.

The A-bomb was a mighty force to be reckoned with, yet it was still technically just a bomb. Within the military, it was considered to be an effective and potentially useful weapon. Shortly after its first test, the weapon would be put to an official military use, bringing a swift resolution to America's war with Japan. Many, including some of the scientists that helped create the bomb, felt it would have been better to stage a second test in the desert and invite various world leaders to witness it. Once having seen the destructive capabilities of the atomic bomb first-hand, coupled with the knowledge that the U.S. intended to use it if need be, many believed an instant truce between the U.S. and Japan would have been forged. Perhaps then the world would have been able to begin discussions on how to control and contain the spread of this awful weapon prior to the arms race that began shortly after the conclusion of World War II. Other atomic scientists and military leaders felt the exact opposite; that the use of the bomb was the only way to ensure peace. Afterwards, it would then be necessary to stash away these atomic secrets from America's enemies to keep the peace through superior firepower and knowledge. As history has proven, it was this second line of thinking that won.

Under the direction of President Truman, the U.S. military used the atomic bomb to destroy two Japanese cities, Hiroshima and Nagasaki. Over 200,000 people were killed. In truth, that was not much worse than the conventional bombing the U.S. had conducted in the final days of World War II. In Tokyo alone, the U.S. killed an estimated 85,000 people during routine bombing. However with those raids, Japanese citizens could hear the armada of U.S. bombers approaching, giving them time to sound the alarm and seek shelter. Over the course of the war, they had become used to this horrific scenario. With the dropping of the A-bomb, however, just one plane with one bomb was able to wipe out an unprepared city. There was no warning, and that upset many Japanese officials more than the actual destruction of their cities. Nonetheless, this was the new fear the world was forced to live with.

Seven short years after the creation of the A-bomb, the first hydrogen-based atomic weapon, the so-called "Super" or H-bomb, was tested on Enewetak, an atoll in the Pacific Ocean. The nice thing about the first H-bomb was the impracticality of it. It weighed some 65 tons; therefore, to put it into position took serious effort. This fact rendered it completely useless as a weapon at that point. The bad part was, well, everything else. The explosion created in that initial test left a crater that exceeded a mile across and was more than 150 feet deep. The island was obliterated. The force of the blast stripped the island clear of vegetation and the resultant fallout left the area contaminated for years. In essence, Enewetak went from being an island to a lagoon as ocean water poured into the crater while at the same time bits of coral landed some 30 miles from ground zero. The estimated strength of the explosion was *450 times* that of either of the atomic bombs dropped on Japan. Why was it so much more powerful? Consider this: the trigger needed to explode a hydrogen bomb is the detonation of an atomic bomb. While the A-bomb requires a heavy and unstable element like uranium to create the needed chain reaction that makes the bomb what it is, in an H-bomb the hydrogen sustains and amplifies that reaction. In essence, that reaction contains the same energy that fuels the sun, hence the resultant power it creates upon detonation. The scary part is the fission reaction created by an H-bomb can be as large or as small as the maker wishes since it all depends on the amount of hydrogen included.

Even prior to that test it was realized that this was not a military weapon—it was truly the first weapon of mass destruction. The H-bomb was good for nothing, unless killing countless people and rendering the remaining land uninhabitable was one's goal. As early as 1949, the Atomic Energy Commission's General Advisory Committee unanimously opposed the development of thermonuclear weapons, arguing, "that the extreme dangers to mankind inherent in the proposal wholly outweigh any military advantage that could come from this development. Let it be clearly realized that this is a super weapon; it is in a totally different category from an atomic bomb….We are alarmed as to the possible global effects of the radioactivity generated by the explosion of a few super bombs of conceivable magnitude. If super bombs will work at all, there is no inherent limit in the destructive power that may be attained with them. Therefore, a super bomb might become a weapon of genocide….In determining not to proceed to develop the super bomb, we see a unique opportunity of providing by example some limitations on the totality of war and thus of limiting the fear and arousing the hopes of mankind." It possessed no practical military application outside of deterrence. Even so, that didn't mean the U.S. military—or any other countries' military—wouldn't use one if push came to shove.

Those were the capabilities over 50 years ago. By 1954, just five years after the first H-bomb test, both the U.S. and the Soviet Union possessed H-bombs that could be transported via aircraft to destinations within each other's country. Soon after, various missiles and shells were created by both sides, giving every country with the know-how and proper resources the ability to launch nuclear weapons to every point on the planet and get its nuclear payload there quickly. In the event of a submarine-based launch, a missile can strike its target in as little as ten minutes. No one was safe. Who knows what sort of unimaginable hell could occur if the modern, up-to-the-minute version of a nuclear device was detonated. For example, consider the "cobalt bomb." While it is believed no country has yet to build such a bomb, it is basically a real life version of the "doomsday device" that finalizes the classic film *Dr. Strangelove: Or How I Learned to Stop Worrying and Love the Bomb*. If one were inclined to do so, coating a hydrogen bomb with cobalt would create the radioactive isotope cobalt-60 upon detonation. This highly radioactive element has a half-life of five years which would allow it to remain lethal as its fallout spread over the entire globe. Potentially, one of these bombs could kill us all.

Most Americans are blissfully unaware of these facts. The prevailing belief is that the "atomic age" is a remnant of history. What they may know comes from grainy black-and-white films showing stock footage of mushroom clouds and school children hiding under desks. Some may be familiar with the buzz words of those bygone days, ideas like civil defense, the Cuban Missile Crisis, atomic mutations, Nike missile sites, etc. But few, if any, recall the actual, palatable fear that accompanied that time in American history. Despite the presence of recent Hollywood films like *The Day After* and *The Sum of All Fears*, nuclear weapons have become in a sense a forgotten menace. Only the renewed threat of terrorism and the possibility of a "dirty bomb" has put a small dose of that fear back into the general public. Although, truth be told, the FBI first issued warnings to local law enforcement officials in 1954 to be on the lookout for "suitcase nukes" (it is quite possible to create a nuclear bomb that fits inside a suitcase). So, while such devices are not really a modern creation, there's an unmentioned difference lurking under the surface. A dirty bomb, that is a bomb packed with radioactive materials, if detonated in New York City would likely barely damage a building while sending a small, yet manageable radioactive cloud into the air. Should a weapons grade nuclear device explode in New York, however, the entire city could/would be wiped off the face of the earth. A radius of ten miles around the epicenter would vanish, and depending on the wind patterns at the time, it's possible that the fallout would kill millions more up and down the Eastern seaboard.

The hope, of course, is that no one has to face such a scenario—ever. Yet as long as America holds a reported stockpile of over 5,100 nuclear warheads (with perhaps upwards of 3,500 more that have been "retired") stashed across the country and continues to spend an estimated *$30 billion* a year on nuclear weapons related projects (according to a study conducted by the Carnegie Endowment for International Peace), sooner or later such a nightmare is likely to come to fruition. While the American public let the fear of a nuclear war drift from its collective conscience as memory of the Cold War faded, the United States government has not. And it will not. Not because the federal government wants to protect its populace from such a horrible fate. No, it's because the government wants to save its own ass.

FEMA's Roots

The Federal Emergency Management Agency (FEMA) was born not by an act of Congress, but much like the super secret

NSA and NRO, it was created by presidential decree. Through the stroke of President Jimmy Carter's pen on March 31, 1979, FEMA came into being via Executive Order 12127. It didn't just spring forth from Carter's head, however. FEMA came about through an arduous process. It wasn't originally a separate entity, but rather a patchwork of several minor agencies, administrations, and congressional acts rolled into one package. Most of these various facets were tasked with disaster recovery, emergency preparations, or civil defense. Perhaps that is why FEMA seems so confused when called in to assist in an operation today—it's still not sure what its primary directive is supposed to be. Is it disaster and emergency response? That's what the public seems to believe, yet FEMA has been closely associated with civil defense (which includes Continuity of Government preparations) since its creation, and it is still called upon to oversee those activities today. Carter's original hope was that by consolidating these tasks within one agency, the better it would be at managing them.

FEMA's own history, as detailed on its website fema.gov, claimed that the agency can trace its origins back to the Congressional Act of 1803. That was considered by many historians to be the first piece of disaster based legislation. Skip ahead another 130 years, and emergency planning and management received a federal kick-start thanks to President Franklin Roosevelt's officially declared national emergency in 1933. In November 1933, FDR organized the National Emergency Council (NEC) through Executive Order 6433A. The NEC was designed to have officers in each state to coordinate federal relief efforts related to the economic depression. FDR didn't stop his emergency efforts there. With Executive Order 6889A in late 1934, he consolidated the NEC with the Executive Council and the National Recovery Administration to create another federal monstrosity named the Industrial Emergency Committee. That committee, along with other such related councils, boards, and administrations, would ultimately result in the Executive Office of the President which is still in operation today.

In May 1940, FDR created the Office of Emergency Management (OEM). While it would seem the OEM was attributed to the Great Depression, in fact the main thrust of the OEM's duties was to prepare the nation for war. That was quite odd considering the nation didn't want to go to war, nor did it pick up a rifle to do so until after the surprise attack at Pearl Harbor in December 1941. Once the OEM did its job, most of its duties were transferred to the Office of War Mobilization; however, while the OEM lies dormant today, it has never been officially terminated. It is the oldest federal emergency agency still in existence.

FDR's initiatives aside, the FEMA of today owes most of its history to the post-World War II era of civil defense. Specifically, it was born out of the historic National Security Act. Signed by President Truman in July 1947, the National Security Act reorganized the entire military apparatus of the country as well as the organizations of foreign policy and American intelligence operations. It merged the Department of War and the Department of the Navy into its modern incarnation of the Department of Defense. It birthed the Department of the Air Force (which was later absorbed by the Department of Defense), the Central Intelligence Agency, and the National Security Council. Also out of the National Security Act sprung two arms related to civil defense. The first was the National Security Resources Board. From that came the Office of Civil Defense Planning, including programs such as CONELRAD. The second was the Office of Civil Defense Preparedness which was closely tied to the White House. In 1948, the Office of Civil Defense Preparedness's Director Russell Hopley devised the idea that his department could be used not just for the expected role of helping protect the nation in its civil defense mission, but it might also be very useful in the mitigation of natural disasters. Soon after Hopley's report, Congress passed the Disaster Relief Act of 1950, a culmination of various aid programs that were consolidated into a uniform disaster relief approach.

At the same time the Disaster Relief Act was being passed, Truman began his undeclared war with Korea. Just a few months prior, the Soviet Union had tested its first atomic bomb. Now the public had a new menace to be concerned about—a war with a communist country tied to the only other nation on Earth in possession of "the bomb." Hopley's ideas of disaster relief were set aside while civil defense took on an entirely new meaning. Americans had already seen what an atomic bomb could do first hand. Now its newly sworn enemy had the same technology. How long might it be before an American city was leveled by a Russian nuke?

Out of this growing fear and panic, Congress began to act. It passed the Federal Civil Defense Act in 1950. From that yet another agency was born—the Office of Defense Mobilization which was based in the Executive Office of the President. This ran concurrent to the pre-existing Office of Emergency Management FDR set up prior to World War II which was also part of the Executive Office of the President. As if to make the whole issue more confusing, another agency was developed at this time, the Federal Civil Defense Administration (FCDA). Begun in 1950 in conjunction with the Korean War, the FCDA ultimately swallowed most of the responsibilities with which the previously existing civil defense agencies were tasked. This was aided by the creation of the Defense Production Administration in 1951. These last few actions did not help end the confusion growing within the government over which agency was assigned which task in both disaster relief and civil defense planning. Too many agencies had been created and assigned conflicting tasks to know who was really in charge of what.

Despite those departmental overlaps, one thing was certain: the government was not messing around in matters of civil defense. What, exactly, was "civil defense?" Perhaps the definition of this term best lay under the heading "Basic Goal of Civil Defense" in the November 1966 Office of Civil Defense handbook titled "Personal and Family Survival." It read:

"The basic goal of civil defense, most simply stated, is to save as many lives as possible in the event of nuclear attack on the

United States. This is not to say that civil defense, even in combination with other elements of strategic defense, could prevent widespread destruction in event of attack. Millions of Americans would die, and there is no point in looking away from this harsh reality of nuclear war. But with proper preparations, which are well within the bounds of technical and economic feasibility, millions of other Americans would live to sustain the life of the Nation."

This sort of preparation took on a variety forms. The federal government's main thrust was the construction of fallout shelters across the nation. It was a remarkable endeavor considering that by 1966 the U.S. public fallout shelter system had space to shield 141.5 million citizens (the estimated population at that time was 197 million), though according to a 1971 report made by the General Accounting Office (GAO), there was a disproportionate amount of fallout shelter space available for urban dwellers (2.5 spaces per person) than country folk (0.4 spaces per person). Yet by 1966, 699 of 763 cities with public shelters were completely supplied and stocked with federally procured goods. This included water, a 2,000 calorie-a-day allotment of food for five days (which the government concluded was "about two-thirds of the average normal intake"), sanitation, and medical supplies at a cost of $2.42 per stocked shelter space.

The government didn't want to just protect its people; it wanted to educate them as well. In 1950, the FCDA began filming of a series of nine movies to be shown in schools nationwide. Featuring the cartoon character Bert the Turtle, it was these films that taught the nation's school kids to "duck and cover" (as absurd as that sounds, prior to Russia's development of its own H-bomb, the duck and cover method would have been a rather effective defensive position should an A-bomb have detonated a few miles from a school. All of the children would have likely survived). Clearly, times have changed in America. Could the federal government today issue a similar set of educational films in this age of political correctness? Wouldn't films describing a nuclear war and how to survive its initial attack by ducking and covering or whatever method was determined best—no matter how cute the animated turtle teaching those instructions was—be considered "too scary" for our modern children? How many protests would there be on school grounds over such a film? Or instead would they be seen as pro-U.S. propaganda films? How many conspiracy theorists would crawl out of the woodwork to proclaim that the only reason the government made those films was because it already had a nuclear war planned? The federal government likely couldn't do right for doing wrong. In those early days of the nuclear program, however, such a response was deemed necessary.

It didn't end with the school kids, either. The FCDA began an informational war, attempting to stamp out the nation's fear. The overriding concern among the government's own reports was that the psychological effects of a nuclear war would cause more damage among the citizenry than the actual bombs. Taking the concerned father approach, the government assumed that panic, rioting, and general chaos would follow any sort of Russian attack. In essence, it was believed that American society would ultimately break down under such stress; mentally collapsing even if a majority of the cities remained standing. To counter that, the FCDA decided to over-prepare America for such a circumstance. Nearly 400 million informational booklets and civil defense-related literature were dispersed across the country. These took a decidedly military-like stance, claiming atomic bombs were just another bomb—hence, nothing to worry about. The FCDA went so far as to sponsor a test published in a 1953 *Collier's* magazine which attempted to prevent readers from becoming victims of "panic" by quizzing readers of the warning signs. There were practice air raids conducted nationwide that voluntarily cleared city streets. Besides the growing call for Dad to build a bomb shelter in the backyard and Mom to stock it with non-perishable goods, all citizens were called upon to take part in the nation's civil defense. Amazingly, people heeded the call. Citizens joined civil defense programs in droves. The hope was the more familiar people became with the bomb and all its surrounding circumstances, the less overwhelming the situation would seem. Comfort was to be achieved through knowledge. To a degree, the government was correct.

As the nation feared the growing "Red Menace" with each passing hour, the notion of disaster relief was not completely forgotten. When Dwight D. Eisenhower became president in 1953, he reorganized most of the disaster relief programs into yet another new agency—the Office of Civil Defense (OCD). Not to be confused with the aforementioned FCDA or the OEM, the Office of Civil Defense was placed in the capable hands of the Department of Defense, specifically the Office of the Secretary of the Army and headquartered at the Pentagon. Why did the Army get control of the OCD when its main purpose was to respond to national disasters? Most likely, it stemmed from the Flood Control Act of 1944 which placed the Army Corp of Engineers in charge of flood control and irrigation projects. Hence, the Army Corp of Engineers had already been established as the go-to group to mitigate any flooding disasters. That experience, Eisenhower assumed, would be useful in covering all national disasters. Shortly after the creation of the OCD, Eisenhower put the office to work when he issued the first ever presidential declaration of a major disaster (and gave birth to the idea of an officially declared "disaster area"). A tornado that struck four Georgia counties in May 1953 was the first disaster to make use of the federal Disaster Relief Act. It would not be the last. Over the following 10 years, the Office of Civil Defense would coordinate over 160 disaster relief efforts across the nation.

Over the ensuing 20 years, both civil defense measures and disaster preparedness and relief efforts were a plentiful, yet unorganized mess. This was due to the inability of the federal government to determine strict roles for the agencies involved. It did not help that the only solution during that time was not consolidation and clarification, but rather creation of newer, overlapping agencies. In the civil defense arena, the Office of Civil and Defense Mobilization (OCDM) was created in 1958. That died in 1961 and was replaced with two separate, yet competing agencies—the aforementioned Office of Civil Defense (OCD) and the new Office of Emergency Planning (OEP). While those two were still in operation, the Office of Emergency Preparedness was created in 1968. All three agencies co-existed through 1972. Then the Defense Civil Preparedness Agency (DCPA) was devised in 1973. During that decades-long process, the growing sentiment within the federal government became the football-like notion that the best defense was a good offense. The idea the United States should prepare its defensive capabilities gave way to stockpiling weapons, basically attempting to scare our enemies away through superior firepower. Deterrence was believed to be the best form of civil defense.

Meanwhile, disaster relief was suffering from the same fate as civil defense. Too many agencies having similar, yet separate roles in mitigating disasters was leading to slow, disorganized relief efforts directed at those in need. When considering the various threats and potential hazards a natural disaster may cause within an area, which included the potential damage of nuclear reactors and the release of chemical or radioactive materials (which was no joke, considering that predicting and spotting tornados didn't become a national interest until the Army feared for the safety of certain vulnerable weapons depots scattered throughout the Midwest in the 1940s), the number of federal agencies that could potentially vie for jurisdiction over a disaster and its relief efforts numbered over 100 separate entities. That did not take into account the various state and local level agencies also tasked with responding to disasters. At the start of the 1960s, however, most of the disaster relief authority on the federal level was handed over to the Department of Housing and Urban Development (HUD). Within HUD was created the Federal Disaster Assistance Administration. It was this administration which oversaw the recovery after such disasters as Hurricanes Carla (1961), Betsy (1965), Camille (1969), and Agnes (1972) as well as the great Alaskan earthquake of 1964 and the San Fernando area earthquake in 1971. In 1974, Congress passed the Federal Disaster Relief Act to attempt to organize the unnecessarily convoluted and multi-pronged approach to disaster preparedness and recovery. At that same time, Congress also authorized the DCPA to prepare the nation for both civil defense as well as natural disaster emergencies.

Coming to the rescue for all of those concerned was President Carter. In 1978, Carter submitted to Congress Reorganization Plan Number 3. From that came the Federal Emergency Management Agency which was made official through Executive Order 12127. Operational as of April 1, 1979, FEMA did not instantly solve all of the previous problems associated with disasters and civil defense. Upon its creation, FEMA absorbed most of the remnant agencies that preceded it, including the Federal Insurance Administration, the National Fire Prevention and Control Administration, the National Weather Service Community Preparedness Program, the Federal Preparedness Agency of the General Services Administration as well as over 100 federal disaster response related programs. Combined, all of these new FEMA sub-agencies and programs had originally reported to over 20 different congressional committees. Of course, with that many people involved—including congressmen—it would take a while for the kinks to be worked out of FEMA.

Two Roads Diverged

Combining all of those once separate agencies and programs into one overarching agency under the FEMA banner posed immediate issues. For one, there was an instant division in personnel. Part of FEMA was comprised of former members of the Department of Defense who had overseen the nation's civil defense. Another subsection came out of HUD's Federal Disaster Assistance Administration who knew only of disaster planning and relief. A third group, and perhaps the lowest on the FEMA totem pole, was comprised from the scientific arm of research and development in such areas as firefighting and flood control. Getting those vastly different disciplines to work together was the job of FEMA's first permanent director, John Macy.

While FEMA became operational April 1979, it wasn't until August that Macy stepped into his appointed position. His efforts were quickly bolstered in 1980 as Congress amended the 1950 Federal Civil Defense Act, pouring over $4 billion into FEMA's coffers over the course of seven years. Macy's plan of attack was to direct FEMA with an "all hazards" approach. He believed the response needed for either a natural disaster or a civil defense emergency was essentially one in the same. An evacuation route developed to escape a hurricane would work just as well to clear people out of the path of a nuclear bomb. While that seemed like a good idea, within FEMA there was a strong division among its staff on the true direction the agency should take.

When Ronald Reagan became president in 1981, everything within FEMA changed. Reagan saw FEMA's role as civil defense first, disaster relief a distant second. The problem was Reagan didn't look at civil defense in the same light as his most recent predecessors. Reagan held two beliefs that contributed to this slanted opinion. One, he believed the Soviet Union was out to get us, and he made the Cold War against the Russians his administration's primary concern. Two, having served as the governor of California from 1967-1975, Reagan had dealt with the "hippie problem" one too many times. He began to conclude those no good beatnik protesters were un-American and comprised a true threat to the country. To be blunt, he viewed them as terrorists. If the homeland was threatened from the outside by the communists while threatened from within by home-grown "terrorists," something had to be done to protect the flag-waving general public.

To oversee FEMA and install this change in philosophy, Reagan appointed "General" Louis O. Giuffrida as FEMA's director in May 1981. A former general in California's state militia, Giuffrida first came to Reagan's attention when he was appointed the head of the California National Guard in 1969. Later, Reagan placed Giuffrida in charge of the California Specialized Training Institute (CSTI) which was a state-based emergency management and counterterrorism training center begun by the governor in 1971. Under Giuffrida's direction, the CSTI ran what was known as "Operation Cable Splicer" which attempted to stop all protests—whether peaceful or violent—prior to them ever beginning through surveillance, intimidation, and if need be, force.

Giuffrida was a bit of a kook. He insisted on being called "general" while director of FEMA. He had himself deputized, and often carried a sidearm while in office. He seemed to be under the delusion that FEMA was simply the CIA's or FBI's little brother and not a disaster relief agency. This ideology carried over from his time directing the CSTI. Having witnessed, as the world did, the terrorist attack on the Israeli wrestling team at the 1972 Summer Olympics in Munich, Giuffrida was determined nothing like that would take place on U.S. soil. His anti-terrorist philosophy peppered his FEMA work, especially with Los Angeles hosting the 1984 Summer Olympics under his watch. Perhaps more to the point, Giuffrida wanted action, and if at all possible, a taste of power as well. This mindset influenced the direction he spun FEMA.

The agency found itself in the worst-case scenario business, often developing plans to save the country from nuclear attack rather than providing any forethought into disaster relief. Where things really got weird within FEMA, and where most of the conspiracy theories surrounding the agency began, was when Giuffrida began developing civil control plans as a response to any sort of emergency. The prevailing attitude Giuffrida imparted upon his agency was that when things go wrong (and they will sooner or later), people will riot and loot. What was the best solution to that? The obvious answer to Giuffrida was to round up those troublemakers along with any likeminded dissenters and lock 'em up. Civil rights be damned; there was a nation to protect. The crazy part was most of Reagan's administration went along with the idea.

What kicked off that insane little enterprise was Giuffrida's meeting with Lt. Col. Oliver North. At the time, North was on the National Security Council's staff leading a group concerned with crisis planning. The pair began developing their own little spinoff within FEMA and the NSC. Their collective attention became focused on Giuffrida's pet project of civil unrest—how it could come about, why it would occur, and of course, what should be done to combat it. Out of these meetings, a national contingency plan was developed. A plan that was to be kept secret, and for good reason. It placed FEMA in charge of virtually all emergency powers, and when enacted, would likely institute martial law over the civilian population while suspending the Constitution. Of course, this was only to occur in the event of a "national emergency," the definition of which was as vague as it always has been. The plan was supposed to be kept on the shelf, ready to be signed into effect on a moment's notice when the proper time came.

Luckily, the *Miami Herald* obtained a copy of a June 30, 1982 memo written by Giuffrida's deputy for national preparedness, John Brinkerhoff. Within the memo Brinkerhoff mentions the use of martial law in mitigating any national crisis. While that was making headlines, Reagan and his staff were busy preparing an executive order to make good on Giuffrida's ideas. This set off alarm bells within Attorney General William French Smith's office. He sent a letter to Reagan's National Security Advisor Robert MacFarlane asking him to step in and stop the lunacy of such an executive order before it was ever written. Smith felt, rightly so, that FEMA was clearly overstepping its boundaries. For one, the five year old agency only had a staff of some 3,000 people, a whopping majority of which were not law enforcement types. This would make it near impossible for FEMA to institute any sort of martial law anywhere. They didn't possess the capabilities, resources, or the muscle to activate any such plans. More importantly, such actions would instantly lead to numerous legal concerns (and the Attorney General realized that the law wouldn't fall on FEMA's side in this matter). The design of the agency was for emergency preparedness, not for stamping out the Constitution at the drop of a hat when an emergency occurred. Reagan wisely listened to his Attorney General and National Security Advisor and backed off pursuing any such Giuffrida-backed executive order.

While that turmoil was whipping around the White House, Giuffrida continued his bizarre preparations. The most notable was Readiness Exercise 1984, better known as REX84. This was not the first, nor the last, readiness exercise FEMA ran, but it has become the most infamous for reasons soon revealed. A staple in conspiracy lore, REX84 was basically a practice run for Giuffrida's master plan. The FEMA exercise took place alongside the military's Night Train 84 operation in April 1984 which inserted troops in Honduras near Contra camps along the Nicaraguan border. This show of force was in preparation for a potential invasion of Nicaragua (prior to the whole Iran-Contra affair blowing up). FEMA's supposed role in this was to support the Department of Defense. How? FEMA was to stem the tide of a mass border crossing of refugees into the United States that would supposedly result from our military's actions in Central America. FEMA simulated rounding up some 400,000 illegal aliens and hauling them off to pre-described detention camps. These holding camps were built on several U.S. bases along the U.S./Mexico border and still exist today. Why hundreds of thousands of refugees would suddenly storm the U.S. border was never really explained (most officials didn't even consider such an invasion possible) which was why the purpose of that exercise was turned around by some and believed not to be an exercise in rounding up refugees, but rather an exercise to prepare for the rounding up of Americans as per Giuffrida's plan.

After REX84 was completed and the *Miami Herald* published its article detailing the Brinkerhoff memo, Giuffrida's hope of making himself (and FEMA) the nation's emergency czar quickly died. The agency took a major publicity hit from which it wasn't able to recover. Federal investigators began looking into Giuffrida for alleged fraud and mismanagement charges. Instead of weathering the storm, Giuffrida resigned in September 1985. He is not mentioned anywhere within FEMA's history on its website.

Immediately after Giuffrida's departure, FEMA floundered. It lacked any sense of structured organization or compelling leadership. In the case of large disasters, such as Hurricanes Gilbert (1988) and Hugo (1989), FEMA's response was slow, disorganized, and often inadequate for the number of people in need of aid. None of that should have been surprising considering the still confused and reeling bureaucracy behind the agency. At other times, when smaller, more regional disasters occurred, FEMA was unsure whether to get involved at all. Was the agency supposed to respond to all emergencies, even when the localities involved didn't ask for it, or was the agency "on hold" until given an official green light to do its thing? There was no clear answer. As a result, for an agency mandated to prepare for emergencies, it proved to be just the opposite. Due to these failures, FEMA began to get a bad name both inside and outside of Washington.

In an attempt to help FEMA, Congress passed the Robert T. Stafford Disaster Relief and Emergency Assistance Act in 1988. The act began with the passage: "The Congress hereby finds and declares that (1) because disasters often cause loss of life, human suffering, loss of income, and property loss and damage; and (2) because disasters often disrupt the normal functioning of governments and communities, and adversely affect individuals and families with great severity; special measures, designed to assist the efforts of the affected States in expediting the rendering of aid, assistance, and emergency services, and the reconstruction and rehabilitation of devastated areas, are necessary." It only took Congress until 1988 to figure that out. The rest of the act was just as enlightening. While the act defined what could be considered an emergency—"'Emergency' means any occasion or instance for which, in the determination of the President, Federal assistance is needed to supplement State and local efforts and capabilities to save lives and to protect property and public health and safety, or to lessen or avert the threat of a catastrophe in any part of the United States"—and what was officially a major disaster—"'Major disaster' means any natural catastrophe (including any hurricane, tornado, storm, high water, wind-driven water, tidal wave, tsunami, earthquake, volcanic eruption, landslide, mudslide, snowstorm, or drought), or, regardless of cause, any fire, flood, or explosion, in any part of the United States, which in the determination of the President causes damage of sufficient severity and magnitude to warrant major disaster assistance under this Act to supplement the efforts and available resources of States, local governments, and disaster relief organizations in alleviating the damage, loss, hardship, or suffering caused thereby"—it did next to nothing to clarify FEMA's already muddied role within that realm. The act did require each state in the country to develop an Emergency Operation Plan. Also, the director of FEMA was mandated to create a Federal Response Plan (FPR). While the FRP was merged with the National Contingency Plan (NCP) that had originally been developed by the Environmental Protection Agency in 1968 to deal with hazardous materials, the FRP was simply that—a plan (and one that would often be updated and rewritten as FEMA continued to fail in its efforts). Even with such a plan in hand, FEMA was uncertain about its role within it. Hence the agency was still rudderless when it ran smack into Hurricane Andrew in 1992.

Prior to Hurricane Katrina nationalizing FEMA's weaknesses, Hurricane Andrew had been the agency's arch enemy. When it struck southern Florida and Louisiana in 1992, FEMA assumed it was ready. Since it knew when and where the hurricane would make landfall, the agency pre-dispatched its emergency responders to be on the scene and ready to go as soon as the storm passed. Little did FEMA realize its responders would be swamped by the same storm from which they were there to aid in the recovery. Since the first responders were also in need of rescue, the entire situation went to hell in a hand basket. The only portion of FEMA's plan that was ready and able to do its duty was its Mobile Emergency Response Support (MERS) vehicles. Of course MERS vehicles aren't your ordinary communications van. They are nuclear-hardened vehicles designed to operate in a post-nuclear war environment. About a dozen of these were deployed to Florida

(FEMA reportedly owns about 300 MERS vehicle spread across the nation). Needless to say, Floridian officials were shocked by the presence of World War III-ready mobile communications vehicles when all they wanted was the ability to coordinate relief efforts in order to supply the population with food and water.

In the midst of his re-election campaign, President George H.W. Bush toured the Hurricane Andrew disaster area with FEMA's director, Wallace Stickney. Seeing the on-going chaotic response first hand, Bush ordered approximately 20,000 Navy, Air Force, and Coast Guard troops into the area to take charge of the relief efforts. Instead of overseeing this effort, Stickney went back to Washington. In his place, Secretary of Transportation Andrew Card took control working alongside the upper echelon of the military commanders on hand.

After all was said and done in response to Hurricane Andrew, the government took a long, hard look at its disaster relief programs. First off, the Federal Response Plan was rewritten in hope of not having to relive the Hurricane Andrew response effort ever again. Then all eyes turned towards FEMA. Twelve years into its existence, it was finally realized that the agency didn't have the suitable resources, staff, or management to respond to the disasters it was mandated to alleviate. Another problem government investigators soon discovered was that too much of FEMA's funding was going into military-like projects (such as the MERS vehicles) and civil defense planning. Unfortunately, that couldn't be avoided. FEMA's charter tasked the agency with national security matters which meant it had to supply those projects whether completely necessary or not. While the Soviet Union had collapsed and the communist threat seemed to subside, there was no mandate for FEMA to halt its civil defense measures, nor was the agency about to, considering half of its staff originated from the Department of Defense.

To survive, FEMA had two basic choices, both of which stemmed from its original creation. Either the militaristic branch of FEMA responsible for civil defense planning had to be separated from the agency so the public could look to what remained when disaster struck, or else the two sides had to learn to work together much more effectively.

New Look, Similar Results

When Bill Clinton became president (which very well may have been aided by FEMA's poor response to Hurricane Andrew as President Bush took the fall for the agency), he installed James L. Witt as FEMA's latest director. Witt had worked under Clinton while he was governor of Arkansas, serving as the head of Arkansas's Office of Emergency Services from 1988-1992. When Witt took over FEMA in April 1993, as shocking as it may appear, he became the first director of FEMA who actually had experience in the role of emergency planning.

Nevertheless, Witt faced an uphill battle. The public saw FEMA as useless, and they were pretty much right. Congress was ready to disband the agency, seeing it as inefficient and a waste of taxpayer money. Witt urged Congress to reconsider, asking for a year to turn the agency around prior to its dismantling. His plan was simple—use an "all-hazards" approach. Of course, this was the exact direction FEMA's original director, John Macy, attempted to install in the agency prior to Giuffrida's corruption of FEMA. The all-hazards approach was the most sensible track to follow. A disaster was a disaster, no matter the cause. While the needed response for such an event could be tailored to each individual incident, the basic needs demanded by those suffering from such a disaster—water, food, shelter, and medical care—would always be the same. Plus, by implementing the all-hazard mentality, the military and disaster relief factions within FEMA could both be appeased (as well as funded).

Given a chance to make it work, Witt stuck to his guns and began to streamline the agency. He brought on experts in disaster related fields (volcanologists, seismologists, etc.) to help FEMA's staff understand what they may be up against and what the proper response to each catastrophic situation should be. At the same time, Witt pushed most civil defense matters to the back burner.

This scaling back in civil defense planning appeared sensible. The nation was not at war, nor was an armed conflict looming. Meanwhile, natural disasters occurred on an annual basis throughout the nation. Aiding in this transformation within the agency, the Civil Defense Act was repealed in 1994. That ended the military's direct involvement in FEMA while freeing up a large portion of the agency's funds. The percentage of money normally delegated to civil defense projects could now be poured into disaster relief efforts.

This influx of money also helped grease a few palms. While Witt's eight-year reign at FEMA was seen as a success revitalizing the agency, Witt was lucky not to have to endure any major U.S. catastrophe. When there was a declared disaster, such as the major Midwestern floods in the mid-1990s, Witt wasn't afraid to freely spend the government's money. During his tenure, there were more federal disasters declared and more relief funding poured into the states that requested it than ever before in FEMA's history. This was done to publicly redeem FEMA as much as anything. If the population saw FEMA actually working for them, then they wouldn't be so rushed in calling their congressmen to place the agency on the chopping block. There was more to it than just saving FEMA's face. While the increase in disaster relief spending was helpful to those who suffered from whatever catastrophe befell them, it also aided the officials who were credited with a quick and decisive response to the emergency in getting re-elected. Those same officials who benefited from Witt's immediate disaster response in turn helped Witt where and when he needed it. This political back scratching did wonders for all involved—even the common folk in need.

While Witt was enjoying FEMA's rebirth, he may have been somewhat responsible for lowering the nation's guard. The National Security Council wanted FEMA to take on more responsibilities, especially those related to preparing for a terrorist attack. It seemed as though the NSC couldn't forget the anti-terrorist ideas planted during the Giuffrida/North marriage in the mid-1980s. There was good reason for that. During Witt's tenure, America endured the bombing of the World Trade Center in 1993, followed by the bombing of the Alfred P. Murrah Federal Building in Oklahoma City in 1995, and the bomb planted at the Centennial Olympic Park in Atlanta during the 1996 Summer Olympics. The powers within the NSC felt more of these terrorist incidents were bound to occur and that FEMA should be the nation's first responders. Witt and FEMA disagreed. The success of their relief programs had pushed the notion of civil defense off their radar (in fact, FEMA had placed most of these programs including Continuity of Government within a completely separate national security entity). Witt didn't feel FEMA had the manpower or the general wherewithal to take on national defense programs such as responding to attacks on the weapons of mass destruction scale. Since those events were technically disasters according to the Stafford Act, that inflexibility threw a wrench into Witt's original hard-line all-hazards approach, yet his stance remained firm.

Those anti-terrorism efforts were then pushed back onto the FBI and the Justice Department, with the Department of Defense helping aid the mission. Even so, FEMA wasn't completely off the hook. A "terrorism annex" was added to the Federal Response Plan in 1997. While the FBI was given the primary tasks involved in response to any such attack, FEMA was forced into the role of consequence management as they should have been; however, the agency made few, if any, real changes to its approach after being given this mandate. Meanwhile, the Justice Department opened their own Office of Domestic Preparedness in 1998 to deal with their newly assigned mission.

Witt's eight year tenure at FEMA quietly ended with George W. Bush's ascension into the White House. Bush's choice to replace Witt at FEMA was his former campaign manager, Joe Allbaugh, who as tradition seemed to hold, had no experience in the emergency/disaster field. Initially all looked well within the agency as Witt had it running like a well-oiled machine when Allbaugh took control. Then the events of September 11, 2001 shook the nation. From that date forward, everything changed.

Its hand forced by the aftermath of 9/11, FEMA had no choice but to alter its mindset. Allbaugh instantly shifted FEMA's gears and placed the agency's focus squarely on civil defense. Terrorism, not natural disasters, became FEMA's prime enemy. The Office of National Preparedness was reopened within FEMA (it had not existed since Witt put the kibosh on the ONP in 1993), and money that originally was put to use preparing the nation for natural disasters now went into counterterrorism. It was a complete flip-flop. The national buzzword of "terrorism" suddenly took precedence over any long-term disaster planning efforts, and not all within the agency were happy with it.

Then at the end of February 2003, the hard work and effort Witt had put into redeeming FEMA went completely up in smoke as President Bush created the Department of Homeland Security through several executive orders. FEMA, along with 22 other agencies, was absorbed by the DHS. Now FEMA was part of an agency that consisted of nearly 200,000 employees working toward four supposedly equal but separate goals. These included emergency preparedness and response as well as border protection, infrastructure protection, and science and technology. Not that the DHS went lacking in terms of funding. Originally in its first year, DHS was given over $14 billion to work with. By 2012, its budget skyrocketed to over $57 billion. Allbaugh was out as FEMA's director, in fact, so was the entire cabinet level post of Director of FEMA. Bush placed Michael D. Brown in Allbaugh's former role, which was now titled Undersecretary of Emergency Preparedness and Response. Brown, like Allbaugh before him, had no real experience for that role. While Brown did serve as Allbaugh's general counsel within FEMA from 2001 to his ascension to undersecretary, prior to that Brown served as the Judges and Stewards Commissioner for the International Arabian Horse Association from 1989-2001.

Brown found himself in an unenviable position. As the newly appointed undersecretary, he no longer had access to either the president or Congress unlike the former directors of FEMA. Instead, the new position reported only to the Secretary of the DHS or other such undersecretaries. In other words, FEMA and its head were pushed further down the bureaucratic ladder. Brown recognized the danger in this and predicted that such an arrangement would not serve the nation's best interest. He openly dreaded a major disaster.

In an attempt to provide more guidance to the DHS (and as an afterthought, to FEMA), the Federal Response Plan was rewritten in 2004 to become the National Response Plan (NRP). The document may have had a different title, yet it possessed the same basic plan. After its refocusing in 2004, the NRP was rewritten again in 2006, and then again in early 2008 when it became known as the National Response Framework (NRF). No one seemed to get the hint that it wasn't the document that was the problem, it was the people tasked with implementing it that couldn't get it straight.

Since the U.S. found itself embroiled in a "war" on "terror," President Bush needed to show the public he was doing something to combat the evildoers. On the home front, this was the creation of the DHS. To steer the DHS, the National Response Plan/Framework was to be that department's guiding principal. For the new version of FEMA existing under the DHS's oversight, the NRF emphasized the old "all-hazards" mantra. To quote from the 2008 version: "This National Response Framework (NRF) is a guide to how the Nation conducts all-hazards response. It is built upon **scalable, flexible, and adaptable coordinating structures** to align key roles and responsibilities **across the Nation**. It describes specific authorities and best practices for managing incidents that range from the serious but purely local, to large-scale terrorist attacks or catastrophic natural disasters. [emphasis in original]." While this looked good, in reality, FEMA found itself back under a militaristically inclined thumb that was focused primarily on terrorists, counterterrorism, and rounding up suspected dissenters rather than disaster relief. The funding for

FEMA was poured into counterterrorism projects while efforts that had proven their worth, such as FEMA's Project Impact which had helped engineers plan and build "disaster proof" cities, were left wanting.

As the DHS-governed FEMA geared up for another 9/11-like terrorist attack (that has yet to materialize), on August 29, 2005, Hurricane Katrina made landfall in Louisiana. The shortsightedness of the government was once again exposed as the relief effort for Katrina was a complete organizational meltdown. Did that come as a surprise to the Undersecretary of Emergency Preparedness and Response, Michael Brown? Not at all. Even though Brown was ill-suited for his position and lacked the political power or insight to change FEMA's role prior to that point, he was still competent enough to recognize the new-look FEMA was nowhere near as prepared as it should have been. Not only had the organizational structure of the agency been completely altered, but a majority of its funding was being utilized for a completely different purpose. Had the government remembered the lesson it should have learned after the debacle that was Giuffrida's reign coupled with the utter failure in the aftermath of Hurricane Andrew, maybe it would have been better prepared to deal with Katrina.

Having grown in size since its merging with the DHS, FEMA itself still possessed a staff of less than 6,000 people. Could a group that size, even if fully trained, funded, and prepared, effectively responded to the massive flooding in New Orleans? The swamping of the city should not have come as a surprise to anyone within the agency. The Weather Channel, in preparing a series of programs titled *It Could Happen Tomorrow* about worst-case disaster scenarios that may someday affect the U.S., created its first episode detailing the results of a category five hurricane striking the city of New Orleans. The show didn't get a chance to air as scheduled because Hurricane Katrina made the show's premise moot. If the Weather Channel had such foresight, then surely FEMA recognized the potential for disaster there. Anyone with common sense could see that a city built below sea level, nestled up against the ocean, and residing in the nation's hurricane belt was major disaster waiting to occur. When New Orleans' levees failed and flooded nearly 80 percent of the city, trapping over 100,000 people that failed to evacuate while displacing upwards of a million more, what could the 6,000 person staff at FEMA really have done to immediately relieve the situation? On top of that, do not forget it wasn't just New Orleans that was affected by the storm. While the city received an overwhelming portion of the media coverage in response to the hurricane, Katrina's devastation was felt all along the Gulf Coast, and many cities, both large and small, were also in need of aid.

Should these facts give FEMA a free pass in the case of Hurricane Katrina? Heavens no. FEMA had over two decades worth of disaster planning and experience—both good and bad—to fall back on. It had the National Response Plan. It knew the hurricane was coming and issued the appropriate evacuation notifications well ahead of the storm's arrival. It was aware from past experience that not all of the people would or could leave as directed and they would be in need of help. Could the agency have been caught by surprise as to the amount of devastation the city of New Orleans felt? Certainly, for had the levees not failed, the amount of damage the city suffered would have been much less. That still doesn't mean an agency devoted to disaster relief, coupled with the support and financing of the federal government, couldn't have been Johnny-on-the-spot when the storm finally passed. Did that mean everyone could have been helped? No. The sheer numbers of people involved coupled with the size of the area affected dictated that some people would inevitably fall between the cracks. It's sad, but true. FEMA even warned of this.

As was usually the case when all hell breaks loose in the aftermath of some major disaster, the government's main response was a lot of finger pointing. It was FEMA's fault. It was President Bush's fault. It was Louisiana Governor Kathleen Blanco's fault. It was New Orleans' Mayor Ray Nagin's fault. It was the citizens' of New Orleans fault. It was America's fault. It was all-of-the-above's fault. None of this did anything to remedy the situation or help in preventing a similar incident from occurring in the future. Michael Brown, who attempted to warn everyone that FEMA wasn't ready for something of the magnitude of Hurricane Katrina, resigned on September 12, 2005 amid the controversy over the relief efforts. He was replaced by R. David Paulison, who was a former fire chief in Miami and served as the DHS's head of the United States Fire Administration. Paulison would serve in this role until President Obama's inauguration in 2009.

In late September 2005, while New Orleans and its surrounding areas were still flooded, the government began its investigation into "what went wrong" in the response to Katrina with the Select Bipartisan Committee to Investigate the Preparation for and Response to Hurricane Katrina. As these members of Congress wrote in their summary, "In crafting our findings, we did not guide the facts. We let the facts guide us." What were these facts? To be brief, the committee found:

"Levees protecting New Orleans were not built for the most severe hurricanes; the failure of complete evacuations led to preventable deaths, great suffering, and further delays in relief [the blame for which fell on Louisiana Governor Blanco and New Orleans Mayor Nagin both of whom delayed ordering a mandatory evacuation in New Orleans until 19 hours before Katrina's landfall]; critical elements of the National Response Plan were executed late, ineffectively, or not at all; command and control was impaired at all levels, delaying relief; the collapse of local law enforcement and lack of effective public communications led to civil unrest and further delayed relief; the military played an invaluable role, but coordination was lacking; medical care and evacuations suffered from a lack of advance preparations, inadequate communications, and difficulties coordinating efforts; long-standing weaknesses and the magnitude of the disaster overwhelmed FEMA's ability to provide emergency shelter and temporary housing; [and] FEMA logistics and contracting systems did not support a targeted, massive, and sustained provision of commodities."

All of which led the Committee to write, "DHS and the states were not prepared for this catastrophic event."

There was more. The committee wrote, "Following Hurricane Katrina, emergency management professionals in the Gulf coast region have questioned whether DHS and state preparedness for catastrophic events has declined over the past years due to organizational changes within DHS and a shift in programmatic priorities. In particular, the decline in preparedness has been seen as a result of the separation of the preparedness function from FEMA, the drain of long-term professional staff along with their institutional knowledge and expertise, and the diminished readiness of FEMA's national emergency response teams." While the Committee wasn't brave enough to give the reasoning as to why that was the truth, they had to be well aware of the facts—that the decline in preparation was directly the result of a large percentage of FEMA's funding going into anti-terrorist efforts. While the scale and related logistics involved in the Hurricane Katrina relief effort easily overwhelmed those tasked with taking part in it, the fact that no one seemed prepared relates directly back to where FEMA's collective brain was: on terrorism. This doesn't mean the relief effort would have been flawless had this not been true, but it certainly would have been much more timely and organized.

Unfortunately, this is where FEMA still stands today. Its role is once again completely confused and somewhat ambiguous. The agency is funded and trained with an eye on terrorism while the public expects it to be there when a natural disaster strikes. While it seems to be pulled in these two opposing directions at once, it's utterly frozen when the call comes in for FEMA to rush into action. That should tell you two things: One, the government isn't about to get its act together any time soon, no matter how much money it throws at the problem which means, two, you better plan on saving yourself because ain't no one else going to do it for you.

S.Y.S. (SAVE YOURSELF)

"The nine most terrifying words in the English language are, 'I'm from the government and I'm here to help.'"
--40th President of the United States Ronald Reagan

There's a disaster looming on the horizon. Don't fool yourself; there is. What form it will take depends on where you live and what America's enemies have in store for her. It could be a tornado. It very well may be a massive tsunami. It might be the detonation of a small tactical nuclear weapon, or all-out nuclear war. Most likely, it will be something you, your neighbors, and the government itself never considered possible (though you'd be surprised what the government considers possible). Chances are, whatever that catastrophe is, you're not prepared to meet it head on. So, when the dust settles, you'll be faced with two options: (A) You can brush yourself off, pull a chair out from under the pile of rubble that was once your house, and have a seat while you wait for the government to come rescue you. Or (B) you can be proactive, prepare a survival kit compatible for any emergency, and have the mindset that you and your loved ones are going to be without any immediate outside help for a significant period of time. Which of these two options do you think gives you the best chance of surviving such a scenario? Here's a hint: It's not A.

The National Response Framework

Mentioned in passing during the previous chapter regarding FEMA, the National Response Framework (NRF) grew out of similarly named plans that were intended as a guidebook for federal government responders in the vast wilderness of disaster possibilities. The first of these response plans was developed in the

1980s, just after FEMA's formation. They have been available to members of our government prior to the San Francisco Bay area earthquake in 1989, Hurricane Andrew in 1992, the 9/11 attacks in 2001, Hurricane Katrina in 2005 and Superstorm Sandy in 2012. It didn't seem to help much though, did it?

That is because as one reads through the current version of the NRF published in January 2008, the reader is quickly struck by how convoluted, overwrought, and complex it is. It's not by any means a simple, straightforward response program. Instead, the NRF spends its 79 pages (that's without the 30 or so annexes the document possesses) setting up nonsensical command posts and operation centers, all of which would take countless hours of effort to perform prior to a single finger being lifted to deliver the necessary aid to those crying out for it.

From the NRF's introduction alone, one should get the sense that we're all in a bit of trouble if one plans on relying on the NRF to facilitate a rescue in an emergency situation. By page 2, the government's already making excuses. **"One of the challenges to effective response is the relatively high turnover and short tenure among elected and appointed officials responsible for response at all levels.** Effective response hinges upon well-trained leaders and responders who have invested in response preparedness, developed engaged partnerships, and are able to achieve shared objectives. The players' bench is constantly changing, but a concise, common playbook is needed by all. [emphasis in original]" Who are our current leaders occupying some of these critical posts? The current FEMA chief is W. Craig Fugate, nominated to the post by President Obama in March 2009. Fugate was a solid choice considering his background in emergency response, including serving as director of the Florida Division of Emergency Management.

His immediate boss, the Secretary of the Department of Homeland Security, whose job description includes overseeing FEMA and its operations, is Janet Napolitano, the former governor of Arizona. As is typical in this role, Napolitano has no disaster-related experience. Could Napolitano be one of those "well-trained leaders" the NRF requests? We can only hope, for the NRF directs that "When the overall coordination of Federal response activities is required, it is implemented through the Secretary of Homeland Security consistent with Homeland Security Presidential Directive (HSPD) 5."

Signed into effect by President George W. Bush in February 2003, HSPD-5's stated purpose is much like the NRF. It is "to enhance the ability of the United States to manage domestic incidents by establishing a single, comprehensive national incident management system." The person responsible for this is the Secretary of the DHS. As HSPD-5 directed, "The Secretary of Homeland Security is the principal Federal official for domestic incident management. Pursuant to the Homeland Security Act of 2002, the Secretary is responsible for coordinating Federal operations within the United States to prepare for, respond to, and recover from terrorist attacks, major disasters, and other emergencies." While Ms. Napolitano's lack of experience should give us pause, perhaps it's not just her past on which we should be so completely focused.

As the NRF makes abundantly clear, "**The President leads the Federal Government response effort** to ensure that the necessary coordinating structures, leadership, and resources are applied quickly and efficiently to large-scale and catastrophic incidents. [emphasis in original]" How is President Obama's record on acting in the face of disasters? Non-existent. In any role prior to and since becoming president, he has yet to face any significant disaster (with the exception of Superstorm Sandy which, at the time of this writing, the Northeast was still recovering from its effects). Luckily for Obama, most of that pressure should be alleviated from his burdened shoulders thanks to the Stafford Act.

The relief funding available under the Stafford Act exists in the official President's Disaster Relief Fund. This isn't some open cookie jar. There are rules (or if you prefer, loopholes) one has to jump through to get at this money. For example, only a

"Presidential major disaster declaration triggers long-term Federal recovery programs, some of which are matched by State programs, and designed to help disaster victims, businesses, and public entities." A simple emergency declaration is "more limited in scope and without the long-term Federal recovery programs of a major disaster declaration." So, how does an "emergency declaration" warrant becoming a "Presidential major disaster declaration?" To become such a "major disaster" as per the NRF, "the event must be clearly more than State or local governments can handle alone." How, or when, do we recognize that situation is occurring? When the governor of the state affected says so, but only if certain requirements are met first.

As per page 41 of the NRF:

"Most incidents are not of sufficient magnitude to warrant a Presidential declaration. However, if State and local resources are insufficient, a Governor may ask the President to make such a declaration. Before making a declaration request, the Governor must activate the State's emergency plan and ensure that all appropriate State and local actions have been taken or initiated, including: Surveying the affected areas to determine the extent of private and public damage, conducting joint preliminary damage assessments with FEMA officials to estimate the types and extent of Federal disaster assistance required, consulting with the FEMA Regional Administrator on Federal disaster assistance eligibility, and advising the FEMA regional office if a Presidential declaration will be requested."

However, "in extraordinary circumstances, the President may unilaterally declare a major disaster or emergency. This request is made through the FEMA Regional Administrator and based on a finding that the disaster is of such severity and magnitude that effective response is beyond the capabilities of the State and affected local governments, and that Federal assistance is necessary." Of course, this could mean that should a particular state's emergency efforts be shoddy and half-assed, they are much more likely to get federal aid as opposed to another state where those same organizations are better staffed and maintained. Should you be a governor with a budget crunch, might not that be an advantageous loophole to exploit in order to shed some state money that could be used elsewhere? As long as you know the federal government's going to come to your (eventual) aid if your (ill-funded) emergency efforts have been "overwhelmed," why bother to pour money into those state agencies? All a governor has to do is simply ask the president to help. What's the president supposed to then do? Say no? Could you imagine the response if the President of the United States came out and said, "I refuse to come to the aid of this state because those dopes refused to properly fund, staff, and prepare for this emergency situation in which they now find themselves. Tough luck, folks, you should've known better." No, the purse strings will open and federal money will pour into the affected state, no matter how likely it is for it to be mismanaged.

Barring the suggested loophole, states are supposed to fend for themselves. The NRF emphatically declares, "States provide the majority of the external assistance to communities." In fact, a large portion of the NRF directs state and other local officials on how they should prepare to deal with disaster scenarios. It provides gems such as a flow chart of "The Response Process" which goes like this: First, "Gain and Maintain Situational Awareness," then "Activate and Deploy Resources and Capabilities," and finally "Coordination Response Actions." The NRF even directs a state in need to ask neighboring states for help prior to tapping the federal government. "If additional resources are required, the State should request assistance from other States by using interstate mutual aid and assistance agreements such as the Emergency Management Assistance Compact (EMAC). Administered by the National Emergency Management Association, EMAC is a congressionally ratified organization that provides form and structure to the interstate mutual aid and assistance process."

There is no doubt your local government is to be the first responder in any emergency, followed by the state's willing assistance. While every state has a general sameness to its disaster relief programs, it is up to each person to know what their state has in mind when catastrophe strikes. All 50 states could not be covered here; however, since those are the people that comprise the first and primary responders to any emergency situation, you may want to take the time to familiarize yourself with their plans and procedures. Your state's plan may be as convoluted as the federal government's. It may not be. Either way, it is your responsibility to know it, especially if you plan on sitting around and waiting for someone else to come to your rescue. Prior to the federal government having to step in and taking charge, relief efforts of some sort should already be underway thanks to state officials. It is only upon these state-level response efforts being overwhelmed (or again, underfunded) that the federal government is to make its presence felt.

Clearly there is a difference between some disaster befalling a state or two as opposed to something clubbing the continental 48 states. The NRF was designed to handle the larger, multi-state or nationwide emergencies which require federal response. While the proverbial buck may stop at the president's desk in declaring a major disaster is occurring, he is allowed to pass that responsibility along. The NRF allows "the President's Homeland Security Council and National Security Council…provide national strategic and policy advice to the President during large-scale incidents that affect the Nation." Both the HSC and NSC have the Secretary of the DHS on its staff, so again Napolitano is effectively on the nation's hook should yet another disaster relief effort be completely mucked up as they have so consistently been in the past.

Or is she? The NRF adds the following on page 24:

"Federal disaster assistance is often thought of as synonymous with Presidential declarations and the Stafford Act. The fact is that Federal assistance can be provided to State, tribal, and local jurisdictions, and to other Federal departments and agencies, in a number of different ways through various mechanisms and authorities. Often, Federal assistance does not require coordination by DHS and can be provided without a Presidential major disaster or emergency declaration. Examples of these types of Federal assistance include that described in the National Oil and Hazardous Substances Pollution Contingency Plan, the Mass Migration Emergency Plan, the National Search and Rescue Plan, and the National Maritime Security Plan."

So, we don't need the DHS to implement the Mass Migration Emergency Plan. Who will we need? It depends. Consider: "Other DHS agency heads have a lead response role or an otherwise significant role, depending upon the type and severity of the event. For example, the U.S. Coast Guard Commandant has statutory lead authority for certain mass migration management scenarios and significant oil/hazardous substance spill incidents in the maritime environment."

Another reason why the DHS may not be needed in such emergency situations comes from the fact that "several Federal departments and agencies have their own authorities to declare disasters or emergencies." Really? "For example, the Secretary of Health and Human Services can declare a public health emergency. These declarations may be made independently or as part of a coordinated Federal response." From that was derived the notion that "under the [NRF], various Federal departments or agencies may play primary, coordinating, and/or support roles based on their authorities and resources and the nature of the threat or incident." Notice here, that by page 26 of the NRF where that statement was made, things are already starting to get a bit willy-nilly. There are rules to be followed, but in certain circumstances, they don't need to be. Instead, some agencies can act independently, but not always because sometimes someone else is to be in charge. Who? What? Where? When?

Maybe you're beginning to understand why the federal response to past disasters wasn't very quick or efficient. Blame the prior incarnations of the NRF all you want, but the current NRF isn't going to make it much easier for these federal level efforts to be organized and put into motion. Try and follow the "structures and staffing" the NRF intends on setting up should it be necessary for the federal government to respond to a major disaster or terrorist attack, and ask yourself where in this chain of command is the whole situation going to get bogged down.

Seated at the top of the food supply chain is the president. He is to be supported by both the National Security Council and the Homeland Security Council. Within both of these entities exists the posts of The Assistant to the President of National Security Affairs (from the NCS) and The Assistant to the President for Homeland Security and Counterterrorism (from the HSC). To support these two positions on "domestic interagency policy coordination on a routine basis, HSC and NSC deputies and principals convene to resolve significant policy issues." These are further supported by two specific groups—the Domestic Readiness Group (DRG) and the Counterterrorism Security Group (CSG)—which are routinely convened to discuss policy and preparedness of related incidents. After that is sorted out, the Secretary of the DHS is to step in and take charge without, of course, trampling upon the president's understood command.

Both the NRF and the HSPD-5 share the definition of when the country will need the Secretary of the DHS to act "when the overall coordination of Federal response activities is required." There are four criteria, only one of which needs to be met for the Secretary of the DHS to jump into action. These are "(1) a Federal department or agency acting under its own authority has requested the assistance of the Secretary; (2) the resources of State and local authorities are overwhelmed and Federal assistance has been requested by the appropriate State and local authorities; (3) more than one Federal department or agency has become substantially involved in responding to the incident; or (4) the Secretary has been directed to assume responsibility for managing the domestic incident by the President."

Directly under the Secretary of the DHS is the FEMA Administrator. "The FEMA Administrator's duties include operation of the National Response Coordination Center, the effective support of all Emergency Support Functions, and, more generally, preparation for, protection against, response to, and recovery from all-hazards incidents." Coming in under the FEMA Administrator is all of the other DHS agency heads who may possess a "lead response role or an otherwise significant role, depending upon the type and severity of the event." Underneath these other DHS agency heads is the DHS Director of Operations Coordination who "is the Secretary's principal advisor for the overall departmental level of integration of incident management operations and oversees the National Operations Center."

In case you were curious as to what the National Operations Center is, one must enter the quirky realm of the Operation Centers. There are a few strata in the Operations Center universe. The overall commanding center is known as the National Operations Center (NOC). The NRF defines the NOC's purpose as "intended to provide a one-stop information source for incident information sharing with the White House and other Federal departments and agencies at the headquarters level." Information sharing is seen as the key to making any relief effort run. "The role of DHS in coordinating Federal response operations must be highly collaborative. There must be excellent, mutual transparency among DHS and its Federal partners into each other's response capabilities. The same is true with regard to States. This requires extraordinarily close, daily operational connectivity among States, DHS, and other departments and agencies at senior levels and at operational levels." Perhaps all of this would be a bit easier if there weren't so many people involved in different levels of response capabilities, but that's just one man's humble opinion.

The general operation of the NOC is explained in the NRF. "The NOC is a continuously operating multiagency operations center. The NOC's staff monitors many sources of threat and hazard information from across the United States and abroad. It is supported by a 24/7 watch officer contingent, including: (1) NOC managers; (2) selected Federal interagency, State, and local law enforcement representatives; (3) intelligence community liaison officers provided by the DHS Chief Intelligence Officer; (4) analysts from the Operations Division's interagency planning element; and (5) watch standers representing dozens of organizations and disciplines from the Federal Government and others from the private sector." If you're willing to believe what you've just read, the NOC—and subsequently, this nation—should never be caught by surprise. Granted, earthquake prediction and other related fields are nowhere near 100 percent accurate, but with the type of surveillance the NOC supposedly provides, as soon as something happens, it should be on top of it. Especially when you consider that the NOC doesn't operate alone.

There are two main Operational Components within the NOC. The first is the National Response Coordination Center (NRCC). "The NRCC is FEMA's primary operations management center, as well as the focal point for national resource coordination. As a 24/7 operations center, the NRCC monitors potential or developing incidents and supports the efforts of regional and field components." The NRCC is also able to expand its staffing and operations "immediately" in preparation or in response to an emergency. The second Operational Component at the NOC is the National Infrastructure Coordination Center (NICC). "The NICC monitors the Nation's critical infrastructure and key resources on an ongoing basis. During an incident, the NICC provides a coordinating forum to share information across infrastructure and key resources sectors through appropriate information-sharing entities such as the Information Sharing and Analysis Centers and the Sector Coordinating Councils."

Moving outside of the NOC, there are several Supporting Federal Operations Centers, all of which contribute to and maintain a "situational awareness" within their specific operational area. Most Cabinet departments and agencies have their own versions of an Operations Center. For example, there is the National Military Command Center (NMCC) which oversees the nation's fighting force worldwide and works with the Joint Chiefs of Staff and the Secretary of Defense among others. Another is the National Counterterrorism Center (NCTC) which organizes and analyzes all terrorism related intelligence as well as conducts counterterrorist strategic planning. Not to be outdone, the FBI possesses the Strategic Information and Operations Center (SIOC). Though separate from the NCTC, the SIOC's role isn't very different, just more focused. The SIOC contends with "domestic terrorist incidents or credible threats." Of course, they work alongside the National Joint Terrorism Task Force (NJTTF) which is supposed to "enhance communications, coordination, and cooperation" across the nation and among the various agencies working to combat terrorism. Lastly, let us not forget the other DHS agencies with their own Operation Centers including the likes of the Transportation Security Administration, the U.S. Secret Service, and U.S. Customs and Border Protection.

Take note that at this point, having gone from the president through the Secretary of the DHS past the FEMA Administrator and various other DHS agency heads to the National and Supporting Operations Centers, we don't have a single federal emergency responder in place to begin any sort of relief effort, no matter if the event took the form of a natural disaster or a terrorist attack. No one, outside of the immediate local and state responders such as the police, fire department, and perhaps National Guard, would be on the scene of said emergency. Instead, everyone at the top levels of the federal government would still be in discussion, contemplating what the proper response should be. Worried yet?

In an effort to cut through some of that bureaucratically mandated red tape, the NRF created something known as Emergency Support Functions (ESF). There are 15 of these scripted response mechanisms to future expected emergencies. These designate who is to be tapped for each specific function needed to respond to each prescribed emergency. "The ESFs serve as the primary operational-level mechanism to provide assistance in functional areas such as transportation, communications, public works and engineering, firefighting, mass care, housing, human services, public health and medical services, search and rescue, agriculture and natural resources, and energy." Each ESF is assigned a coordinator as well as primary and support agencies, and these may be activated in both Stafford Act and non-Stafford Act incidents. FEMA is even allowed to pre-plan for such deployments in an expected disaster, such as an approaching hurricane, even though its presence isn't officially allowed until a governor makes such a request and the president declares an official emergency. The NRF provides an example of how these ESFs should operate: "If a State requests assistance with a mass evacuation, the [Joint Field Office] would request personnel from ESF #1 (Transportation), ESF #6 (Mass Care, Emergency Assistance, Housing, and Human Services), and ESF #8 (Public Health and Medical Services). These would then be integrated into a single branch or group within the Operations Section to ensure effective coordination of evacuation services." To accompany the ESFs, the NRF's annexes feature similar pre-planned support outlays to be used upon each specific emergency that may be at hand. These include everything from nuclear war to cyber attacks, as well as various natural disasters or even a worldwide pandemic. So, there is an official game plan prepared. The question is can anyone implement it?

In order to do so, the actual field-level response is likely to flow out of one of the 10 FEMA regional offices. The breaking up of the 50 states into specific regions isn't FEMA's or the NRF's creation. Back in the late 1950's, the Office of Civil and Defense Mobilization divvied up the nation into eight regions. Today, the DHS through FEMA has divided the nation into 10 regions with a headquarters somewhat centered within the area of command. These are located in Boston, New York City (which only has to deal with the states of New York and New Jersey, plus the far flung U.S territories of Puerto Rico the U.S. Virgin Islands), Philadelphia, Atlanta, Chicago, Kansas City, Denver, Seattle, Oakland (which is tasked with overseeing not just California, Arizona, and Nevada, but Hawaii, Guam, and various other US territories scattered throughout the Pacific Ocean), and Denton, TX (which was one of the original eight cities the Office of Civil and Defense Mobilization designated as a headquarters). Each of these offices maintains a Regional Response Coordination Center (RRCC). These are staffed 24/7 and may be filled with ESF teams prior to an anticipated event as well as in response to one that already occurred. Also flowing out of these regional offices are the various Incident Management Assistant Teams (IMATs) FEMA has at its disposal. These include the Hurricane Liaison Team, Urban Search and Rescue Task Forces, and Mobile Emergency Response Support (which include the nuclear hardened communication vans that unexpectedly showed up in response to Hurricane Andrew).

Since most emergencies won't be centered in the exact city where FEMA has its regional offices, the initial response to any disaster requires the setting up of a Joint Field Office (JFO). This is where the rubber meets the road…well, almost. As the NRF states, "the JFO does not manage on-scene operations." Even so, the JFO is "the primary Federal incident management field structure." It is to be the "temporary Federal facility that provides a central location for the coordination of Federal, State, tribal, and local governments and private-sector and nongovernmental organizations with primary responsibility for response and recovery." Again remember, it does not manage on-scene operations. "Instead, the JFO focuses on providing support to on-scene efforts and conducting broader support operations that may extend beyond the incident site." Confused?

The basic make-up of the JFO is as follows. The JFO is led by the Unified Coordination Group (UCG) which is comprised of specified leaders on federal and state or local levels. This can include a Principal Federal Official (PFO). By law, the Secretary of the DHS is the PFO, yet the Secretary can transfer that role to someone else. Even so, the PFO is supposed to be "a senior Federal official with proven management experience and strong leadership capabilities." When a PFO deploys, he will be accompanied by a "small, highly trained mobile support staff."

Why this is necessary is hard to determine, since the PFO doesn't really have any true duties and no authority. "The PFO does not direct or replace the incident command structure established at the incident. Nor does the PFO have directive authority over a Federal Coordinating Officer, a Senior Federal Law Enforcement Official, a DOD Joint Task Force Commander, or any other Federal or State official. Other Federal incident management officials retain their authorities as defined in existing statutes and directives. Rather, the PFO promotes collaboration and, as possible, resolves any Federal interagency conflict that may arise. The PFO identifies and presents to the Secretary of Homeland Security any policy issues that require resolution." So why is this role necessary? Turns out, it isn't. PFOs are not always required. They are only appointed for "catastrophic or unusually complex incidents that require extraordinary coordination." That is probably a good thing since they don't seem to be able to do much of anything.

Directly under the PFO, or should one not be required, taking command of the Unified Coordination Group is the Federal Coordinating Officer (FCO). Should the emergency in question be a true Stafford Act incident, the president appoints the FCO. This can't be some name just pulled from a hat, however. The FCO is to be a senior FEMA official and is authorized to lead all FEMA-related efforts and responsibilities. The reason why this role isn't simply filled by the FEMA Administrator is because the FCO is supposed to be a person trained to deal with a specific emergency. The FCO can be aided by deputy FCOs should the disaster area be widespread. Many times FCOs (and the unnecessary position of PFOs) are predetermined, again based upon the disaster. As the NRF points out, "beginning in 2007, the [DHS] Secretary pre-designated a national PFO and five regional PFOs together with a national FCO and regional FCOs, who will serve in the event of a nationwide outbreak of pandemic influenza or other similar nationwide biological event."

The rest of the Unified Coordination Group falls under the FCO's lead. This includes the State Coordinating Officer, which is determined by the state in question and based upon each state's own criteria. Following from this position is various other senior officials including law enforcement, health officials, and even Department of Defense officials. After this group, the most significant role is held by the Infrastructure Liaison. It is that person's job to know the disaster area's key infrastructures and resources while advising the UCG on these matters. Not to be forgotten is the Safety Officer, whose job is rather self-explanatory.

Moving ever closer to the goal of getting someone, anyone on the scene to help those in need, the final rung in the UCG's ladder are the four basic sections. First is the operations section which oversees the coordination of the "on-scene incident management efforts." Second is the planning section which—surprise—plans everything as well as collects the vital information needed to make said plans. Third is the logistics section. Its job is more detailed and includes "control of and accountability for Federal supplies and equipment; resource ordering; delivery of equipment, supplies, and services to the JFO and other field locations; facility location, setup, space management, building services, and general facility operations; transportation coordination and fleet management services; information and technology systems services; administrative services such as mail management and reproduction; and customer assistance." Last is the finance and administration section. This is the section the taxpayers should have their collective eye on, since they manage all of the money flowing into the relief effort.

While that may close the door on the JFO, that is by no means all, folks. There may be other field structures and officers involved in implementing the NRF. The two most likely field offices that may be formed in conjunction with the JFO are the Joint Operations Center (JOC) and the Joint Information Center (JIC). The JOC would be an FBI created entity to deal with some form of terrorist incident. As for the JIC, it would basically be a branch of the JFO designed not for the collection of information, but rather the dissemination of information to the public.

There are six types of JICs. The most common is known as an Incident JIC. This is created at the emergency site (yes, actual people on site—but not to help in disaster relief) and is run in conjunction with the JFO. According to FEMA's *Basic Guidance for Public Information Officers* handbook from which most of the following information on JICs and Public Information Officers (PIOs) was taken, having an Incident JIC on-site is supposed to provide "easy media access, which is paramount to success." (That is success in media relations, and little else). Below these are Satellite JICs, which are intended to support the Incident JIC and are typically located closer to the disaster epicenter than the Incident JIC. Both the Incident and Satellite JICs can be augmented with Support JICs; however, these support people would be located outside of the disaster area. If the disaster is more widespread or covers multiple states, then an Area JIC would be activated. This, too, would likely be located outside the affected area and set up in the largest media market near the disaster. It would oversee the on-the-scene JICs while helping to spread the word nationwide via its close knit media connections. Lastly, there is a National JIC which would only be established should the incident require "Federal coordination and is expected to be of long duration (weeks or months)." Such an entity will be staffed with "numerous Federal departments and/or agencies." The sixth form of a JIC is that of a Virtual JIC. It is to be established "when a physical co-location is not feasible." As it further explains about Virtual JICs, "for a pandemic incident where PIOs at different locations communicate and coordinate public information electronically, it may be appropriate to establish a virtual JIC."

There are really two facets to Joint Information Centers and the Public Information Officers staffed within them. The first should be rather helpful, yet it doesn't appear as if anyone is actively performing this duty. This would be in the realm of public education and preparedness. As the handbook on PIOs states, "Preparedness is essential for an effective response to an incident or planned event. Public information efforts should begin well in advance of an incident or planned event and may involve a combination of planning, resource gathering, organizing, and training and exercises. Public information planning allows for lifesaving measures such as evacuation routes, alert systems, and other public safety information, to be coordinated and communicated to diverse audiences in a timely, consistent manner. Public education contributes to preparing citizens to respond to a variety of hazards." The handbook goes so far as to define public education for the ill-informed PIO as "the process of making the public aware of risks and how they can prepare for all hazards in advance." How is the PIO supposed to educate the public? Examples of educational campaigns include "hurricane preparedness; personal preparedness and developing family or business emergency plans; hazardous materials awareness; tornado and severe weather awareness; and special needs population awareness." If you believe you fall into any of these potential disaster categories and haven't heard a word from your local PIO, then ask yourself, why?

The second facet, which is the most emphasized role in the 29 page handbook, is media relations. The handbook instructs a PIO to make well-connected media contacts. "Working relationships with media will help during an incident. Establish a media contact list with after-business hours contact information. Keep media aware of all preparedness/awareness campaigns. Invite local media to the Emergency Operations Center (EOC), JIC, or other areas prior to any incident or planned event to show them the location and to answer questions about how information will be disseminated during an incident or planned event. Positive media relationships built during normal day-to-day activities will be valuable during emergency situations. Do not wait until an incident to make first introductions to the media."

This is because the role of the PIO is to be the chief propagandist for the disaster at hand. Imagine that an unexpected disaster strikes. Most, if not all, true disasters cut both power and communication lines in the affect areas. What good will a PIO serve for those suffering from a disaster? Most likely, the answer is not at all since none of those affected may be able to receive any outside communications (though PIOs are instructed on how to reach those unreachable people. This includes using reverse 911, amateur radio, loud speakers, reader boards, filers and factsheets, and going door-to-door among other methods). However, the PIO will be in direct and immediate contact with the major U.S. media and be able to shape and control the message coming from the disaster area instantaneously. What the country will know about a disaster will be filtered through a PIO. The handbook makes this quite clear. For example, PIOs are directed to have "Go Kits" ready and waiting should a disaster strike. What's in a PIO's "Go Kit?" According to the handbook, "office supplies such as pens, paper, stapler, tape, etc.; laptop computer and portable printer with an alternate power source(s), including accessories (e.g., memory stick, CDs, mouse, etc.); maps; television, radio, and/or broadcast recording equipment; cell phones/Personal Data Assistants (PDAs); fax machine; agency letterhead; PIO and other emergency operations plans; camera; contact lists; battery powered radio; and pre-scripted messages and template releases." What was that last item again? Pre-scripted messages and template releases? Hmmm.

Actually, that should not come as a surprise. The further one delves into the PIO's role in an emergency situation, the more the role clarifies itself. The PIO is instructed that "all information in the field must be cleared by the [Information Center] prior to release." Meanwhile, the first box available in the "PIO Major Responsibilities Checklist" is "determine from the [Information Center] if there are any limits on information release." Elsewhere in the handbook, the Lead PIO's "Common Roles and Functions" is listed, in part, as "provides overall communication policy direction; recommends and develops strategy for messages, briefings, and news releases; obtains approval from those in authority before releases are made." Just so that's straight—not all of the available information regarding a disaster may be made public and nearly everything will need to be cleared by a "those in authority" prior to public dissemination. Should there be some blowback as to the official line in handling either the "Escalating Incident" or the "Large Scale Incident," the Lead PIO has at his disposal an unexplained or defined office available titled "Media Monitoring and Analysis." You can fill in your own definition of that office here.

Returning to the NRF itself, outside of the Joint Field Office and its PFO or FCO, the incident may require the presence of yet another type of commander or lead officer. Besides any number of particular federal agency heads that may be needed depending on their field of expertise as compared to the emergency at hand, the NRF allows for the establishment of four other titled officers. The first is a Federal Resource Coordinator (FRC). The FRC is only activated in non-Stafford Act emergencies when another federal agency requests help from the DHS. The FRC may be someone pulled from the same pool as FCOs should that person possess the proper skills for that particular situation. Should the incident be a terrorist situation, a Senior Federal Law Enforcement Official (SFLEO) may be appointed. If terrorism is suspected, the SFLEO is likely to be a high ranking member of the FBI and assigned to oversee and coordinate the entire law enforcement activities of the incident.

The other two posts are appointments from the Department of Defense. This is a very interesting predicament in which the country may someday find itself. While the ability and legal ramifications of the U.S. military operating within the borders of the United States will be probed in a moment, know the NRF takes the position that the military's presence may be both wanted and required, depending on the circumstances. In fact, the DOD has already assigned a Defense Coordinating Officer (DCOs) to each of the 10 FEMA regions. The DCOs are the DOD's liaisons to FEMA and would be the ones to request military aid if a situation demanded. According to the NRF, "specific responsibilities of the DCO (subject to modification based on the situation) include processing requirements for military support, forwarding mission assignments to the appropriate military organizations through DOD-designated channels, and assigning military liaisons, as appropriate, to activated ESFs." The other DOD entity within the NRF is the Joint Task Force (JFT) Commander. "Based on the complexity and type of incident, and the anticipated level of DOD resource involvement, DOD may elect to designate a JTF to command Federal (Title 10) military activities in support of the incident objectives." The JTF Commander would not replace the active DCO; rather the JTF Commander "exercises operational control of Federal military personnel and most defense resources in a Federal response."

With those final assigned roles, the NRF effectively brings to a close the federal government's responsibility to respond to any such emergency or disaster. It does so without specifically defining how it will actually help people. Rather, it simply defines the federal power and command structure to be implemented to get these relief efforts under way. Remember, it is only when a state is overwhelmed and officially requests the federal government's assistance that it will show up and get down to business—after it first sets up its elaborate commander structure.

Your Friendly, Neighborhood Army Brigade

The U.S. government is a bit paranoid. Since the 9/11 attacks, the main thrust of its emergency planning has focused primarily on counteracting another terrorist event. When or if such a scenario of that magnitude will ever take place on U.S. soil again is completely debatable. At the same time, we know without doubt that another category 4 or 5 hurricane will make landfall somewhere along the Southeastern U.S. coastline. Sooner or later a major earthquake will rock the West Coast (or maybe the Midwest). Every year, wildfires burn hundreds of thousands of acres in the arid Southwest. Volcanoes are continually erupting in Hawaii, and are likely to do so elsewhere along the Pacific Coast. Tornados touch down on U.S. soil in every month of the year. None of these events receive nearly the amount of attention or money the simple *threat* of terrorism does. Does that mean we shouldn't have some sort of response plan in place in the event terrorists do indeed again strike the U.S.? Of course not. Yet what sort of capabilities or attack plan would a terrorist organization need to possess to actually disrupt the entire nation?

There is a reason to ask that question. Think back to the tragic events of 9/11. That was the largest terrorist attack not just in U.S. history, but in the world's history, and how long did it last? The terrorist action began that morning upon the first plane being hijacked and officially ended when the last plane crashed into that empty field in Pennsylvania. Those actual terrorist driven events spanned the course of less than four hours. The aftermath, which included the fall of the three World Trade Center buildings and the clearing of all air traffic over U.S. soil, lasted for days. The attack, like all terrorist attacks, was swift, explosive, and painful. In nearly all cases, such terrorist activity is over in minutes, if not seconds. It was not a protracted war with land, air, and sea battles. It was not intended to be. It could not be. Such a thing is an impossibility in that realm. It was a snake bite, a moment of pain followed by the agony of feeling the venom seep throughout the body. That is the nature of terrorism.

This truth has not stopped the U.S. government from preparing for an unlikely outbreak of terrorist events spreading across the country. Despite the fact that in the case of 9/11 (or even the Oklahoma City bombing in 1995) the first and main responders were local police and fire units, the federal government no longer wishes it to be that way. Even though in a future attack those same local departments will again be the first on the scene due to simple logistics and response time, from this day forward the government fully plans on stepping in and taking control of such a situation on a federal level. Not with the likes of FEMA, the DHS, or even the FBI leading the way, however. Today's plan, as found within the confines of the National Response Framework, clearly shows that the right people for this job are none other than the U.S. military.

This is preposterous. One would be hard pressed to determine a need for U.S. military units to become active and involved in what would very likely be—even in the event of a nuclear explosion—a local event. There is an already established and well trained military group ready and willing to deploy in these disaster scenarios. They are known as the National Guard. For years, the National Guard has lent itself on numerous occasions to assist in a wide variety of disaster relief efforts. The problem for the federal government seems to be that the National Guard is a state level organization, overseen by the state's governor. Since, as we've already seen, the federal government likes to have its contingency plans in place well ahead of time, the thought process has turned to consider what would happen if a state's National Guard couldn't control whatever situation it was tasked with? What then? Who should step in to help?

The answer, of course, is the Department of Defense and all of its military subsidiaries. As the NRF explains, "Many DOD components and agencies are authorized to respond to save lives, protect property and the environment, and mitigate human suffering under imminently serious conditions, as well as to provide support under their separate established authorities, as appropriate." While DOD forces are "providing Defense Support of Civil Authorities," they are primarily under the command of the Secretary of Defense. It is made clear within the NRF that "for Federal military forces, command runs from the President to the Secretary of Defense to the Commander of the combatant command to the DOD on-scene commander. Military forces will always remain under the operational and administrative control of the military chain of command, and these forces are subject to redirection or recall at any time."

The reason why the DOD should become involved is not made clear. The excuse put forth within the NRF is "the primary mission of the Department of Defense (DOD) and its components is national defense." That rings a tad hollow when one considers the recent history of this country. Since the attack on Pearl Harbor in 1941, the United States has not had to make any sort of defensive stand against a foreign attack or invasion. Of course, the argument could be made that 9/11 was the second such "surprise" attack. But there's a clear difference. The military base at Pearl Harbor was attacked by the Japanese and the defense of the naval fleet docked there was reliant on the U.S. military personnel stationed in Hawaii. The attack of 9/11 was launched by a terrorist network with no known or specific country supporting it. While it was charged with protecting the nation from foreign attack (though why the hijacked planes were not intercepted by armed Air Force jets remains an unanswered question), the military itself was not attacked. The U.S. citizenship was. The protection failure of 9/11 was the fault of both the intelligence community as well as the investigative arm of the FBI. Somehow the federal government now believes the DOD can accomplish this protective task against a faceless enemy.

The idea as proposed within the NRF is that should an emergency occur a governor will send in the National Guard to help. The governor is allowed to order a Guard member to active duty to "conduct homeland defense activities for the military protection of the territory or domestic population of the United States, or of the infrastructure or other assets of the United States determined by the Secretary of Defense to be critical to national security, from a threat or aggression against the United States." If that fails, or if the National Guard is overwhelmed in the same fashion a state's emergency response efforts may be, then the U.S. military can be called to assist. If that occurs, the two entities are supposed to work together. "DOD elements in the incident area of operations and National Guard forces under the command of a Governor will coordinate closely with response organizations at all levels."

Should the National Guard get in the way and/or not follow the mandate coming from its big brother the U.S. Army, the fact is "in rare circumstances, the President can federalize National Guard forces for domestic duties under Title 10 (e.g., in cases of invasion by a foreign nation, rebellion against the authority of the United

States, or where the President is unable to execute the laws of the United States with regular forces (10 U.S.C. 12406)). When mobilized under Title 10 of the U.S. Code, the forces are no longer under the command of the Governor. Instead, the Department of Defense assumes full responsibility for all aspects of the deployment, including command and control over National Guard forces." So, in the event of a "rare circumstance" like a terrorist attack—it's only happened twice on U.S. soil in 230+ years which makes it pretty rare—the president could federalize National Guard troops and hand over their command to either himself or the Secretary of Defense. Theoretically, that action is supposed to follow pre-written law. That law, the above mentioned Section 12406 of Title 10, however, contains the opened ended phrase "…is in danger of invasion by a foreign nation…" not mentioned in the NRF. Couldn't a terrorist attack, if "state sponsored" (proof could come later when needed), be considered a potential invasion threat? Certainly the right spin master could make it appear so.

Posse Comitatus

The question that immediately follows becomes is it legal for the military—that being the Army, Navy, Air Force, Marines, or some unit contained within those branches—to operate within the borders of the United States? The answer is simple: yes. As written in the Joint Chiefs of Staff *Joint Publication 3-26* titled "Counterterrorism," "The President has the authority to direct the use of the military against terrorist groups and individuals in the United States for other than law enforcement actions (i.e., national defense, emergency protection of life and property, and to restore order)." The reason the "other than law enforcement" distinction is made is due to the notion of "posse comitatus," a term and idea in need of clarification.

Translated from its original Latin, posse comitatus literally means, "Attendants with the capacity to act," but has taken the meaning, "The power (or force) of the country." In essence, it is the use of the military by the government as a police force over the citizens they are charged with protecting. The Posse Comitatus

Act, officially known as 18 U.S.C. 1385, was an outgrowth of the reconstruction period following the Civil War. After the Union had been reunited, the federal government stationed army troops in the Southern states to maintain civil order, oversee elections, and generally quash any lingering Confederate sentiments. Once order and peace were achieved, some members of Congress (mainly Southerners) worried that the Army was acting outside of its original intent. To eliminate those fears, the Posse Comitatus Act passed in 1878. This was not a constitutional right—nor based upon one—but rather a simple act of Congress. Today this law reads much like it did when originally passed: "Whoever, except in cases and under circumstances expressly authorized by the Constitution or Act of Congress, willfully uses any part of the Army or the Air Force as a posse comitatus or otherwise to execute the laws shall be fined under this title or imprisoned not more than two years, or both." What the act did, and what it was intended to do, was to prevent the military from acting as a police force, especially a private one for the likes of a power mad general or president. It never was to completely stop the military from operating within the borders of the United States.

Even though it was a congressional act, the Posse Comitatus Act has several exceptions. The primary one is that two branches of the military do not have to adhere to it. The first is the U.S. Coast Guard. While the Coast Guard performs a variety of services, one of its main tasks is to curb criminal violations, a power it was granted via a direct act of Congress. The other military branch is the National Guard. The National Guard operates under a separate set of laws (Title 32 of U.S. Code) from its brethren in the other military branches (Title 10, though the Coast Guard operates under Title 14). As such, the National Guard is free from posse comitatus restrictions. In fact, during emergencies, one of the Guard's primary objectives is to maintain law and order since often times in major emergencies local law enforcement officials are spread too thin to accomplish their duties.

Other military branches were granted congressional exemptions from posse comitatus beginning in the 1980s in order to help fight the "war on drugs." Both the Navy and Air Force are allowed to provide equipment and personnel in a preemptive way to stop smuggling prior to drugs or drug runners breaching the nation's borders. The Army is also allowed around posse comitatus in providing training and "military advice" to law enforcement agencies. In fact, the Army's Domestic Preparedness Team has trained law enforcement officials in over 120 cities across the United States. The standing rule for the U.S. military as defined by the federal courts has been that they may partake only in a "passive" role in aiding law enforcement, not an "active" one while within the confines of the country.

The "war on drugs" excuse helped open a secondary loophole in this active/passive argument with the creation of Joint Task Force North (JTF-N) in 1989. Originally called Joint Task Force 6, JTF-N consists of 150-200 military operatives from all sections of the DOD. It was first assigned to support law enforcement officials in the border states of California, New Mexico, Arizona, and Texas and was headquartered at Fort Bliss in El Paso, TX. By 2004, its mission was expanded to cover the entire nation. To legally operate within the U.S., a request must be made by local or state law enforcement officials for JTF-N's assistance. These commando-like squads run out of JTF-N have often been seen patrolling along the U.S./Mexico border, and despite needing the official request to operate, they appear to be in constant use.

Another hole in the Posse Comitatus Act lies in the ability of the Attorney General to seek help from the Secretary of Defense in the case of rogue nuclear weapons. According to 18 U.S.C. 831, which details the illegality of nuclear "materials and by-products," "(e)(1) The Attorney General may also request assistance from the Secretary of Defense under this subsection in the enforcement of this section. Notwithstanding section 1385 of this title [which is the Posse Comitatus Act], the Secretary of Defense may, in accordance with other applicable law, provide such assistance to the Attorney

General if - (A) an emergency situation exists (as jointly determined by the Attorney General and the Secretary of Defense in their discretion); and (B) the provision of such assistance will not adversely affect the military preparedness of the United States (as determined by the Secretary of Defense in such Secretary's discretion)." An "emergency situation" as defined by this subsection of Title 18 is "a circumstance—(A) that poses a serious threat to the interests of the United States; and (B) in which—(i) enforcement of the law would be seriously impaired if the assistance were not provided; and (ii) civilian law enforcement personnel are not capable of enforcing the law." As far as research would reveal, this has never been enacted or utilized; however, such an imminent situation may be exactly the sort of incident that even the most paranoid person out there would want the military to step in and help.

A Posse Comitatus Act exception also exists in the Robert T. Stafford Disaster Relief and Emergency Assistance Act. The authors of this act slipped an interesting little posse comitatus caveat into its wording. Under the "Utilization of DOD Resources" in Section 403, it reads:

"General rule - During the immediate aftermath of an incident which may ultimately qualify for assistance under this title or title V of this Act, the Governor of the State in which such incident occurred may request the President to direct the Secretary of Defense to utilize the resources of the Department of Defense for the purpose of performing on public and private lands any emergency work which is made necessary by such incident and which is essential for the preservation of life and property. If the President determines that such work is essential for the preservation of life and property, the President shall grant such request to the extent the President determines practicable. Such emergency work may only be carried out for a period not to exceed 10 days." Notice that it does not mention the abilities or the overwhelming of the National Guard. A governor can simply make a request of the president, should the disaster at hand qualify as a

Stafford Act incident, to have the DOD step in and help in seemingly any number of roles. Many would argue that this does *not* include law enforcement and could *not* be used to circumvent posse comitatus. Yet, it clearly states "if the President determines that such work is essential for the preservation of life and property…." Wouldn't the "preservation of life and property" demand some form of law enforcement, given the disaster scenario necessary for a Stafford Act incident to be mandated? Since a law enforcement role was not specifically ruled out, it appears it would. If the DOD would not be allowed to operate in any type of law enforcement endeavor, then the question remains why would the DOD—if not acting outside the constraints of posse comitatus—be allowed to operate in the disaster area for only 10 days?

The final exception to the Posse Comitatus Act, and by far the most controversial aspect to it, is the fact that the U.S. government can call in the military to save itself when it fears for its life (or jobs). In other words, to combat a "civil disturbance." There is no clear definition of what a civil disturbance actually is. It is most often equated with an open or armed rebellion against the government of the United States, but sometimes simply refers to a breakdown in law and order (never mind if such "law" is deemed unjust and is the cause of the rebellion in the first place). This is why the following set of laws as laid out in Title 10 U.S.C. Sections 331-335 is commonly known as The Insurrection Act.

The Insurrection Act originated in 1807. This goes to show you that even our Founding Fathers, having themselves rebelled against an "unjust" ruling power, worried about maintaining their own rule over the land. In 200+ years, not much has changed as those in power seek to maintain their control over the common people no matter the price. It is very conceivable that in the near future our government will anger enough of the populace to the point they take up arms to overthrow their duly elected representatives. If the local law enforcement community cannot quash the rebellion, or if they instead decide to join up with the dissenters, the president is allowed to send in the military to do the job for them thanks to the Insurrection Act.

As clearly stated in Title 10 U.S.C. 332, "Whenever the President considers that unlawful obstructions, combinations, or assemblages, or rebellion against the authority of the United States, make it impracticable to enforce the laws of the United States in any State by the ordinary course of judicial proceedings, he may call into Federal service such of the militia of any State, and use such of the armed forces, as he considers necessary to enforce those laws or to suppress the rebellion." Of course, since this is America, there are rules and regulations for sending in the troops. Well, *a* rule. This lies in Title 10 U.S.C. 334: "Whenever the President considers it necessary to use the militia or the armed forces under this chapter, he shall, by proclamation, immediately order the insurgents or those obstructing the enforcement of the laws to disperse and retire peaceably to their abodes within a limited time." So listen up, you potential rebels: you'll be given a warning to return to your "abode" prior to the jackbooted "peace keepers" stepping in and forcefully attempting to take control back from the mob. How effective such a "go home or else" warning would be once the point of rebellion was reached remains to be seen.

Other than in an open rebellion, there was—for about a year—a second option available to the president via the Insurrection Act in which he could have used the military outside of the constraints of posse comitatus. This would have been in the case of a "major public emergency" in which to "restore public order." This loophole was not originally included within the Insurrection Act of 1807. Instead, this rewording of Title 10 U.S.C. 333 was controversially added by Congress in the John Warner Defense Authorization Act of 2007 which clearly broadened the president's authority in any such "emergency" situation. The reworded version read:

"(a) Use of Armed Forces in Major Public Emergencies. (1) The President may employ the armed forces, including the National Guard in Federal service, to

"(A) restore public order and enforce the laws of the United

States when, as a result of a natural disaster, epidemic, or other serious public health emergency, terrorist attack or incident, or other condition in any State or possession of the United States, the President determines that

"(i) domestic violence has occurred to such an extent that the constituted authorities of the State or possession are incapable of maintaining public order; and

"(ii) such violence results in a condition described in paragraph (2); or

"(B) suppress, in a State, any insurrection, domestic violence, unlawful combination, or conspiracy if such insurrection, violation, combination, or conspiracy results in a condition described in paragraph (2).

"(2) A condition described in this paragraph is a condition that

"(A) so hinders the execution of the laws of a State or possession, as applicable, and of the United States within that State or possession, that any part or class of its people is deprived of a right, privilege, immunity, or protection named in the Constitution and secured by law, and the constituted authorities of that State or possession are unable, fail, or refuse to protect that right, privilege, or immunity, or to give that protection; or

"(B) opposes or obstructs the execution of the laws of the United States or impedes the course of justice under those laws.

"(3) In any situation covered by paragraph (1)(B), the State shall be considered to have denied the equal protection of the laws secured by the Constitution. (b) Notice to Congress. The President shall notify Congress of the determination to exercise the authority in subsection (a)(1)(A) as soon as practicable after the determination and every 14 days thereafter during the duration of the exercise of that authority."

This reworking of section 333 basically nullified the Posse Comitatus Act. The president would have been able to use the military almost at his whim to police the country "in times of emergency" (and at the time, the U.S. was under 20+ national emergencies) and do so as long as he notified Congress. It completely stripped states of their rights and would have allowed the president to strip the state of its National Guard units as well.

Many concerned citizens and a few politicians including some very peeved state governors noticed this incredibly unpublicized shift in U.S. domestic policy. Led by the efforts of Senator Patrick Leahy (D-VT), these concerned citizens attempted to repeal the new version of section 333 by the passage of Leahy's U.S. Senate Bill 513 which would have restored the Insurrection Act to its original wording. While Senator Leahy's bill was introduced in February of 2007, it never progressed beyond that point. Luckily, an alternative bill, H.R. 4986, was introduced in the House of Representatives by Ike Skelton (D-MO) and did exactly what Senator Leahy's bill could not. Passed in 2008, H.R. 4986 eliminated the new version of section 333 of the Insurrection Act and restored its original wording to once again read:

"The President, by using the militia or the armed forces, or both, or by any other means, shall take such measures as he considers necessary to suppress, in a State, any insurrection, domestic violence, unlawful combination, or conspiracy, if it (1) so hinders the execution of the laws of that State, and of the United States within the State, that any part or class of its people is deprived of a right, privilege, immunity, or protection named in the Constitution and secured by law, and the constituted authorities of that State are unable, fail, or refuse to protect that right, privilege, or immunity, or to give that protection; or (2) opposes or obstructs the execution of the laws of the United States or impedes the course of justice under those laws. In any situation covered by clause (1), the State shall be considered to have denied the equal protection of the laws secured by the Constitution."

Notice that in comparing the two versions of section 333, the 2007 version was nowhere near the wording of the original 1807 copy. In fact, how the 2007 version could have been considered part of the Insurrection Act was rather questionable. What was perhaps even more remarkable was that Congress actually acted to strip some power away from the executive branch rather than blindly handing it over to the president as it had done with the passage of the John Warner Defense Authorization Act.

So has such a situation occurred in the U.S. in which the military needed to respond either in a public emergency or to quell a potential rebellion? The answer is a resounding yes. Two immediate examples are the already discussed Whiskey Rebellion and the American Civil War in which the Southern states were deemed to be "in open insurrection." In both circumstances, federal troops were used to put down the rebellion. The first instance took just a few days, while the other lasted four years. Those events aside, there are more recent situations in which the government felt compelled to send in its military to keep the peace. Author and historian Howard Zinn in his bestseller *A People's History of the United States* repeatedly cited incidents when federal troops were used to quell both rioters and strikers, often in the collective interests of the government and big business. One of the most blatant and curious examples of the U.S. military strong-arming citizens occurred during the Great Depression.

Few people today know the story surrounding the Bonus Expeditionary Force or more quaintly, the Bonus Army. After the end of World War I, the U.S. government found itself with some 4.5 million veterans, most of whom had returned home unemployed. During the war, the under-funded military scantly paid its servicemen to the point that soldiers had to pay for their own uniforms. To alleviate their post-war financial burdens, Congress passed a bill in 1924 to retroactively pay WWI veterans. Soldiers were to get $1 a day for every day they had served, bumped up to $1.25 for every day served overseas. As with all great government deals, there was a huge catch—the veterans couldn't collect this money until 1945 (some 21 years after the bill's passage). The only exception was if the unfortunate veteran died prior to that date, then the deceased's family was allowed collect the amount due. This became colloquially known as the "tombstone bonus."

Once the depression hit, those veterans desperately wanted the money Congress had promised. A Portland, Oregon veteran by the name of Walter Waters decided to attempt to force Congress's hand. Along with 300 other veterans, Waters set off on a cross-country train trek to round up supporters. By the time they arrived in Washington, DC in 1932, they had tens of thousands of veterans backing them. This huge congregation set up shanty towns outside the White House to wait for a bill to pass to immediately grant them their bonuses. President Hebert Hoover was rattled by the presence of the so-called Bonus Army. He called in his Army Chief-of-Staff, General Douglas McArthur, to assess the situation. McArthur's response was to station army personnel armed with bayonets, tear gas, and even tanks in and around Washington to police the shanty towns and the growing Bonus Army (this action alone seemed to violate the Posse Comitatus Act, but Washington DC is a federal district and not subject to the act).

In June, the bill the Bonus Army had pressed for failed in Congress. Many members gave up and returned home, but some 10,000 or more continued to live in the shanty towns while demanding their just dues. When DC police attempted to relocate people from their shanties, a riot broke out. In the ensuing chaos, police shot and killed two of the WWI veterans. That's when it got really rough in the streets of the nation's capital. General McArthur, under Hoover's orders, sent in the Army to completely squash the Bonus Army. Tanks under command of General George S. Patton rumbled through the shanty town, smashing any of the makeshift homes in their path. The federal troops physically pushed the Bonus Army out of the city, and then burnt down the remnants of the shanty towns.

Needless to say, that action raised the ire of the rest of the nation. By 1935, Congress wisely relented and passed the bill. Hoover's successor, Franklin Roosevelt, vetoed the bill—twice. He refused to pay out the nearly $2 billion due to the veterans during the depression. Congress, still under pressure from the Bonus Army and their supporters, passed another bill to pay the veterans again in 1936. FDR vetoed that as well. By then Congress had reached its breaking point, and later in the year overturned FDR's veto to pay the Bonus Army what they were promised some 12 years prior.

Soon after the Bonus Army was appeased World War II erupted and Americans came together to support the cause. By the 1960s however, that rah-rah American spirit was in shambles. As protests and riots broke out in major cities and college campuses, the government began to fear the possibilities of American citizens running lawlessly in the streets. California witnessed the devastating effects of the Watts riots in 1965 and again in 1966. During that turbulent time in Los Angeles, over 30 people were killed, nearly 1,000 were injured, and more than 3,500 were arrested in connection with the riots. It took the efforts of the National Guard to restore peace. In 1967, a riot in the city of Detroit killed more than 40 people and injured over 1,100. When both the police and National Guard couldn't restore order, the Army's 82nd Airborne division was deployed to the city—a major turning point in the use of the Posse Comitatus Act as it was the first time since the Bonus Army's march on Washington that federal troops were sent into an American city to act as peace keepers. When all was said and done in Detroit, over 7,000 people were arrested. That was just the tip of the iceberg. In the first nine months of 1967 there were more than 160 incidents of "civil disorder" in over 120 different American cities according to the Kerner Commission.

Established by President Johnson's 1967 Executive Order 11365, the Kerner Commissioner as it became known was chaired by then-governor of Illinois and former Army Major General Otto Kerner. Its official title was the National Advisory Commission on Civil Disorders. LBJ's goal for the Commission was to learn three things: how did riots start, how to contain them once they had started, and how to eliminate them from occurring in the future. The commission's final recommendation, once one looked past the racially charged language contained within it (its most famous line being, "Our nation is moving toward two societies, one black, one white—separate and unequal") was rather simple: get the Army involved.

The report did admit, "The commitment of federal troops to aid state and local forces in controlling a disorder is an extraordinary act." That didn't mean it couldn't, or even shouldn't be done if the need arose. Prior to being called into action, the Army could not only aid in training police forces (which was allowed under the Posse Comitatus Act as long as their actions were "passive'), but they could "investigate the possibility of utilizing psychological techniques to ventilate hostility and lessen tension in riot control, and incorporate feasible techniques in training the Army and National Guard units." The Army could also "participate fully in efforts to develop nonlethal weapons and personal protective equipment appropriate for use in civil disorders."

Less than a year after the Kerner Commission released its report, the Army was following the commission's recommendations and more. It began the Directorate of Military Support (DOMS) run out of the Pentagon in the summer of 1968. Its primary mission was to monitor all civil disturbances in the nation and was run like a war room. Due to the political turbulence of the era, it was staffed 24/7 and ready to deploy troops wherever and whenever the call came. Despite all of this preparedness and staffing, such a call was rarely made. Even so, the unit is still operational today.

Out of those beginnings came a larger, more overarching plan to control all forms of civil unrest in what was supposed to be a democratic society. This plan was officially labeled the Department of Defense Civil Disturbance Plan 55-2. It's better known by its code name, Operation Garden Plot. Garden Plot was the general Operations Plan for the U.S. military to support local law enforcement agencies in responding to civil unrest. It drew on participants from the U.S. Army, the National Guard, and local law enforcement among other similar themed agencies in an attempt to quell any potential riot-like situation. Operating much like counterterrorism programs do today, Garden Plot even went so far as to draw on members of the intelligence community including the NSA and CIA which, by law, are not supposed to operate within the nation's borders.

Much of the operational aspects of Garden Plot remain classified to this day. What little is known about the plan comes by way of an Air Force version of the plan which was released via the Freedom of Information Act some time ago. This Air Force copy was dated June 1, 1984, but it was not the original version, nor is it likely to be the current version either. Prior to the date of that FOIA copy, the Air Force had twice been called upon to act under the guidance of Garden Plot to assist in controlling what was deemed "civil disturbance conditions" (CIDCON). The first incident occurred upon the assassination of Dr. Martin Luther King Jr. on April 4, 1968. Two Air Force reserve units were enacted to help contain and control the civil unrest that broke out upon the broadcast of King's death. Two years later, between April 30 and May 4, 1970, the Air Force was again called in to aid in Garden Plot operations after the U.S. invasion of Cambodia. During the resultant protests on various college campuses, Air Force units airlifted "civil disturbance control forces" to destinations across the eastern U.S. It was during that same time that four college students were shot to death on the Ohio campus of Kent State (May 4, 1970).

When the "Rodney King riots" broke out in Los Angeles in 1992 following the acquittal of the police officers charged in the video-taped beating of Rodney King, Garden Plot was again enacted. The interesting aspect of this was the exacting structure the federal response took because it contained elements of the Insurrection Act.

The riot began on April 29, 1992 in a few different locations within Los Angeles. As it intensified in both force and violence, a group of protesters actually stormed and damaged L.A. Police Headquarters. Needless to say, the LAPD's response was instantly overwhelmed and disorganized. Arsonists started over 4,000 fires which burned portions of some 10,000 buildings and businesses while angry mobs would sometimes attack the firemen called into to contain the blazes (one fireman was actually shot while attempting to fight a fire). As the rioting continued into the following day, California Governor Pete Wilson called in both the California State Police and the National Guard to restore law and order. When that effort proved to be slow and disorganized upon implementation, President George H.W. Bush stepped in to take command.

Bush issued Proclamation 6427 on May 1, which stated:

"Whereas, I have been informed by the Governor of California that conditions of domestic violence and disorder exist in and about the City and County of Los Angeles, and other districts of California, endangering life and property and obstructing execution of the laws, and that the available law enforcement resources, including the National Guard, are unable to suppress such acts of violence and to restore law and order;

"Whereas, such domestic violence and disorder are also obstructing the execution of the laws of the United States, in the affected area; and

"Whereas, the Governor of California has requested Federal assistance in suppressing the violence and restoring law and order in the affected area.

"Now, therefore, I George Bush, President of the United States of America, by virtue of the authority vested in me by the Constitution and the laws of the United States, including Chapter 15 of Title 10 of the United States Code, do command all persons engaged in such acts of violence and disorder to cease and desist therefrom and to disperse and retire peaceably forthwith."

Notice this was the "cease and desist" order needed to precede any military involvement in matters of civil unrest via the Insurrection Act. This was issued simply in a procedural manner. It's highly doubtful that any of the rioters got wind of Bush's official proclamation. Even if it had, would Bush's veiled threat really have stopped anyone?

Almost immediately after issuing his proclamation Bush then issued Executive Order 12804. In it, Bush federalized the California National Guard troops already in place attempting to quell the riots while "authorizing" the Secretary of Defense (at the time, future Vice President Dick Cheney) to "call into the active military service of the United States units or members of the National Guard, as authorized by law, to serve in an active duty status for an indefinite period and until relieved by appropriate orders." Their goal was "to suppress the violence described in the proclamation and to restore law and order in and about the City and County of Los Angeles, and other districts of California." Thus, Garden Plot was officially enacted via use of the Insurrection Act.

The Joint Task Force—Los Angeles was formed and on the scene in L.A. in just 24 hours. It coordinated the efforts of the approximately 1,500 U.S. Marines and 2,000 Army troops from Fort Ord called to assist in stopping the riots. This military force was added to the 10,000 National Guardsmen plus the LAPD and California state troopers already attempting to maintain peace. The effort was a success. Three days after Bush's order, on May 4 the mayor of Los Angeles lifted the city's curfew. Less than 48 hours later, with order completely restored, the federal troops left the city.

Garden Plot would be enacted one more time following the L.A. riots, but that wouldn't be the result of civil unrest. This last implementation of Garden Plot would be as a result of the attacks on September 11, 2001. Three days after 9/11, Operation Noble Eagle was begun under the command of the North American Aerospace Defense Command (NORAD). This operation was an effort by the military to patrol the nation's airspace and was allowed to circumvent posse comitatus restrictions thanks in part to Garden Plot. While Noble Eagle watched the skies, thousands of National Guard troops were mobilized to act as a national security force on the ground in an attempt to prevent any further terrorist attacks. Many of these troops were deployed at major airports to aid in security while others were utilized to inspect and protect other potential targets.

The reason developments like the rewording of section 333 of the Insurrection Act and Operation Garden Plot are so threatening to the American population is not just the readiness but the seeming eagerness of the government to implement martial law upon its citizens. Such an extreme action on a national level has occurred on numerous occasions in an untold number of other countries throughout history. When that has happened, it changed not just the history of the nation involved (and rarely for its betterment) but of the entire world. The recent example most often cited is the rise of the Nazi party in Germany prior to World War II which was aided by the implementation of martial law. Here in America, the obvious fear is that martial law would not be a temporary situation brought about by a legitimate national emergency, but would become the permanent structure of our nation's law enforcement. Doing so would lead to the cessation of our personal liberties and our democratic nation. We would no longer be a country "of the people, by the people, for the people," but rather a nation ruled over by a dictator in command of the world's most elite military structure. Once under such rule, there would be no coming back to a constitutional government.

How likely is this to happen? Who can say? This is why the paranoia of the situation has grabbed a hold of many Americans. Who can blame them? While such widespread martial law has not occurred on a large scale since the Reconstruction Era in the American South after the Civil War, even the small scale implementation of it in situations like the L.A. riots in 1992 do impede on the civil rights of everyone—good and bad—that happen to come under its umbrella. Most Americans, given such an extreme situation as a city-wide riot or worse, would welcome military aid to restore peace and order even if it meant temporarily limiting one's own rights. The scary part is once you willingly give up those right in the assumption that they will be returned to you, how are you to know they will indeed be given back? Another worrisome aspect of the potentiality of martial law in the United States is that every facet of such an overthrow of the Constitution has already been planned by the very government that is supposed to ensure this never happens. While this has been done under the guise of contingency planning by a bloated federal government which tends to leave no idea unexplored no matter how radical or absurd it seems to the average person, the truth is the wrong person in the proper position of power does have the ability to enact an awful lot of awful legislation that could clamp down on a once free American society. Even worse, such scenarios have even been and continue to be trained for, all in the name of protecting national security.

The RAND Corporation

While posse comitatus restrictions seemed to ebb away as more and more emphasis was placed on a looming national emergency by way of terrorist attack, the federal government was spurred on by the DOD to create a permanent entity within the country to coordinate this slow joining of the military and law enforcement. The DOD was not alone in that line of thinking. They had backing by way of the Rand Corporation.

RAND is short for Research and Development. Since its founding in 1946 by five-star Air Force General Henry "Hap" Arnold, the Rand Corporation has become the U.S. government's #1 think tank. It is not a government-owned agency, though at the same time, many of its ideas become official U.S. policy. The people working at Rand have lent their opinions and research to the government on issues ranging from nuclear war strategies to communication systems to welfare reform to whether or not the World Series had been fixed (seriously). Approximately half of Rand's $200+ million annual funding comes from the federal government which helps keep its 1,000 or more researchers employed.

On December 15, 2001, just a scant few months after the 9/11 attacks, Rand issued its *Third Annual Report to the President and the Congress of the Advisory Panel to Assess Domestic Response Capabilities for Terrorism Involving Weapons of Mass Destruction.* One chapter of the report was focused on "Clarifying the Roles and Missions of the Military." Within it, Rand hit all of the same posse comitatus bullet points this book has. It made sure to emphasize the protection of civil liberties and even to "establish a reasonable budget balance" for preparing the military for civil support missions in emergency settings. It also made two key recommendations. The first was, "We recommend that the Secretary of Defense seek and that the Congress approve the authority to establish a new under secretary position for homeland security." Of course, shortly after that report was published, President Bush bypassed Congress and by executive order made the Department of Homeland Security a reality. This was more than the Rand report suggested, but it accomplished the goal nonetheless.

The other primary suggestion Rand made was, "We recommend that the National Command Authority establish a single, unified command and control structure to execute all functions for providing military support or assistance to civil authorities." That suggestion also didn't go unnoticed. In October 2002, the Pentagon established its U.S. Northern Command (USNORTHCOM). Its primary mission was to defend the land, sea, and air approaches to the United States. USNORTHCOM was also tasked with protecting all U.S.-based military forces and their associated bases of operation. Headquartered alongside NORAD in Colorado Springs, CO, USNORTHCOM's area of operations was deemed to be "America's homefront."

Despite this admission, USNORTHCOM's own website emphatically stated that USNORTHCOM was not involved in law enforcement nor did it exceed any posse comitatus restrictions. If true, then why did USNORTHCOM see the arrival of the first ever actively deployed army unit since the Civil War to be stationed within the U.S. on October 1, 2008? The First Brigade of the Third Infantry Division was originally deployed in Iraq and was in fact a combat unit. In an *Army Times* report dated September 8, 2008, it stated that these 3,000 troops were stationed at Fort Stewart, GA under USNORTHCOM's command to be a "federal response force for natural or manmade emergencies and disasters, including terrorist attacks." As the *Army Times* went on to claim, this "response force" was able to assist "with civil unrest and crowd control or to deal with potentially horrific scenarios such as massive poisoning and chaos in response to a chemical, biological, radiological, nuclear or high-yield explosive, or CBRNE, attack." Officials at USNORTHCOM responded by emphatically stating (again) that this unit would not exceed their posse comitatus bounds, though they did concede that the unit was trained and equipped with both lethal and nonlethal (often deemed "crowd control") weapons.

They did not say, however, what that unit would be allowed to do in the event Operation Garden Plot was again enacted. This was a key question no one bothered to ask since control over Garden Plot was transitioned from the Secretary of the Army to USNORTHCOM in August of 2003. Garden Plot is now officially known as USNORTHCOM FUNCPLAN 2502, the details of which remain classified.

In 2008, it was reported by several sources that two more military units would be assigned to USNORTHCOM in addition to the First Brigade. Unlike the First Brigade, though, these units would be stationed there on a permanent basis. This would bring the total number of actives up to nearly 5,000 by 2010. Would that be enough troops to establish martial law within the entire country? No, but it could do the trick within a large city based upon training and equipment. Given the "right" circumstances, such a military presence may be quite necessary in an emergency or disaster situation. But herein begins the slippery slope.

The First Brigade's original orders were a one year mission within the U.S., not a permanent station forever assigned to USNORTHCOM. In a December 1, 2008 article in the *Washington Post*, Pentagon officials are sourced as saying that by 2011, they hoped to have 20,000 uniformed troops stationed within the U.S. "trained to help state and local officials respond to a nuclear terrorist attack or other domestic catastrophe." It's amazing, considering that the nation had no troops assigned to the U.S. for over 200 years, then 3-5,000 troops were given that mission beginning in 2008 (which have yet to be needed in any capacity), and now the DOD wanted 20,000 troops prepared and ready to go at a moment's call.

Why? Preparedness against disaster is one thing, but the military already possesses small and well-trained response teams ready to deploy for all sorts of terrorist or weapons of mass destruction situations.

The biggest of these is the Special Operations Command, better known as SOCOM. SOCOM is more than just a popular video game title. It has control over all U.S. special operations forces and is headquartered at MacDill Air Force Base in Tampa, FL. Its command mission is rather straightforward: "Provide fully capable Special Operations Forces to defend the United States and its interests. Plan and synchronize operations against terrorist networks." One of the entities SOCOM oversees is the Joint Special Operations Command (JSOC) which is based at Fort Bragg in North Carolina. JSOC has been operational since 1980 and includes several counter-terrorism units with specialties ranging from hostage rescue to nuclear weapon recovery. According to author William Arkin in his book *Code Names*, "JSOC is, by secret executive orders, exempt from the Posse Comitatus statutes in the conduct of certain duties." What "duties" are allowed around Posse Comitatus and to what extent remains unknown.

SOCOM is just the tip of the anti-terrorism sword. In just the area of weapons of mass destruction, the United States has a multitude of units ready and willing to storm into action. For example, there are the U.S. Army's Response Task Force East, Response Task Force West, four Special Improvised Explosive Device companies, 35 Biological Integrated Detection System Teams, the Soldier Biological Chemical Command (with its own 24-hour hotline), and the Madigan Army Medical Center Disaster Assistance Response Team among others. The Air Force has a

Radiation Assessment Team, the Navy has the Naval Medical Research Institute Bio-Defense Research Program, and the Marines have the USMC Chemical/Biological Incident Response Force. This doesn't include the various factions set up within the FBI, the Bureau of Alcohol, Tobacco, and Firearms (ATF), FEMA, the EPA, the Secret Service, and the Department of Energy that are also tasked with responding to weapons of mass destruction incidents.

So, what are those extra 20,000 troops stationed at USNORTHCOM supposed to be used for?

The Great Roundup

The buildup of USNORTHCOM has led some to wonder if the military is training to counteract terrorists or instead preparing to police and/or round up average citizens. Seems like crazy talk, doesn't it? Think again.

In a 1975 Senate investigation, California Senator John V. Tunney discovered the Federal Preparedness Agency (the immediate forerunner to FEMA) possessed a list of some 100,000 Americans who were being continually monitored by the federal government. On that computerized list held in the confines of the secret base located within Mount Weather were the names of 15,000 people to be immediately rounded up and detained in a national emergency. They were considered "dissenters." Never mind that they hadn't necessarily done anything wrong; they were still under the government's close scrutiny. The fear was that these "anti-American" types would seize upon a national emergency to further disable the nation's stability, doing anything from protesting to engaging in open revolt. The government believed these citizens would have to be removed/arrested to ensure tranquility for everyone else; civil rights be damned. While that seems like the ravings of a conspiracy theorist, it is a confirmed truth.

Yet the real depths of that program remained secret…until 2011.

What follows is based upon a FBI file released via the Freedom of Information Act in early 2011. Within this once secret file were FBI memoranda dating between 1967 and 1968 regarding the Emergency Detention Act (EDA), the Emergency Detention Program (EPA), and Presidential Emergency Action Document (PEAD) A1-8. PEAD A1-8, to quote one of the FBI memorandums, "Suspends the privilege of the writ of habeas corpus and authorizes apprehension and detention of certain persons, the search of persons and premises, and the seizure of property."

The FBI was apparently a bit concerned with certain PEADs, including A1-8. It wrote, "With respect as to whether the language of these documents will withstand current constitutional tests and adequately protect the constitutional rights of individuals involved, this is a matter which will have to be decided by the Department of Justice." When that would occur, they didn't say. But the FBI did realize what was at stake. It wrote, "This is a drastic program set up under the assumption that drastic steps will be necessary to protect the national security of this country so that efforts can be made to remove from circulation individuals determined to be potentially dangerous to the national defense and public safety of the United States by engaging in espionage, sabotage and/or subversion in the event an attack is launched against this country."

How would the FBI "remove from circulation" these questionable characters? Through the use of the Emergency Detention Program which was based on the Emergency Detention Act included within the Internal Security Act of 1950. However, in early 1968 there was a debate between the FBI and the Office of Legal Counsel over the effectiveness of the program. The Office of Legal Counsel was of the belief that the EDP needed to be revised and "bring the program under courts of law." The FBI disagreed, writing, "Office of Legal Counsel fails to recognize that at time of an emergency, survival as a nation is utmost. Extreme measures are needed to preserve the internal security of the Nation and summarily, those individuals who are deemed dangerous should be apprehended and detained. The EDA is unworkable and would not provide the security of the Nation. It would not allow us to immediately detain those individuals who seek to overthrow or destroy the Government." To end this debate, PEAD A1-8 was rewritten to have the Emergency Detention Program fall under the Emergency Detention Act while only suspending the writ of habeas corpus for a "period not to exceed 30 days."

At the end of January 1968, "There are 10,109 individuals currently in the Security Index who are considered dangerous." Who were these people and how were they to be rounded up? By May 1968, the FBI wanted to establish a "new Priority Apprehension Program" with three "priority levels" based on the individual's "potential dangerousness." The "first priority apprehension list" was to consist of "hardcore national and state basic revolutionary organization leaders, leaders of other subversive organizations and anarchistic groups and individuals who have indicated a propensity for violence and/or have received special training in sabotage, espionage and/or guerrilla warfare." Level two contained "the second level leadership of basic revolutionary organizations and other subversive organizations or other individuals who present significant threat but are in less influential positions than those in Priority 1." The third level consisted of, well, everyone else on the list. All the FBI needed was the Attorney General's approval to begin. Of course, "These plans are not scheduled to be implemented unless a massive surprise nuclear attack is launched against the United States." Then again, "By letter 4/24/68, the Department advised that the President, when approving the new documents, also directed the committee to develop emergency plans specifically designed to be implemented in the event of a 'light' or 'limited' nuclear attack on the United States or its allies."

Despite all of that planning, the Emergency Detention Act was repealed in September 1971. Along with the Immigration and Naturalization Service (INS), the FBI continued to monitor aliens, creating a constantly updated "Administrative Index" of those individuals. Even this was cancelled by early 1976. Yet two Presidential Emergency Action Documents still in circulation at that time required the FBI to round up and detain persons of interest. The FBI, however, "has no means of providing a readily retrievable list of 'alien enemies'…additionally, the Bureau has no means of providing such a list of 'citizens…or aliens…prejudicial to the national security and public safety'…should the Bureau be called upon to provide such." Don't think the FBI had softened. It was still all for the program; it just wanted "specific guidelines as to the type of information to be maintained and how it is to be maintained."

Despite Senator Tunney's public revelation of such a program and the apparent fizzling out indicated in the FBI's own files, the practice never ceased. In fact, it has increased exponentially. Today there is a government database known as the Terrorist Identities Datamart Environment used by both law enforcement and the major U.S. airlines. It's from this database the famous and often erroneous "no-fly list" has been created. There are 1.1 million identities contained on that list, 400,000 of which are used to screen airline passengers as of January 2010. Supposedly of those 400,000 identities, 3,400 people are actually on the "no-fly list" and of those, only 170 are American citizens.

The U.S. government also possesses another database known ominously by its code name: Main Core. Some reports have stated that within Main Core, which reportedly tracks nearly every Americans' personal yet public information (and perhaps then some), the government lists over 8 million Americans as potential terrorist suspects. "Terrorists" to the government are not just the radical Islamic types; they are now deemed to be anyone with "anti-American" tendencies—including those simply doing their patriotic duty in protesting the government's actions. Again, while under the pressure of a national emergency, the federal government may turn to these lists and databases to begin rounding up those perceived enemies of the state. Far-fetched? Do not forget the similar action taken in World War II to round up thousands of innocent American citizens of Japanese descent conducted exclusively under executive order and rubber stamped by the Supreme Court.

To aid in stoking such rightful paranoia, in April of 2005 the Army released *U.S. Army Field Manual FM 3-19.15*. The subheading of the manual was "Civil Disturbance Operations." For those working on the assumption that the manual was intended only for soldiers stationed overseas, the preface quickly dispels any such notion in its first sentence, "Field Manual (FM) 3-19.15 addresses continental United States (CONUS) and outside continental United States (OCONUS) civil disturbance operations." The preface goes on to give a good idea of what's contained within the 250+ pages of the manual:

"In addition to covering civil unrest doctrine for OCONUS operations, FM 3-19.15 addresses domestic unrest and the military role in providing assistance to civil authorities requesting it for civil disturbance operations. It provides the commander and his staff guidance for preparing and planning for such operations. The principles of civil disturbance operations, planning and training for such operations, and the [tactics, techniques, and procedures] employed to control civil disturbances and neutralize special threats are discussed in this manual. It also addresses special planning and preparation that are needed to quell riots in confinement facilities are also discussed. In the past, commanders were limited to the type of force they could apply to quell a riot. Riot batons, riot control agents, or lethal force were often used. Today, there is a wide array of nonlethal weapons (NLW) available to the commander that extends his use of force along the force continuum. This manual addresses the use of nonlethal (NL) and lethal forces when quelling a riot."

It is safe to assume that the U.S. military is not a bunch of dopes. Its first and foremost job is to protect the Constitution, and most, if not all, of our service men and women take that task very seriously. Field Manual 3-19.15 also recognizes that mandate. In Appendix B, titled "Operations and Legal Considerations in the Continental United States," FM 3-19.15 takes into consideration all of the laws of the U.S. including both Posse Comitatus and the Insurrection Act that control the use of the armed forces within the country. It states, "Providing military assistance to state and local governments to assist them in quelling a civil disturbance or riot requires close coordination through a host of state and federal agencies. It requires a thorough briefing of soldiers at all levels on what they can and cannot do with respect to law enforcement. Civil authorities must be briefed on the restrictions placed on federal forces by the Constitution of the United States and federal statutes and laws."

It is quite healthy to fear and question the unprecedented military build-up within this nation since there is no solid rationale for it to be occurring. There are excuses made to justify it, but when pulled apart, the unseen and often unfounded threats of terrorism or a civil disturbance do not equate with the vast amounts of spending and training that are slowly transforming our military into becoming peace keepers for our own nation. No U.S. citizen wants to see martial law implemented, no matter the situation, scale, or timeframe. The hope is that the constant training and command structure within the military has not brainwashed our soldiers into becoming automatons where they will follow any order given, even if it is counterintuitive to their core beliefs. While those brave enough to serve have the power to tear this country apart, they may just be the glue that holds it together. Given the right disaster or national emergency, we all may be very happy to have our military directly involved in mitigating the situation.

Disaster Scenarios

The National Response Framework doesn't exist alone on an island. It actually falls under what is known as the National Preparedness Architecture. Besides the NRF, the Architecture includes the National Preparedness Guidelines, the National Infrastructure Protection Plan (NIPP) as well as 17 "sector-specific" plans related to what has been deemed critical infrastructure, the Protected Critical Infrastructure Information Regulations, the National Incident Management System (NIMS), various Continuity of Government programs, and a coordinated National Exercise Schedule which includes updated and re-imagined versions of Giuffrida's highly debated REX84 program with names such as Determined Promise. As the NRF states, "A national focus on preparedness is imperative to develop the capabilities that empower the Framework and response planning. The National Preparedness Guidelines and the NIPP focus on preparedness activities conducted in the absence of a specific threat or hazard. The Framework uses these programs and investments to build the capacity to respond to all manner and magnitude of threats and hazards." It goes on to boast, "Publication of these strategic documents—supported by others developed at the Federal, State, tribal, and local levels—defines the essential architecture of our national preparedness system and marks a significant milestone in post-9/11 preparedness."

What is the federal government planning for? To answer that question, one has to turn to the official National Planning Scenarios. As the NRF states, "the **National Planning Scenarios are the focus of Federal planning efforts.** They represent examples of the gravest dangers facing the United States **and have been accorded the highest priority for Federal planning**. Using a shared set of scenarios provides a common yardstick for determining how to achieve expected planning results....The 15 scenarios have been grouped into 8 key scenario sets that reflect common characteristics in order to integrate planning for like events, and to conduct cross-cutting capability development. The scenarios will be updated and amended on a biennial basis using risk-based analysis to ascertain the most likely or most dangerous threats to the homeland. [emphasis in original]"

Each of these 15 scenarios is supposed to require three levels of planning and preparedness. The first is a Strategic Guidance Statement coupled with a Strategic Plan. According to the NRF, the Statement and Plan "together define the broad national strategic objectives; delineate authorities, roles, and responsibilities; determine required capabilities; and develop performance and effectiveness measures essential to prevent, protect against, respond to, and recover from domestic incidents." Next in line is the National-Level Interagency Concept Plan (CONPLAN) which "describes the concept of operations for integrating and synchronizing Federal capabilities to accomplish critical tasks, and describes how Federal capabilities will be integrated into and support regional, State, and local plans to meet the objectives described in the Strategic Plan." The last stage of this federal planning structure is the Federal Department and Agency Operation Plans (OPLANs). These are "developed by and for each Federal department or agency describing detailed resource, personnel, and asset allocations necessary to support the concept of operations detailed in the CONPLAN."

Now if one is to believe the National Response Framework as well as its sister publication the National Preparedness Guidelines, there is already a deeply measured and planned response in place, ready to become operational if and when any of the following 15 pre-determined disasters strike. While we as a nation may be caught off-guard as to the exact timing of any such disaster, the federal government cannot have any excuse as to why it wasn't prepared to deal with these scenarios. Remember that when any of the following may unfortunately occur:

- Scenario 1 – Nuclear Detonation – Improvised Nuclear Device
- Scenario 2 – Biological Attack – Aerosol Anthrax
- Scenario 3 – Biological Disease Outbreak – Pandemic Influenza
- Scenario 4 – Biological Attack – Plague
- Scenario 5 – Chemical Attack – Blister Agent
- Scenario 6 – Chemical Attack – Toxic Industrial Chemicals
- Scenario 7 – Chemical Attack – Nerve Agent
- Scenario 8 – Chemical Attack – Chlorine Tank Explosion
- Scenario 9 – Natural Disaster – Major Earthquake
- Scenario 10 – Natural Disaster – Major Hurricane

- Scenario 11 – Radiological Attack – Radiological Dispersal Device
- Scenario 12 – Explosives Attack – Bombing Using Improvised Explosive Device
- Scenario 13 – Biological Attack – Food Contamination
- Scenario 14 – Biological Attack – Foreign Animal Disease
- Scenario 15 – Cyber Attack

Notice that 12 of these 15 scenarios are some form of attack which likely will be committed on a terrorist level. This is why nuclear war, once the primary concern of this nation's civil defense planning, is not among the 15 scenarios. There are various other annexes that detail other chemical and biological attacks as well as other natural disasters, but these don't qualify for the official list since most of the planning and responses are redundant. What is interesting is that this sort of terrorist-laden planning harkens back to the argument of whether FEMA was to be a disaster agency or a civil defense/counterterrorism entity. Clearly most of the forethought has gone into a variety of attacks upon the United States—something that is very unlikely to occur.

The certainty of that statement is backed by the government's own studies. In 2001, the Rand Corporation issued a report entitled *Preparing the U.S. Army for Homeland Security: Concepts, Issues and Options* written by Eric V. Larson and John E. Peters. While the political slant of this report leaned heavily in the "America needs to strengthen homeland security because the terrorists are coming to get us" vein, the authors wrote on page 48, "the actual incidence of terrorism remains quite low." Obviously, one terrorist attack is one too many. There is no denying that. Yet, even on a worldwide scale, they rarely occur. On U.S. soil, there have been two attacks in the past 20+ years attributed to foreign terrorists, both of which were focused on destroying the World Trade Center. Fewer than 4,000 people died in those two incidents. Not to belittle those unnecessary deaths, but according to U.S. fire department officials more than 4,000 people die *every year* from residential fires. National mandates and funding have not been distributed to equip every home in the nation with smoke detectors and fire extinguishers even though such spending would lower American fatalities more than the billions of dollars spent on anti-terrorism measures.

In continuing to prepare for a looming terrorist attack, there are a couple of important aspects the government and people in general seem to forget. Number one, coming straight from the U.S. Government Accountability Office (GAO) in its 2008 report titled *Risk Management: Strengthening the Use of Risk Management Principles in Homeland Security* is the fact that "the nation can neither achieve total security nor afford to protect everything against all risks." Perhaps no department of the federal government has ever communicated a more honest statement. The only alternative would involve the complete cessation of our freedom and liberties which no sane person would agree to, and even that measure would not completely rule out some sort of future terrorist activity.

According to another GAO report published in December 2008 and titled *Global War on Terrorism: Reported Obligations for the Department of Defense*, it was written:

"Since 2001, Congress has provided the Department of Defense (DOD) with about $808 billion in supplemental and annual appropriations, as of September 2008, primarily for military operations in support of the Global War on Terrorism (GWOT). DOD's reported annual obligations for GWOT have shown a steady increase from about $0.2 billion in fiscal year 2001 to about $162.4 billion in fiscal year 2008. The United States' commitments to GWOT will likely involve the continued investment of significant resources, requiring decision makers to consider difficult trade-offs as the nation faces an increasing fiscal challenge."

Just shy of a trillion dollars has been spent to fight the global war on terror in a 10 year span. Despite this fact, Americans are supposed to fear another terrorist attack? If a trillion dollars plus the efforts and untold billions of dollars that fund the CIA, NSA, FBI and other non-DOD agencies can't clamp down terrorism, then nothing is going to do the trick. There have been significant results attributable to this vast spending including the capture or death of many known and/or suspected terrorists as well as the destruction of a significant portion of those terrorists' supposed capabilities. As the 10 year anniversary of 9/11 passed without a single terrorist attack on U.S. soil, was the mission actually accomplished?

There may be a very valid reason why that is true beyond the government's massive spending spree. The 2001 Rand report quoted from above also sourced a 1999 GAO report titled *Combating Terrorism: Observations on the Threat of Chemical and Biological Terrorism.* In this report, the GAO stated on page 2, "Terrorists face serious technical and operational challenges at different stages of the process of producing and delivering most chemical and all biological agents." Did it state such an attack was impossible? No, but the GAO described the difficulty any terrorist would face in manufacturing such chemical or biological weapons.

For example, in discussing nerve agents, the GAO wrote:

"Most chemical nerve agents such as tabun (GA), sarin (GB), soman (GD), and VX are difficult to produce. To begin with, developing nerve agents requires the synthesis of multiple chemicals that, according to the experts we consulted, are very difficult to obtain in large quantities due to the provisions of the 1993 Chemical Weapons Convention, which has been in force since April 1997. In addition, a 1993 Office of Technology Assessment report on the technologies underlying weapons of mass destruction indicated that some steps in the production process of these nerve agents are difficult and hazardous."
They concluded:

"In general, production of chemical nerve agents could be technically unfeasible for terrorists without a sophisticated laboratory infrastructure because their production requires the use of high temperatures and generates corrosive and dangerous by-products….Even if chemical agents can be produced successfully, they must be released effectively as a vapor, or aerosol, for inhalation exposure, or they need to be in a spray of large droplets or liquid for skin penetration. To serve as terrorist weapons, chemical agents require high toxicity and volatility (tendency of a chemical to vaporize), and need to maintain their strength during storage and release."

As for biological agents, the GAO was equally as dismissive, writing: "Causing mass casualties with biological agents also presents extraordinary technical and operational challenges for terrorists without the assistance of a state-sponsored program….Although most biological agents are easy to grow if the seed stock can be obtained, they are difficult to process into a lethal form and successfully deliver to achieve large scale casualties. Processing biological agents into the right particle size and delivering them effectively requires expertise in a wide range of scientific disciplines."

If that weren't enough, the GAO concluded by adding:

"Terrorists have additional hurdles to overcome. For example, outdoor delivery of chemical and biological agents can be disrupted by environmental (e.g., pollution) and meteorological (e.g., sun, rain, mist, and wind) conditions. Once released, an aerosol cloud gradually dissipates over time and as a result of exposure to oxygen, pollutants, and ultraviolet rays. If wind conditions are too erratic or strong, the agent might dissipate too rapidly or fail to reach the desired area. Indoor dissemination of an agent could be affected by the air exchange rate of the building. In addition, terrorists risk capture and personal safety in acquiring and processing materials, disposing byproducts, and releasing the agent. Many agents are dangerous to handle. In some cases the lack of an effective vaccine, antibiotic/antiviral treatment, or antidote poses the same risk to the terrorist as it does to a targeted population."

What the GAO made abundantly clear—two years prior to the 9/11 attacks—was the threat from terrorist biological or chemical agents was minimal at best. Such agents are complex to manufacture, hard to maintain and stabilize, and difficult to release to render them useful in killing large numbers of people. While the U.S. did see the highly unusual anthrax letters sent to various public figures in 2001 (a case that has not been satisfactorily explained even though the investigating officials were able to track the anthrax spores to an exact test tube that had been contained within a U.S. government laboratory), since then nothing resembling such an attack has been knowingly attempted or perpetrated. There have been scares and hoaxes which tend to keep the public on edge, but none of these have contained true chemical or biological agents nor has anyone fulfilled on such horrific promises.

Sensible talk like that, however, is often shunned by the powers that be. Instead, fear mongering rules the day. In the previously mentioned Rand report *Preparing the U.S. Army for Homeland Security: Concepts, Issues and Options*, the authors included a specially designated box on page 54 under the ominous heading "Not If But When" to illustrate how certain another terrorist attack was. Their reasoning was:

"Although the probability of successfully acquiring or manufacturing, weaponizing, and employing WMD is presently low, the probability of an attack increases over a longer time span. An illustration:

• Assume that 25 terrorist groups are seeking to acquire and employ WMD.

• Assume furthermore that each group has an independent probability of .01 annual chance of acquiring and successfully employing WMD.

• The probability of a successful attack in the next year is $(1 - (1 - 0.01)25) = 0.222$, or a little over one in five.

• The probability of a successful attack in the next 10 years is $(1 - (1 - 0.01)25 \cdot 10) = 0.918$, or about nine in 10.

• If one assumes that the probability of success is increasing each year (e.g., through a learning curve phenomenon or through diffusion of learning among WMD-intent groups), the probability is even higher."

The authors literally stated that the chances of another terrorist attack are 9 in 10 *or higher* within the next ten years. That was written at the end of 2001, meaning if the authors weren't

215

simply out to scare the public, then another significant attack was almost certain to occur by the end of 2011….yet one never materialized.

Following a similar line of reasoning, the GAO reviewed the Department of Homeland Security's risk assessment methods in 2008. In the ensuing report titled *Homeland Security: DHS Risk-Based Methodology Is Reasonable, But Current Version's Measure of Vulnerability is Limited*, the GAO determined "measuring vulnerability is considered a generally-accepted practice in assessing risk; however, DHS's current risk analysis model does not measure vulnerability for each state and urban area. Rather, DHS considered all states and urban areas equally vulnerable to a successful attack and assigned every state and urban area a vulnerability score of 1.0 in the risk analysis model, which does not take into account any geographic differences." In other words, the DHS determined that for the 60 urban areas they considered, each was equally vulnerable to a terrorist attack. Not one was safer than another, no matter its location or population. According to the DHS then, almost all of us are continually locked in the terrorists' crosshairs.

The reason the DHS conducted that analysis was to determine how its grant program money should be distributed. As the GAO's report explained, "since 2002, the Department of Homeland Security (DHS) has distributed almost $20 billion in federal funding through various DHS grant programs that provide funding to public jurisdictions and private owners/operators for planning, equipment, and training to enhance the nation's capabilities to respond to terrorist attacks and, to a lesser extent, natural and accidental disasters." Notice once again terrorism was highlighted over and above any natural disaster. While the DHS's conclusion was that all 60 metropolitan areas it considered for that yearly grant money were equally vulnerable, it did make one concession. Seven of those 60 were deemed "Tier 1" areas and granted 55 percent of the nearly one billion dollars in funding to be doled out by the DHS. The other 53 "Tier 2" areas had to share in the remaining 45 percent.

Even as that money was passed around, the GAO wrote, "As inherent uncertainty is always associated with estimating risk of terrorist attack, policy and analytic judgments are required." No kidding. The question remained; whose judgment? Hopefully not the GAO's, for just 10 years prior, it seemed to believe that even the threat of major terrorist attack based on either chemical or biological weapons was nearly nonexistent. The GAO did report in 2005 that "according to the International Atomic Energy Agency, between 1993 and 2004, there were 650 confirmed cases of illicit trafficking in nuclear and radiological materials worldwide. A significant number of the cases involved material that could be used to produce either a nuclear weapon or a device that uses conventional explosives with radioactive material (known as a "dirty bomb")." Even with "650 confirmed cases" of nuclear and/or radiological trafficking, nothing along the lines of the detonation of a dirty bomb has seemingly even come close to fruition anywhere in the world. Of course, it may be that the "significant number" the report threateningly mentions wasn't really all that significant. Maybe it's two (it doesn't specifically say), which would be significant in a sense, but perhaps not all that frightening. While the threat remains that a dirty bomb certainly could be detonated at any time, no one's willing to guess when—or if—such a day will ever come. Yet the government is hedging its bets by gambling billions of dollars in taxpayer money, plunking it down on the assumed fact that a massive terrorist attack *will* happen.

Many questions remain unanswered though. How much preparedness is enough? How much money would ensure the country is in fact prepared for any such occurrence? How much of a threat really exists? And perhaps strangest of all: are we even preparing for the right circumstances?

Returning once again to the 2001 Rand report *Preparing the U.S. Army for Homeland Security: Concepts, Issues and Options*, in Chapter Eight the authors offered "Illustrative Planning Vignettes." There were nine of these which were supposed to "assist in thinking through the key consequences, key tasks, key Army tasks, and current and needed Army capabilities…" since the authors' argument was that America needed its Army to be among the nation's first responders. The authors' pro-military stance aside, what these vignettes showed was that there are countless ways in which terrorists could attack this nation and no one would see it coming. Whether any of these scenarios are actually probable or even possible, however, is debatable.

The authors' first example was rather mundane. It involved a fertilizer-diesel fuel bomb hidden in a sports arena concessionaire truck. Parked inside a 17,000 seat stadium, the bomb explodes during a collegiate basketball game. The results are as you would imagine. While that sort of attack is one of the most likely scenarios depicted in the Rand report due to its straightforwardness, it isn't very original. The United States had already been on the unfortunate end of two such truck bombs, one in Oklahoma City and the other at the World Trade Center. Neither of those required a military response, and even the authors of the Rand report didn't call for the military's aid outside of sending in medical support teams to assist the wounded.

The next vignette also focused on an attack on an enclosed sports stadium. This time, however, the attackers weren't just faceless, but deemed "a domestic millenarian group." Their weapon of choice? A release of sarin gas via a number of small canisters attached to the bottom of seats spread out through the arena. Timers would coordinate the release of the gas while the perpetrators fled the scene. When the gas is released, the ensuing panic causes a human stampede. Ultimately, by Rand's assessment, 2,500 people die from the gas while another 1,000 suffer injuries.

This vignette was interesting in a few different areas. For one, the authors labeled the attackers. Why they did that wasn't explained (or even necessary). Perhaps the authors made their terrorists a domestic group to run a parallel to the sarin gas attacks that occurred in Japan. In 1995, members of the Japanese religious cult Aum Shinrikyo released sarin gas in a coordinated attack on

Toyko's subway system during the peak of the morning rush hour. The attack sent some 6,000 people to area hospitals, yet in the end, only about a dozen unfortunate souls perished. Not too bad an outcome considering the potential lethality of sarin gas coupled with the approximately 12 million people that call Tokyo home. While it's easy to notice the similarities between the real and imagined attacks, note the incredible difference in the death toll. Both the subway and the sports arena were enclosed areas filled with thousands of people, but in the real attack only 12 died, whereas in Rand's scenario 2,500 die. The numbered of injured was also flip-flopped with 6,000 injured in Tokyo, and only 1,000 in the vignette. This vast discrepancy was not addressed. In all likelihood, that was because in the scenario the attackers were assumed to be able to get their sarin to vaporize, something the real attackers could not do. That would definitely increase the lethality of the gas. Another key point not brought up was that the GAO specifically listed sarin gas as one of the chemical agents terrorists would find extremely difficult to produce and utilize. The real attacks in Tokyo backed the GAO's findings while the Rand report shunned them.

Within that vignette, the authors did point out one key fact that should put to rest their own argument that the military should be among the nation's first responders. What the Rand report declared was, "The first Army elements (WMD CSTs) on the scene are intended to respond within four hours. In four hours, most of the chemical victims will have died or received other care." That statement could be made about nearly any and all terrorist attacks. The Army is designed to fight wars, not to combat an incident that can be over within seconds. In the vignette, even if the incident occurred during an Army-Navy basketball game, the military could do little to alleviate the situation. Once an attack occurs, in nearly all such situations, the only thing left to do is help the wounded and bury the dead. Sure, you can secure the area and hopefully track down the perpetrators, but how does the military fit into that equation? When did that become its duty?

Vignette number three again involved the attack on a sports

arena, this time during a hockey game with 17,000 in attendance. A "foreign terrorist organization" places anthrax in the stadium's air ducts and silently infects the hockey fanatics while they watch the game and eat their hot dogs. The authors pick up the action from there: "Within three days, many experience flu-like symptoms and seek treatment. Six days after exposure, some 3,200 have died and another 4,250 are seriously ill. As news of the illness circulates through the population, hundreds of people begin flooding emergency rooms complaining of flu-like symptoms. Most of those seeking treatment are completely healthy and complicate the work of health care providers." This simulated attack also flies in the face of the GAO report on chemical and biological weapons that the authors themselves cited. The GAO report clearly stated that biological weapons like anthrax are even more difficult to produce than chemical weapons. Yet in this scenario, not only are the terrorists able to produce (or at least, procure) anthrax, they are able to successfully distribute it among an arena full of hockey fans, killing nearly 20% of them.

The Rand report's fourth scenario appeared more realistic, not because of the damage done, but due to the assessment of the public's reaction. Once again, terrorists are armed with a truck bomb. Rather than blow up a stadium full of sports fans, the terrorists detonate their bomb at "the loading dock of the reactor building at a major metropolitan university." The explosion cracks open the nuclear reactor and in the ensuing fire, radioactive particles escape into the atmosphere. Since the authors could dream up whatever they desired, they place their fictitious college in the heart of a major city so when the radioactive materials start falling, havoc ensues. The authors stated "the news media cover the story as if it were Chernobyl" which is highly probable given the media's often hyper-excited and exaggerated nature, and because of this, people panic and immediately attempt to escape the city. The uncontrolled exodus clogs the streets and subways, not only causing a new set of problems but making it difficult for the emergency crews to get to the scene of the radiation leak. While the scenario claimed that only a few die—and not from radiation poisoning, but from heart attacks—it is the panic surrounding the situation that is perhaps more of a threat than the actual source of the chaos.

Another vignette in the Rand report also sounded eerily familiar to a previous, or at least supposed, terrorist attack. In this situation, terrorists smuggle nine Stinger missiles purchased off the black market into the United States. Armed with the anti-aircraft missiles and trained on how to use them thanks to the army's own field manuals downloaded from the internet, the terrorists set up camp outside a few key Air Force bases and a civilian airport. At the proper time, the terrorists shoot down not just Air Force cargo planes, but a passenger airliner as well. Flights are then shut down nationwide, much like during 9/11 when all air traffic was cleared from the nation's skies. This missile attack on a passenger jet sounded exactly like what many believe brought down TWA's Flight 800 which mysteriously crashed into the Atlantic Ocean just after its take off from New York City. While the circumstances surrounding the downing of TWA 800 are both controversial and debatable, this similar scenario put forth in the Rand report appeared to be quite plausible. It's is a simple plan, easily executed, and capable of causing mass panic, yet once again, nowhere within this scenario is the Army's involvement warranted.

While a missile attack is as straightforward as a terrorist could get, the next vignette was the complete opposite as it appeared to be ripped from the playbook of a James Bond-esque super villain:

"It is winter, and the Washington, D.C., area is experiencing periodic snowstorms. In anticipation of another snowstorm, the enemy contaminates with plutonium oxide the Pentagon's supply of salt and sand used for clearing walkways. When the next storm occurs, the regular maintenance personnel salt and sand the sidewalks. Pentagon workers subsequently track the contamination throughout the building. The contamination spreads to individual cars and homes as workers leave at the end of the day. Some employees inadvertently inhale small amounts of plutonium oxide while others ingest contamination after handling their shoes. The conspirators announce their attack to CNN. Subsequent investigation confirms their allegations."

What happens next in the minds of the Rand authors was just as nefarious. "It is not only a military attack, it is also an area crisis. All facilities—automobiles, the Metro (subway and bus) system, homes, convenience stores, dry cleaners—that Pentagon employees may have visited after becoming contaminated must be screened for plutonium. Contaminated areas must be cleaned up. Everyone who entered the building after the contamination must be decontaminated and medically examined to ascertain the level of plutonium exposure they have experienced." While there was an inherent evil genius-ness to this plot, how high could this rank on the possibility scale?

It may sound frightening, but just how dangerous would plutonium oxide actually be? According to the U.S. Nuclear Regulatory Commission:

"The most common form of plutonium, plutonium oxide, is virtually insoluble. The behavior of plutonium oxide in the body varies with the way in it is taken. If one drinks or eats it, a very large percentage will be eliminated quite rapidly in bodily wastes. If plutonium oxide is inhaled, part of it, usually between 20 and 60 percent depending upon such factors as the size of the particles, is retained in the lungs. The rest is eliminated from the body within several days. Of that remaining in the lungs, about half will be removed each year, some to be excreted, some to lodge in the lymph nodes, and a very small amount will be deposited in other organs, mainly bone. If plutonium enters the body through an open wound, depending on its form, it may move directly into body organs, mainly bone and liver."

While the U.S. Nuclear Regulatory Commission stated that such ingestion of plutonium oxide could—not will—lead to cancer/tumors, the likelihood of mass causalities from the Rand authors' plot appeared rather low. Add on top of that the fact that plutonium of any sort is almost an entirely man-made substance which is covered under the Nuclear Non-Proliferation Treaty, and the chances of your average terrorist getting a hold of a significant amount of such radiological materials are very slim.

Even so, it goes to show you that with the right plan and imagination, as the GAO themselves reported, nothing would ever be completely safe.

The Pandemic

In 1918-1919 the United States suffered through three waves of what was then commonly dubbed the Spanish Flu. This influenza epidemic took the lives of approximately 675,000 Americans—a causality amount greater than that of every American war during the 20th Century combined—at a time when the country's population was just over 100 million people. Worldwide, the death tolls were much higher with estimates ranging from 20 to 50 million people killed (some sources claim an even higher death toll). Despite the fact that in 1918 there was not a network of commercial airliners to transport thousands of people across the globe daily as there is today, this potent little virus managed to spread itself around the world in a matter of months. Much of that transmission was thanks to World War I. Early reports of a "bad case of the flu" began to crop up in the Midwest in the spring of 1918. As U.S. soldiers were shipped to Europe to fight in the war, the flu quickly spread from infected soldiers to civilians living in Europe throughout the summer. Within a few short months, the flu bug mutated itself into a killer and spread from Europe to Asia, Africa, South America, and back home to North America.

In America, the major outbreak site of the killer form of the virus was in Boston, Massachusetts. In late summer, a large number of dockworkers there reported severe flu-like symptoms, with some five to 10 percent suffering a secondary reaction that included a deadly pneumonia. Less than two months later, the flu was reported in all corners of the country. No segment of the population appeared safe as the flu favored infecting young adults, something uncommon with most viruses of this type which normally attack the very young or the very old.

As the pandemic spread, so too did the panic associated with it. Healthcare workers, already stretched thin due to significant numbers of their rank serving the military in the war effort, were either overwhelmed by the numbers of the sick or found themselves incapacitated from the flu. Schools emptied of both students and teachers. Many businesses went short staffed. Both the telephone and telegraph companies faltered due to lack of operators. Garbage went uncollected and mail was undelivered. Areas were quarantined and many public gatherings were either suspended or outright banned. Bars and theaters were closed. There was even a law passed to stop spitting in public as fear of the disease's transmission was widespread. Despite thousands wearing masks, nothing the public attempted to do to stop the spread of the flu proved effective.

Medical officials at the time did not completely understand the outbreak. It was originally thought to be brought on by a bacterial infection. When that was proven false, some believed the flu to be either a variation of cholera or the plague. When the idea that this medical disaster was created by a mutant strain of the flu, vaccines were created and tested. None of them proved to be effective. It was understood the flu spread much like the common cold, yet medical officials could not find a solution to stop it. Luckily for the world, by the spring of 1919 the flu seemed to burn itself out. While the great pandemic of 1918-1919 was seemingly forgotten as it coincided with the end of World War I, both health officials and insurance companies continued to seek its cause and work on various methods of prevention. Despite all best efforts, two more outbreaks of a worldwide flu epidemic occurred—once between 1957-1958 and again between 1968-1969. The combined death tolls from these two outbreaks reached 100,000 people in the U.S.; not nearly as brutal as the 1918-1919 flu, but significant nonetheless.

As the global population continues to surge with no end in sight, the fear has become that another great, lethal worldwide pandemic is certain to occur. The belief is that most major, deadly viruses begin their existences in animals only to later jump to humans in a mutant form. With such a large percentage of the world still living in squalor, the worry is the overcrowded and unsanitary conditions in many Third World areas will become hotbeds of such viral mutations. Since the world is growing more interconnected with each passing day, when such a virus does manifest itself, the trip from being an isolated Third World entity to a major worldwide pandemic could take an extremely short time. Many healthcare officials point a knowing finger at the H5N1 virus, better known as Avian Influenza, or simpler still, the "bird flu" as being the likely culprit of this soon-to-be pandemic. The truth is every year we are all faced with various strains of the flu, including even a less pathogenic strain of the 1918 Spanish Flu (a.k.a. H1N1), any of which could one day mutate into a very potent and lethal form. When and where that will occur, no one can say.

Unless this potentially lethal pandemic outbreak is noticed upon its inception and is immediately contained, we may all face an unusual set of circumstances. As the new killer flu spreads, it will inevitably lead to suspicion, paranoia, and eventual panic. Media reports will fuel this growing fire. The early warning signs of infection may be quite similar to the common cold and the transmission of the virus could be just as easy, but no one would immediately know for certain. Anyone who sneezes around you— be it on the train, at work, or during the backyard BBQ—may be just clearing their sinuses, or they may be spreading the growing plague. Who can you trust *not* to be infected? Your closest friends cannot be completely believed, for you can't be certain who they have come in contact with as anyone could potentially be a carrier of this virus. You even have reason to fear your own family. While you may love your spouse and children to death, either may be bringing home your demise with them thanks to an infected co-worker or schoolmate. What can and should be done?

The obvious answer would seem to be to quarantine those

infected. With a nation of 300+ million interconnected people, where would be the best place to start? Who are the proper people to lock down and keep out of society at large? And for how long? What if the flu takes a toll on local fire or police departments, since they are the people who work the closest with the general public? Who fills those roles? Or any of the public service departments? What happens to a corporation if a large percentage of its employees are among those forced to stay home? What becomes of those jobs? Who is responsible to the stock holders if no one is able to work and the business flounders?

Consider your own situation in a public health emergency. If you happen to fall under that quarantine zone, what then? If you can't get to work, how will you make money? If you don't get paid, how can you buy food or pay your mortgage? What if a family member gets sick? Do you take them to the over-burdened and under-staffed hospital or do you care for them yourself? Or should you instead treat the ill as an outcast to save yourself or the other healthy members of your family?

A quarantine by definition requires the surrendering of certain rights and liberties we take for granted as American citizens. Are you willing to sacrifice those rights for the greater good, even if you yourself are not one of the infected living in the quarantine zone? Is that fair? If such a quarantine is mandated, who is going to hold you to it? Are you willing to police your own neighborhood? While it would most likely be the government backed by local law enforcement, if not the military, which enforces the quarantine, would you be willing to look the other way when someone else breaks it? Or would it be you who attempts an escape? There are many unanswered and unknown "what ifs" created by a pandemic scenario. No one has all the answers to these questions, but if one digs through the government's own plans created to combat such an outbreak, you might be able to find one or two.

Be Prepared

As we've already seen, the U.S. government of late has become a lot like the Boy Scouts of America, living by the notion "be prepared." This mindset has not been lost when considering the possibility of a pandemic influenza outbreak. The federal government has already set up a website with the semi-alarming name www.pandemicflu.gov for the occasion. At the end of 2008, Secretary of Health and Human Services (HHS) Mike Leavitt posted a "Message from the Secretary" on the site. In his address, he made a valid and keen observation, writing, "Today, many people mistakenly think influenza pandemics are a thing of the past, but influenza has struck hard in the era of modern medicine—much harder than most people realize. And it will strike again. Pandemics are hard things to talk about. When one discusses them in advance, it sounds alarmist. After a pandemic starts, no matter how much preparation has been done, it will be inadequate." This damned-if-you-do-damned-if-you-don't position is quite true.

In the conspiracy circles, much has been made of the nation's preparedness against the outbreak of a pandemic flu. The resounding question always asked is, "Why would the government bother to spend all that money and engage in so much preparation if they didn't already know it was coming?" That is usually followed by, "it will probably be the government—thanks to all their secret experimentation—that will be the cause of such an outbreak anyway." While I won't (and really can't) debate the second point since it is true such controversial viral experiments are in fact ongoing, the first position is worth looking at a little closer.

Much like the civil defense preparedness the nation endured for decades, planning for a pandemic flu may be all for naught. While it seemed certain at particular points in history that nuclear war would start, it never actually did. Fallout shelters across the nation sat unused while the canned rations and medical supplies stored within them either rotted or expired. The nuclear weapons themselves were never launched and are now in need of continuous maintenance with the hope that the radioactive material contained inside doesn't contaminate the land or water. Was it all just a colossal waste of money? Was it a dumb thing to prepare for?

Considering the times, no. So, is preparing for a pandemic that may not occur wasteful?

Secretary Leavitt's 2008 message on the pandemicflu.gov website generated a lot of facts and figures to consider. He wrote, "In November 2005, President Bush mobilized the nation to prepare for an influenza pandemic. He called for the deployment of a $7.1 billion national pandemic plan. Congress responded quickly." That's a lot of money to develop a national "pandemic plan" when one considers that Secretary Leavitt went on to write that such preparedness wasn't just an American initiative, but one in which the entire world needed to participate. Highlighting America's plan, Secretary Leavitt wrote, "One of our highest priorities is to enhance and expand U.S.-based vaccine production capacity to the point that it can generate enough pandemic influenza vaccine for every American within six months of the time that the actual pandemic virus is identified, wherever in the world it is identified." To do that, the government granted $1 billion to six different companies to develop "commercial grade" manufacture of such a vaccine. This was hoped to be completed by 2011. By the end of 2008, "We have now procured 12.2 million treatment courses (each course provides a full treatment for one person) of H5N1 pre-pandemic influenza vaccine. If the virus mutates to where it has pandemic properties, a new vaccine will be developed to match it exactly, but this stockpiled vaccine will provide some protection in the interim." Those 12.2 million courses are stockpiled to be used for first responders and medical workers. If you don't happen to fall within the category, fear not, for, "We have reached our goal of stockpiling enough pandemic influenza antivirals to cover 44 million people, which will help slow the spread of an emerging pandemic." Over three-fourths of these have been purchased by individual states along with another 22 million treatment courses of Tamiflu and Relenza. On top of all of that, "We purchased more than 150 million masks and respirators. We have obligated $100 million for the purchase of ventilators, syringes, intravenous antibiotics, and other supplies for potential distribution in case of an influenza pandemic. We have developed a highly sensitive rapid diagnostic test for avian and seasonal influenza. This will serve as the gold standard worldwide for confirming the first cases of avian or potentially pandemic influenza."

It appeared as if the federal government had its population covered, yet not all was as it appeared in the virus world. For one, through the end of 2008, 67 countries around the world had reported cases of animals with Avian Influenza (the H5N1 virus). Despite this, only about 250 people had actually died from it. That's an average of less than 4 deaths per country. Wasn't this supposed to be the cause of the great worldwide pandemic? How can there only be 250 deaths caused by the H5N1 virus if it's going to be the plague of the 21st Century? Maybe that is the problem. Maybe H5N1 isn't the virus we should worry about.

In 2009, another virus—the H1N1 "swine flu" virus (which is a mutant form of the 1918 Spanish Flu)—became a media darling due to its pandemic-like properties. The virus began its path of infection in Mexico in the spring and quickly circled the globe. America was quick to react, and at times, overreact to its arrival. On April 26, the Secretary of Health and Human Services declared a public health emergency related to the virus's spread. It was renewed twice, once on July 24 and again on October 1. During this time, myths and rumors regarding the virus spread as fast as the disease. People were unsure of the infection's symptoms. Many did not believe the vaccine rushed to the public was safe. Estimates on how lethal the virus was fluctuated widely. Medical officials disagreed on what safety precautions were best. Meanwhile, the media only seemed to feed the H1N1 frenzy, airing every school closing or outbreak cluster associated with the virus.

In an attempt to combat the virus and the paranoia associated with it, President Obama issued Proclamation 8443 on October 23, 2009 declaring the "H1N1 Influenza Pandemic" a national emergency. Obama wrote, "Given that the rapid increase in illness across the Nation may overburden health care resources and that the temporary waiver of certain standard Federal requirements may be warranted in order to enable U.S. health care facilities to implement emergency operations plans, the 2009 H1N1 influenza pandemic in the United States constitutes a national emergency." In issuing this proclamation, Obama freed the Secretary of Health and Human Services from some of the position's usual constraints in order to combat the virus's spread. This included the ability "to temporarily waive or modify certain requirements of the Medicare, Medicaid, and State Children's Health Insurance programs and of the Health Insurance Portability and Accountability Act Privacy Rule throughout the duration of the public health emergency declared."

Whether this worked or not was difficult to determine. In a *New York Times* article written by Donald G. McNeil Jr. in December 2009, questions still lingered as to the potency of H1N1. McNeil wrote that an October report from the Centers for Disease Control and Prevention (CDC) listed only 4,000 deaths from the virus. Just over a month later, unidentified "federal health officials" claimed the death toll had reached over 10,000 in the U.S., though the numbers are hard to prove because not everyone who supposedly died from the virus was actually tested for it. These same officials stated that over 50 million Americans (one sixth of the nation) had been infected with over 200,000 requiring hospitalization by the end of 2009. While these appear to be stunning numbers, an average of 36,000 people dies each year during the typical flu season.

The H1N1 outbreak of 2009 seemed to render President Bush's and former HHS Secretary Leavitt's $7.1 billion pandemic plan from 2008 moot. Even the pandemicflu.gov website was completely stripped of all mention of the H5N1 Avian Influenza because it wasn't the problematic outbreak as expected; swine flu was. So, while the 12.2 treatment courses for H5N1 sat and collected dust, over 50 million vaccines for H1N1 were rushed into people's arms, and in some cases, noses. Such are usually the pitfalls when preparing for a worst case scenario. What one expects to be the problem ultimately isn't.

The world may have dodged a bullet with the swine flu. Had the pandemic been a mutant form of ebola or SARS or even some unknown virus, vaccines may have been a long time in coming. Should this ever be the case, the backup plan seems to rely heavily on four main antiviral drugs. These are Oseltamivir (the brand name of which is Tamiflu), Zanamivir (its brand name is Relenza), Amantadine, and Rimantadine. These drugs neither are total preventatives nor are they cures. Used as a preventative, such antiviral drugs are deemed by the CDC to be anywhere from 70-90% effective. As a treatment once infected, such an antiviral can help the body minimize the flu-like symptoms, usually cutting the recovery time by a day or two. It is believed these drugs, if administered properly in the absence of a true vaccine, could help control an outbreak. Whether they could effectively contain one is a completely different and unanswered question.

Another concern surrounding antiviral drugs is that they might not be effective against particular virus strains. As flu viruses often mutate, this year's major strain may be completely different from next year's. Which one will the antiviral beat, and which will beat the antiviral? No medical official can say for certain. Already some strains of the flu seem to have become resistant to certain antiviral medications. And Tamiflu came under scrutiny in November 2012 when British medical researchers announced their findings that "no evidence" exists that the drug can stop the influenza virus *at all*. Despite this fact, both countries like America and groups such as the World Health Organization (WHO) are hedging their bets and stockpiling large quantities of antiviral medications.

It's All Part of the Plan

In an effort to both prepare for and combat any major pandemic, the U.S. government has issued three primary documents that outline its plan. These are the *HHS Pandemic Influenza Plan* issued by the Department of Health and Human Services in November 2005, the Department of Defense's

Department of Defense Implementation Plan for Pandemic Influenza released in August 2006, and the *North American Plan for Avian and Pandemic Influenza* which was released in August 2007 and was co-sponsored by the Public Health Agency of Canada. Of the three, the Department of Health and Human Service's plan was the largest, covering nearly 400 pages.

While lengthy to the point of becoming mind-numbing, the HHS's plan is as straightforward as one might hope. As it begins in the executive summary:

"An influenza pandemic has the potential to cause more death and illness than any other public health threat. If a pandemic influenza virus with similar virulence to the 1918 strain emerged today, in the absence of intervention, it is estimated that 1.9 million Americans could die and almost 10 million could be hospitalized over the course of the pandemic, which may evolve over a year or more. Although the timing, nature and severity of the next pandemic cannot be predicted with any certainty, preparedness planning is imperative to lessen the impact of a pandemic. The unique characteristics and events of a pandemic will strain local, state, and federal resources. It is unlikely that there will be sufficient personnel, equipment, and supplies to respond adequately to multiple areas of the country for a sustained period of time. Therefore, minimizing social and economic disruption will require a coordinated response. Governments, communities, and other public and private sector stakeholders will need to anticipate and prepare for a pandemic by defining roles and responsibilities and developing continuity of operations plans."

The HHS has already determined when a pandemic is considered to be in effect, at least officially for the United States. It states, "Sustained human-to-human transmission anywhere in the world will be the triggering event to initiate a pandemic response by the United States." Such a declaration will result in three primary responses once it is believed that the virus has invaded the country. First, "When possible and appropriate, protective public health measures will be employed to attempt to reduce person-to-person viral transmission and prevent or delay influenza outbreaks." If such an outbreak cannot be prevented within the U.S., then secondly, "At the onset of a pandemic, vaccine, which will initially be in short supply, will be procured by HHS and distributed to state and local health departments for immunization of pre-determined priority groups." This is immediately to be followed by the final response which is, "At the onset of a pandemic, antiviral drugs from public stockpiles will be distributed to health care providers for administration to pre-determined priority groups."

Who are in these "pre-determined priority groups" and who exactly pre-determined them? The answer lies in the HHS's booklet, under appendix D. "Two federal advisory committees, the Advisory Committee on Immunization Practices (ACIP) and the National Vaccine Advisory Committee (NVAC), provided recommendations to the Department of Health and Human Services on the use of vaccines and antiviral drugs in an influenza pandemic." Their findings may surprise you. A chart contained within the booklet lays out their recommendations along with the two committees' rationale. The order of importance for the distribution of a vaccine is as follows. Tier 1 persons are: the vaccine and antiviral manufactures themselves. Can't make these needed medical supplies without them, right? Next in line are the medical and public health workers who are in direct contact with patients. These two groups are followed by those thought to have the highest risk conditions including those over 65 years of age as well as those in any age range with more than one "influenza high-risk condition" or previous history of hospitalization for pneumonia. The next subsection includes pregnant women, children under 6 months of age, and "household contacts of severely immunocompromised persons who would not be vaccinated due to likely poor response to vaccine" which includes caregivers for transplant, cancer, and AIDS patients (but not those suffering from these conditions). The last members in this tier are public health emergency response workers "critical to pandemic response" followed by "key government leaders." In the end, Tier 1 alone covers approximately 45 million people according to the HHS.

If there are enough doses of the vaccine to cover those first 45 million, the rest of us are placed in the following order of importance. Tier 2 consists of: healthy persons 65 or older, persons under 65 with one high-risk factor, and healthy children 6-23 months of age. These are followed by other public health emergency responders, public safety workers (including police, firemen, and correctional facility staff), utility workers, transportation workers, and lastly telecommunications and IT staff "for essential network operations and maintenance." Tier 2 contains nearly 68 million people. Tier 3 is rather small, consisting of "other key government health decision-makers" and funeral directors and embalmers. The final tier is everyone else—some 174 million people by the HHS's estimations.

The HHS realized that certain subsections of the population were not covered in its four tiers. This included U.S. citizens overseas, non-U.S. citizens living within the U.S., and specifically "other groups providing national security services such as the border patrol and customs service." But the primary group missing is the military. The HHS's expanded on this omission, stating, "ACIP and NVAC recognize that Department of Defense needs should be highly prioritized. DOD Health Affairs indicates that 1.5 million service members would require immunization to continue current combat operations and preserve critical components of the military medical system. Should the military be called upon to support civil authorities domestically, immunization of a greater proportion of the total force will become necessary. These factors should be considered in the designation of a proportion of the initial vaccine supply for the military." It is interesting that the HHS does not specifically place the military anywhere within its four tier system. While it admits that should the military be needed to support law enforcement officials a greater number of soldiers would require immunization, the HHS doesn't necessarily say that the military would be in the same place in line—deep within tier 2—as police and fire officials are. Who would get their shots first?

What the DOD may be lacking in immunizations, they make up for in antiviral medications. According to a 2009 Congressional Research Service paper titled *The Role of the Department of Defense During a Flu Pandemic*, the DOD reported having 8.2 million courses of Tamiflu in its reserves. It also claimed to have an 80-day supply of personal protective equipment for its medical providers.

As for the rest of the nation, the procedure for administering antiviral medications takes a different course than the vaccination program. It isn't divided into specific tiers; rather it appears to be mandated based upon immediate needs. The first group is comprised of patients admitted to hospitals. This follows the basic medical service mandate to treat those who are sick first and foremost. The second group consists of the very caregivers treating those in the first group. From that point onward, the recommendations follow the level of risk involved with no surprises. The HHS does suggest that "Sufficient drugs should be stockpiled to address top priorities. NVAC recommends that the minimum stockpile size be about 40 million courses, allowing coverage of the top 7 priority groups."

If a vaccine cannot be found or made in vast enough quantities while none of the expected antiviral medications can do the job they were expected to do, perhaps the only other option to halt the spread of such a killer disease will be to quarantine people. For many, a quarantine order brings up images of people locked away in their homes while the sick are forcefully removed from their families by armed soldiers protected in biohazard suits. While such actions make for great movies or books, in reality, this could only occur in extreme cases, if they would ever be needed at all. As the HHS handbook states, "The negative connotations associated with quarantine likely stem from its misuse or abuse in the past. Although inappropriate use of quarantine, either voluntary or mandatory, would not and should not be accepted by the public, efforts should be made to gain public acceptance when use of this measure is indicated."

There are different variations of quarantines. The first would attempt to isolate the U.S. from the rest of the world. "Individuals may be denied admission to the U.S. if thought to have a communicable disease of public health significance, as defined in CDC regulations." This is allowed not just in CDC regulations, but is stated clearly in the Public Health Service Act in Title 42 U.S.C. 264. It is a sensible reaction. If there was an outbreak of the avian flu somewhere outside the U.S., the best way to prevent American casualties would be to stop an infected individual from entering the country. Of course, this is much more difficult in practice than it sounds. The borders of the country could not and would not be completely closed at any point. Even if they were sealed up as best as believed possible, the HHS plan states, "Preliminary mathematical modeling results suggest that travel restrictions would need to be about 99% effective to delay introduction into a country by one to two months." Notice that they suggest it would merely delay introduction, not completely prevent the virus from spreading into the nation.

Once the virus achieved a foothold here in the U.S. without immediate medical controls available, quarantine may be necessary. There are statues and laws that need to be followed and consulted prior to the implementation of quarantine, however. Most of these are state level actions. Governors are allowed to restrict travel within their state or prevent travel to or from their state as well. They are also allowed to implement quarantines. As the HHS plan points out, however, "Current quarantine laws, regulations, and enforcement procedures vary widely from state to state. Many of these laws date to the 19th century."

While the HHS plan suggests updating those quarantine laws in states that haven't considered the subject in decades, it also suggests not overlooking the constitutional notion of "due process" within those laws. It states:

"Procedural due process is implicated when the government seeks to deprive an individual of 'liberty' interests within the meaning of the Due Process Clause of the Fifth or Fourteenth Amendment to the U.S. Constitution. Many states, through statute or regulation, have established specific administrative and judicial schemes for affording due process to a person subject to a quarantine and/or isolation order. Schemes in other jurisdictions may not directly address this issue. Although due process is a flexible concept and calls for procedural protections as the particular situation demands, the basic elements of due process include: adequate notice (typically through written order) of the action the agency seeks to compel; right to be heard (typically through the right to present evidence and witnesses and to contest the government's evidence and witnesses); access to legal counsel; and a final administrative decision that is subject to review in a court of law. These due process protections should not impede the immediate isolation or quarantine of an individual for valid public health reasons in an emergency situation." Notice that the HHS recommends that an individual's right to "due process" be tossed in the backseat should an "emergency situation" be at hand because of "valid public health reasons." While you may find such a suggestion to willingly violate the Constitution deplorable, the HHS does not appear to be advocating the complete elimination of due process. It merely suggests the potential need to wave it—temporarily—in such an emergency situation.

The HHS also suggests that the courts be made aware of these health-related statues in advance of a potential pandemic situation so they can properly interpret the law. "Judges who may be called upon to review a public health order may not be familiar with the state or local health authority's broad public health powers. During the 2003 SARS outbreak in Toronto, Canada, for example, many judges were unaware of the health officer's broad ex parte authority to compel isolation/quarantine under rarely used laws." One such law that may raise an eyebrow is that in some states, depending on the circumstances, an individual may be required (read: forced) to take either an antiviral medication or to be vaccinated. Any objection to compliance with such an order would likely go unheard. You could not argue your religious stance or personal freedoms at that point in time. You may refuse to vacate your home in event of a volcanic eruption and be willing to die if the lava flow heads your way, but such a refusal for treatment in a time of pandemic could render you lethal to those around you. There is little legal wiggle room when your unwillingness to cooperate may make you an instrument of death, but there is little doubt such objections will be heard should such a time come. You may wish to check your own state to see when the last time these laws were updated and just what they may do to you own "due process" should such an infectious disease make itself present.

Prior to armed soldiers from USNORTHCOM invading your town to prevent an infectious disease from becoming a nationwide epidemic (and we'll get to USNORTHCOM's plan of action momentarily), there are smaller, less threatening quarantines possible. The primary version is playfully termed a "snow day." Per the HHS handbook:

"Implementation of 'snow days'—asking everyone to stay home—involves the entire community in a positive way, is acceptable to most people, and is relatively easy to implement. Snow days may be instituted for an initial 10-day period, with final decisions on duration based on an epidemiologic and social assessment of the situation. States and local authorities may wish to consider recommendations to the public for acquisition and storage of necessary provisions including type and quantity of supplies needed during snow days. Snow days can effectively reduce transmission without explicit activity restrictions (i.e., quarantine)." The HHS handbook goes on to state, "Closure of office buildings, stores, schools, and public transportation systems may be feasible community containment measures during a pandemic…Anecdotal reports suggest that community influenza outbreaks may be limited by closing schools. Results of mathematical modeling also suggest a reduction of overall disease, especially when schools are closed early in the outbreak."

If we ever did reach a quarantine situation, it is doubtful it would entail a nationwide lockdown. As the HHS states, "Modern quarantine is more likely to involve limited numbers of exposed persons in small area, than to involve large numbers of persons in whole neighborhoods or cities." There is a valid reason for this line of thought. "Modern quarantine does not have to be absolute to be effective. Modeling exercises suggest that partial quarantine can be effective in slowing the rate of smallpox spread, especially when combined with vaccination."

If you happened to be one of the unlucky few to be quarantined, it may not be as horrible as you imagined. While no one wants their personal freedoms stripped from them, quarantines are not just about turning the sick into outcasts, separating them from society and leaving them to rot. In fact, the opposite is true. The HHS claims, "Quarantined individuals will be sheltered, fed, and cared for under the supervision of trained healthcare professionals. They will also be among the first to receive all available medical interventions to prevent and control disease, including: vaccination (e.g., in the case of smallpox); antibiotics (e.g., in the case of plague); early and rapid diagnostic testing and symptom monitoring; [and] early treatment if symptoms appear." The people quarantined may in fact be the first healed. On top of this perk, those in line for these first treatments may not even have to leave their own homes for some science-fiction inspired tent city to receive them. The idea behind quarantining people is to keep them separated, not herded together like cattle. Staying in one's own home accomplishes that better than anything else. The fear that some may have from being quarantined may be completely unfounded, unless you fear your own home or family.

Turning from the state to a national level response, there are two main justifications for implementing a quarantine situation. The first comes from the aforementioned Public Health Service Act which resides in Title 42 U.S.C. 264. In subsection b, it states "Regulations prescribed under this section shall not provide for the apprehension, detention, or conditional release of individuals except for the purpose of preventing the introduction, transmission, or spread of such communicable diseases as may be specified from time to time in Executive orders of the President upon the recommendation of the Secretary, in consultation with the Surgeon General." Subsection d clarifies the matter by stating, "Regulations prescribed under this section may provide for the apprehension and examination of any individual reasonably believed to be infected with a communicable disease in a qualifying stage and (A) to be moving or about to move from a State to another State; or (B) to be a probable source of infection to individuals who, while infected with such disease in a qualifying stage, will be moving from a State to another State. Such regulations may provide that if upon examination any such individual is found to be infected, he may be detained for such time and in such manner as may be reasonably necessary." It could be worse. You could be an animal. In subsection a, the Surgeon General is allowed to "provide for such inspection, fumigation, disinfection, sanitation, pest extermination, destruction of animals or articles found to be so infected or contaminated as to be sources of dangerous infection to human beings, and other measures, as in his judgment may be necessary."

President George W. Bush issued two executive orders deeming which infectious diseases were capable of providing "the apprehension, detention, or conditional release of individuals to prevent the introduction, transmission, or spread of suspected communicable diseases." The first order, EO 13295, was published on April 4, 2003. It singled out the following diseases as those that met the national requirements: "Cholera; Diphtheria; infectious Tuberculosis; Plague; Smallpox; Yellow Fever; and Viral Hemorrhagic Fevers (Lassa, Marburg, Ebola, Crimean-Congo, South American, and others not yet isolated or named)." It also added to this list "Severe Acute Respiratory Syndrome (SARS), which is a disease associated with fever and signs and symptoms of pneumonia or other respiratory illness, is transmitted from person to person predominantly by the aerosolized or droplet route, and, if spread in the population, would have severe public health consequences." SARS was singled out because it was that virus and not the dreaded bird flu that first brought the world the closest it has come to a pandemic since the late 1960's. The SARS outbreak lasted from late 2002 to mid-2003 and infected nearly 9,000 people in 16 different countries of which 775 died. There were actually over 25 cases of SARS reported within the U.S. during that time, but none resulted in a fatality. The fear surrounding the virus was well-founded enough to give the virus a special designation, making a person suffering from its effects able to be quarantined. Two years after EO 13295 was published, President Bush amended the order in EO 13375 which added just one sentence to the original: "Influenza caused by novel or reemergent influenza viruses that are causing, or have the potential to cause, a pandemic." This, of course, was justified by the fear of the Avian Influenza.

Should one of those diseases indeed emerge within the nation, there is a potential for the enforcement of quarantine restrictions to become federalized. If that was to happen, guess who would manage the quarantine? The Department of Defense utilizing its forces stationed at USNORTHCOM. It is at this point that we leave the realm of the HHS's plan and turn to the DOD's variation on it, titled *Department of Defense Implementation Plan for Pandemic Influenza* issued in August 2006.

Not surprisingly, the DOD's take on the subject varies in tone from the Department of Health and Human Service's. The DOD states in its plan, "If efforts to contain human-to-human transmission of a potential pandemic influenza outbreak at its source fail, the resources of the [United States Government] will not be sufficient to prevent the spread of a pandemic across the nation. Accordingly, the [United States Government] will use all instruments of national power to address the pandemic threat."

That "instrument of national power" is none other than USNORTHCOM. If called into action, it will operate under Concept Plan (CONPLAN) 3551 titled "Response to Pandemic Influenza." Though released in a heavily redacted form, CONPLAN 3551 is still insightful, especially in reading how the military views a potential pandemic. "A pandemic differs from most natural or manmade disasters in nearly every respect. The impact of a severe pandemic is more comparable to a global war or a long term environment than an isolated disaster such as a hurricane, earthquake or an act of terrorism. It will affect all communities. Exact consequences are difficult to predict in advance because the biological characteristics of the virus are not known. Similarly, the role of the Federal government in a pandemic response will differ based on the pandemic's morbidity and mortality rates."

Beyond those generalities, the DOD's implementation plan willingly makes certain assumptions (which it actually labels as "assumptions"), but the curious part is the exacting nature of them. For example, the plan states, "A pandemic outbreak will last between 6-12 weeks and multiple pandemic waves will follow." This is followed by such statements as "a vaccine (pandemic specific strain) will not be available for distribution for a minimum of 6-9 months after the clinical confirmation of sustained human-to-human pandemic influenza transmission" as well as "a pandemic in the United States could result in 20-35% of the population becoming ill, 3% being hospitalized, and a fatality rate of 1%." This prediction is interesting considering the fatality rate of the 1918 influenza outbreak has never been fully determined (though it was likely much higher than 1 percent) while the 2003 SARS outbreak's fatality rate was a whopping 9 percent. Of course, the DOD's prediction regarding the fatality rate is followed by the happy thought that "DOD can expect requests from interagency partners to support civilian mortuary affairs operations." It states further within its plan, "Mortuary Affairs (MA) capabilities within DOD are extremely limited. When directed by the President, or upon approval by the Secretary of Defense, of a request from a Federal department or agency, DOD can provide search, recovery, receiving, processing, and can coordinate evacuation of remains of the deceased." With only an expected 1 percent fatality rate, would the military really need to come in to clean up the deceased?

In the meantime, CONPLAN 3551 has its own set of "Assumptions" which vary considerably from the DOD's official plan. These are:

"(1) USNORTHCOM's Homeland Defense mission will remain first priority.

"(2) A critical priority will be to sustain the health and safety of DOD key population in order to accomplish all DOD missions.

"(3) Protection of the Nation's critical infrastructure and key resources will be required to accomplish force projection.

"(4) Support of essential government functions will be as requested and performed within capabilities.

"(5) Authorities will remain the same, consistent with existing laws of the US Government, including as primary considerations, the Posse Comitatus Act (PCA) and DODD 5525.5. Title 10 DOD forces do not have the authority to provide law enforcement in support of movement restrictions or enforcement of civil law, unless the [President of the United States] asserts his authorities under the Constitution and directs Title 10 DOD employment in accordance with the 'Insurrection Act,' or another exception to the PCA applies."

The DOD seems to be of the belief that any such "pandemic" will result in nothing short of the worst case scenario. This may just be contingency planning at work, but its assumptions support this notion. The DOD states, "Military and civilian medical treatment facilities will be overwhelmed." Not only that, but "State, tribal and local jurisdictions will be overwhelmed and unable to provide or ensure the provision of essential commodities and services." This expected breakdown in public services would result in the military coming to our rescue. "Under applicable authorities, DOD will assist civil authorities in the event of a pandemic."

This response would come in two different forms. The first would be in aiding local enforcement of quarantine orders:

"When directed by the President, DOD may assist U.S. civil authorities responsible for isolating and/or quarantining groups of people in order to minimize the spread of disease during an influenza pandemic. Isolation is a commonly used public health practice for the separation and restriction of movement of ill persons to stop the spread of a contagious illness…Isolation is primarily used on an individual level, but may be applied to populations. It is often voluntary, but may be mandatory. Quarantine, in contrast, applies to the separation and restriction of movement of well persons presumed to have been exposed to a contagion. Quarantine may be enacted at a home or other residential facility. It may also be voluntary or mandatory."

The second form would arrive when panic hit the population and civil disorder erupts. "When directed by the President, DOD will provide support to civil authorities in the event of a civil disturbance. DOD will augment civilian law enforcement efforts to restore and maintain order in accordance with existing statutes."

The DOD doesn't necessarily need to wait for a presidential order to jump into action. It possesses an "immediate response" authority which it can enable in a "limited manner." As written in the 2003 *Department of Defense Directive 3025.1* titled "Military Support to Civil Authorities," certain local military commanders and DOD civilians can act immediately "to save lives, prevent human suffering, or mitigate great property damage" if they receive an emergency request from a local authority and not enough time exists for the commander to receive clearance from headquarters prior to entering the fray. Of course, any commander engaging in such a situation is supposed to seek official approval as soon as it can be readily secured. Once again, this military support is to be limited in both ability and time frame, sticking to the system as set up in the National Response Framework and as limited by the Posse Comitatus Act. In an immediate epidemic situation, the military's role here should include such support roles as medical assistance, distribution of food and supplies, and the restoration of critical public services.

In the case of a pandemic, the Department of Defense has already implemented plans to take care of its own:

"In November 2005, the Deputy Secretary of Defense

directed that a pandemic task force be established within DOD. The Assistant Secretary of Defense for Homeland Defense (ASD(HD)) was named as the lead for the Pandemic Influenza Task Force (PITF). The Assistant Secretary of Defense for Health Affairs (ASD(HA)) is supporting the effort as the Department's lead for health service support for pandemic influenza preparedness and response. The PITF is charged with the coordination and implementation of policies and plans which will (1) prepare for, detect, respond to, and contain the effects of a pandemic on military forces, DOD civilians, contractors, dependents, and beneficiaries; (2) ensure the Department's continued ability to protect American interests at home and abroad; and (3) be prepared to render appropriate assistance to civilian authorities in the United States (to include Commonwealths, Territories, and Possessions)."

Not only is the DOD ready and willing to aid both the civilian and military population of this country when the pandemic arrives, but it is also ready to lend its assistance to other nations as well. This isn't necessarily a humanitarian effort. The DOD's primary goal is to stop any such potential pandemic virus from reaching our nation's shores. While the DOD's work would undoubtedly aid those suffering from whatever disease makes up the growing pandemic, the main thrust of that effort would be to contain the virus, with the former effect simply being a consequence of that work.

"Preparing and responding to a pandemic influenza will require an active, layered defense. This active, layered defense is global, integrating seamlessly, U.S. capabilities in the forward regions of the world, in approaches to the U.S. territory, and within the United States. It is a defense in depth. It will include assisting partner countries to prepare for and detect an outbreak, respond should one occur, and manage the key second-order effects that could lead to an array of challenges. The top priority is the protection of DOD forces, comprised of the military, DOD civilians and contractors performing critical roles, as well as the associated resources necessary to maintain readiness. Also, it is critical to ensure DOD is able to sustain mission assurance and the ability to meet our strategic objectives. Priority consideration is also given to protect the health of DOD beneficiaries and dependents."

The main cooperation in that worldwide attempt to hopefully prevent, or at the very least, contain a potential pandemic will be between the U.S. and its border allies Canada and Mexico. This plan was laid out in the publication *North American Plan for Avian and Pandemic Influenza* which was released by the Security and Prosperity Partnership of North America (SSP) in August 2007. The SSP was established in 2005 by an agreement between the President of the U.S., the Prime Minister of Canada, and the President of Mexico "to increase security and enhance prosperity among the three countries through greater cooperation and information sharing." In the case of a potential pandemic, this agreement makes sense. Preventing a virus from reaching any portion of North America would likely keep all three nations safe. If the virus breaks out in one country, it's 99.9% likely it will spread to the other two as well. Working together to establish guidelines and response efforts may ensure North America remains pandemic free.

The SSP's plan was developed from a meeting of the partners in Cancun in March 2006. The goals of their collaboration were quite straightforward: "detect, contain and control an avian influenza outbreak and prevent transmission to humans; prevent or slow the entry of a novel strain of human influenza to North America; minimize illness and deaths; and sustain infrastructure and mitigate the impact to the economy and the functioning of society." The hope was to be able to accomplish this "with minimal economic disruption" and "in the best interest of all three countries."

To achieve these goals, the agreement allowed for the coordination of all three countries' emergency management agencies. "The three countries share a common approach based on the four pillars of emergency management: prevention and mitigation, preparedness, response and recovery. Canada, Mexico and the United States intend to work collaboratively in each of these areas to manage the threat of avian and pandemic influenza." This massive effort would tap the resources of several different agencies within each country. In Canada, that would include Public Safety Canada which is akin to the U.S. Department of Homeland Security, the Canadian Food Inspection Agency, the Public Health Agency of Canada, Health Canada, and the Department of Foreign Affairs and International Trade. For Mexico, those efforts would task their General Coordination for Civil Protection, the Ministry of Agriculture, the Ministry of Health of Mexico, and the Secretariat of Foreign Affairs. Of course for the United States, this response effort would involve the usual suspects: the Department of Homeland Security, the Department of Health and Human Services, the State Department, the Department of Agriculture, the Department of Transportation, and the Department of Defense. Those efforts also plan to take into account such documents as the U.S. National Response Framework, Canada's Emergency Management Framework, and each nation's own variation of a predetermined pandemic emergency plan (such as the HHS's plan previously discussed).

"Accurate and timely information before and during an outbreak of avian or pandemic influenza will be critical to the successful management of the situation. The public, governments and their key stakeholders need appropriate information to make effective and timely decisions." Among these necessary communication lines is an effective notification system capable of alerting each of the countries that one of its partners is in need of help. The SSP has already set up guidelines allowing a country in need to seek emergency response assistance from the others. This includes "when national human or material resources are overextended; when an avian or pandemic influenza event in any of the three countries poses a potential threat to either of the other two countries; or when an avian or pandemic influenza outbreak requires robust coordination of the North American response in order to minimize the risk to animal and public health, minimize damage, and provide the basis for long-term social and economic recovery."

Of course, to effectively coordinate such emergency response activities, there would be a need to practice them. "The authorities of Canada, Mexico and the United States intend to conduct trilateral or bilateral exercises to assess and strengthen their emergency response and contingency plans. In addition, each country intends to design and deliver training to maximize the effectiveness of its respective emergency response and contingency plans. Wherever possible, training and exercises should be designed to maximize stakeholder involvement." These international exercises have already taken place and were implemented during the 2009 swine flu epidemic.

While their emergency response efforts may be able to be coordinated, the laughable portion of the SSP's plan comes in the subject of border control. To ensure a pandemic virus doesn't enter North America (assuming it doesn't originate here in the first place as both the 1918 Spanish Flu and the 2009 swine flu appeared to do), controlling the influx of potentially infected people is key. Yet even the SSP's plan makes some assumptions regarding this step which are highly debatable. For one, the plan states, "It is expected that travelers departing for North America from affected countries will be screened prior to departure in accordance with guidance from [the World Health Organization] and the International Civil Aviation Organization (ICAO)." It is then noted, "ICAO recently adopted guidelines regarding communicable disease/avian influenza that include provisions for exit screening of international travelers from affected areas." Now if one country, or even a compartmentalized section of the globe, experiences a true outbreak of a killer virus, it is highly probable that any persons capable of leaving the area will do so rapidly. Such a potential outpouring of people would likely overwhelm a country's ability to control this exodus. If control is lost, then how likely is the country in question going to maintain the WHO's strict guidelines for infection screening? Chances are infected people—especially ones who don't even realize they are carrying the virus—will make it out of such an international quarantine. If this were to happen, the SPP assumes, "Given the short incubation period of influenza and the length of some international flights, one can assume that some travelers with influenza will develop their first symptoms during the journey. It is possible that additional training of flight and cabin crews to detect and manage ill travelers may decrease the risk for others on board, as well as at the point of arrival in North America." Obvious arrivals of infected people will be quarantined as need be, but those who may be arriving by air anywhere in North America from a country or region where the flu is active may not be detained in any way. "Canada, Mexico and the United States intend to employ a risk-based approach to screening and intend to collaboratively establish common criteria and protocols for entry screening of all travelers on flights bound for North America during a pandemic. The three countries intend to minimize arrival screening measures and maintain existing pre-clearance arrangements employed for air travelers within North America to the extent practicable."

Should these efforts not prevent the pandemic from reaching North America, which is something the Department of Health and Human Services sees as being inevitable no matter the measures taken, the hope then becomes to keep the virus contained within the outbreak country. This means tighter control between the land borders of the U.S., Canada and Mexico. Considering the ease both illegal immigrants and illegal narcotics seem to flow between the three nations, this effort seems doomed before it even begins. The SSP agrees. Even worse, it believes that commerce is more important than the control of a deadly virus. "Canada, Mexico and the United States intend to share and coordinate common triggers, criteria and protocols for screening of travelers at land borders when certain conditions are met. These triggers, criteria and protocols should be balanced against the necessity to maintain the flow of persons, cargo and trade across North American borders."

This attitude is echoed by the defeatist sentiment written just a few sentences later, "Once pandemic disease is common in all three North American countries, Canada, Mexico and the United States mutually understand that exit screening at our shared land borders may no longer be necessary.

So much for containing the pandemic.

You and Your Own

"Everyone should have a plan." That is how the *Preparing Makes Sense. Get Ready Now.* booklet the Department of Homeland Security produced and made available via its ready.gov website begins. Despite the DHS having a yearly budget of over $46 billion, despite the National Response Framework and its associated documents, despite the existence of USNORTHCOM, and despite governmental preparedness plans that are supposed to cover every disaster or terror attack thought imaginable, the federal government wants you to know that your survival depends not on them, but on yourself. So, while they hold up all of their shiny toys with one hand, the other remains hidden behind their back, unwilling to completely reveal that all of the money you've provided them with through your taxes isn't really going to save you when disaster strikes. You're going to have to spend a little more of your hard earned cash to prepare yourself for any catastrophe ahead.

Many books have recently been published focusing on different aspects and techniques of survival. Popular television programs like *Doomsday Preppers, Survivorman* and *Man Vs. Wild* also highlight a variety of survival techniques. While much of this information may be beneficial to know, most involve circumstances that may come along once in a lifetime, if that often. Chances are, even if you did study these survival manuals, when the time came to put that knowledge into use, the finer nuances may continue to elude you. Many of the people responsible for these guides and programs are professionals for good reason; they've made it their life's work to learn it.

Setting that sort of survival knowledge aside, what we'll delve into here is the federal government's own ideas on what the average person needs and what it believes one should do if any of the following disasters come to fruition. Most of this information will come from two main sources. The first is the DHS's *Preparing Makes Sense. Get Ready Now.* booklet. The other is a FEMA produced booklet titled *Are You Ready? An In-Depth Guide to Citizen Preparedness.* Your author went a step further and completed the independent study course offered by FEMA associated with the *Are You Ready?* booklet. In passing the course, FEMA awarded an official certificate that stated your author has "reaffirmed a dedication to serve in times of crisis through continued professional development and completion of the independent study course."

The federal government warns you that in an emergency situation, you are going to have to fend for yourself. It makes this point abundantly clear in the second sentence of the *Preparing Makes Sense. Get Ready Now.* handbook: "Be prepared to improvise and use what you have on hand to make it on your own for at least three days, maybe longer." To do this, the government suggests that you make two survival kits. One kit should be packed and ready to go at a moment's notice while the other kit should be larger and stashed away should you decide (or be forced) to stay at home for the duration of the emergency. What should be in each kit? Basic supplies including, "A flashlight, battery powered radio, extra batteries, a first aid kit, utility knife, local map, toilet paper, feminine hygiene products, soap, garbage bags and other sanitation supplies, plastic sheeting, duct tape, as well as extra cash and identification." On top of this, it is recommended you store one gallon of water per person per day for drinking and sanitation. Also, food may come in handy. This should be "food that won't go bad and does not have to be heated or cooked." Remember, "Choose foods that your family will eat."

One thought that may not cross your mind in an emergency is the cleanliness of the air you breathe. In the aftermath of 9/11, the air quality in and around the World Trade Center site was horrific.

Ten years later, residents and workers that were in that area are still suffering from the effects of the airborne particles they inhaled (don't forget that it was government officials that gave the "all clear" for people to reenter the area so soon after the buildings collapsed). It is likely with this in mind that the authors of the booklet wrote, "Many potential terrorist attacks could send tiny microscopic 'junk' into the air...Many of these agents can only hurt you if they get into your body, so think about creating a barrier between yourself and any contamination." Besides face masks (or for the survivalists out there, gas masks) to keep any fine particulate out of your lungs, there is still the classic and controversial suggestion of using trash bags and duct tape to seal up your home. "Have heavyweight garbage bags or plastic sheeting, duct tape and scissors in your kit. You can use these things to tape up windows, doors and air vents if you need to seal off a room from outside contamination. Consider precutting and labeling these materials. Anything you can do in advance will save time when it counts." For all the brouhaha surrounding that suggestion, it would actually work. For how long, though, is debatable.

Perhaps the most important question you may have to ask yourself in an emergency setting is whether to stay home or head for the hills. The government gives you some, but not much, guidance in making this decision. "Depending on your circumstances and the nature of the attack, the first important decision is whether you stay put or get away. You should understand and plan for both possibilities. Use common sense and available information...to determine if there is immediate danger. In any emergency, local authorities may or may not immediately be able to provide information on what is happening and what you should do. However, you should watch TV, listen to the radio or check the Internet often for information or official instructions as it becomes available. If you're specifically told to evacuate or seek medical treatment, do so immediately." If you decide to get out of town with your trusty, pre-packed survival kit in hand, the question remains where to go? The government doesn't specifically say. It simply instructs, "Choose several destinations in different directions so you have options in an emergency. If you have a car, keep at least a half tank of gas in it at all times. Become familiar with alternate routes as well as other means of transportation out of your area. If you do not have a car, plan how you will leave if you have to." This last suggestion directed at those lacking an automobile is a major kink in any evacuation plan. It was an Achilles heel in evacuating New Orleans prior to Hurricane Katrina. How do people effectively clear out of a city if they don't have their own transportation? Trains seem like a good idea, but people still have to get to the stations. What other options are there? Buses? Taxis? Boats?

What the ready.gov booklet doesn't mention is the evacuation plans FEMA developed in the 1980s. Deemed "Crisis Relocation Planning," FEMA devised a way to move some 150 million people out of so-called "risk areas" to safer "host areas" in the event of a nuclear war. The feeling was (and likely remains) nuclear war would only begin after an escalation in hostilities between the U.S. and some foreign power. Given time by that presumed heightened state, FEMA assumed it would be able to relocate nearly half of the population of the entire country from major U.S. cities and other risk areas (such as those living around potential targets like major military bases) within 24 to 72 hours, prior to any nukes being launched. This would accomplish two things. One would be to show the foreign nation opposing America that the U.S. was committed to staging a nuclear war. If we're clearing out our cities in preparation for an attack, then it follows that we'd be ready to launch our missiles…or so our enemy would believe. Of course, the other outcome of that mass exodus would be to save lives. Without a doubt, since the dawn of the nuclear age, the most dangerous place to reside is in a major city. There has been a crosshair targeting every major population center all day, every day since the Cold War began. The best way to save the lives of those people is to move them out of harm's way. The government went so far as to create pamphlets that would be distributed on every doorstep informing the residents "this area *will* be evacuated" when a nuclear war seemed apparent. These pamphlets included maps directing the people where their specific "host area" was located based upon their home address. Yes, we were *that* prepared for a nuclear war.

While such nuclear war preparedness by way of civil defense planning has given way to the preparations for a terrorist attack since 9/11, the idea of host areas has not completely vanished. In early 2009, Representative Alcee Hastings (D-FL) introduced a bill, H.R. 645, which calls for the establishment of at least six "National Emergency Centers" on military bases scattered within the ten FEMA regions. These were quickly dubbed "FEMA camps." The fear was that these camps would be used to round up dissenters (perhaps for Main Core's list of 8 million "terrorists") during times of national emergency when martial law was declared; effectively making them prisons for those deemed to be un-American. Without a doubt, by reading the wording of the bill as it was introduced, this would be a possibility, but only due to the vagueness of the following passage in Section 2, part b of the bill: "The purpose of a national emergency center shall be to use existing infrastructure... to meet other appropriate needs, as determined by the Secretary of Homeland Security." Never mind posse comitatus, "appropriate needs" was seen by some as the ability to use these facilities as makeshift concentration camps, especially considering their likely location within military bases.

That idea is not without some basis in fact. A May 15, 2008 article in the *San Antonio Express-News* written by Lynn Brezosky discussed a similar situation, albeit directed at non-U.S. citizens. Brezoksy wrote, "Ending speculation about the fate of the Rio Grande Valley's undocumented immigrants during a hurricane evacuation, U.S. Customs and Border Protection has confirmed it will check the citizenship both of people boarding buses to leave the Valley and at inland traffic checkpoints. Those determined to be in the country illegally will be taken to detention centers away from the hurricane's path and later processed for deportation."

While Brezosky reported that a spokeswoman for Texas Governor Rick Perry stated that it was the state's position not to implement such checks during an evacuation, the U.S. Customs and Border Protection Agency wasn't backing off its stance. It already had two detention centers in place. One is located in Laredo, the other in San Antonio. When asked about encountering a situation in which some family members were U.S. citizens and others were not, Dan Doty, a spokesman for the agency told Brezosky, "We try to keep families together, but I can't put a U.S. citizen in a detention center."

In all likelihood, what was intended with the introduction of the "FEMA camp" bill was what immediately preceded that questionably vague passage that has many people up in arms. It described the emergency centers' purpose as, "(1) to provide temporary housing, medical, and humanitarian assistance to individuals and families dislocated due to an emergency or major disaster; (2) to provide centralized locations for the purposes of training and ensuring the coordination of Federal, State, and local first responders; (3) to provide centralized locations to improve the coordination of preparedness, response, and recovery efforts of government, private, and not-for-profit entities and faith-based organizations."

The introduction of this bill stemmed from FEMA's horrific handling of housing accommodations post-Hurricane Katrina. To shelter the thousands rendered homeless after the storm ravaged the Gulf Coast, the government housed people haphazardly. Some were put up in hotels at the government's expense while others were given trailers to live in which later were discovered to have formaldehyde fumes up to five times the safe level. To prevent such a mess in the future, the government planned to create these "emergency centers" to house those needing help after a disaster. This makes sense. If another major metropolitan city suffers as New Orleans did, whether it is from a natural disaster or from a terrorist attack, those people will need somewhere to recuperate. A military base set up to accommodate a large number of people provides protection, medical assistance if needed, and the infrastructure to feed and house the common folk while recovery operations take place. Considering that few people will have heeded the government's warning about being prepared to make it on one's own for a few days should disaster strike, there may be thousands of gracious people happy to have "emergency centers" available to flee to when their hometown is devastated.

The HEPA Solution

Besides those generalities, the government does offer some advice on what to do in specific disaster scenarios. Most of this advice is common sense and should have been picked up by people by the time they finished grammar school. Much of it relates to natural disasters—tornados, hurricanes, earthquakes, etc.—which one can prepare for rather easily, even if there is no way to stop them from occurring. There is another set of advice; however, one should take with regards to the government's pet peeve—terrorist attacks. Some of this may seem counterintuitive or just flat out weird, yet it is worth considering.

FEMA's booklet *Are You Ready? An In-Depth Guide to Citizen Preparedness* lays out some general information regarding terrorism. It explains to the reader that "Terrorism is the use of force or violence against persons or property in violation of the criminal laws of the United States for purposes of intimidation, coercion, or ransom." While this statement seems to link basic criminality with terrorism, it goes on to explain what sort of behavior are official forms of terrorist acts. These include: "Assassinations; kidnappings; hijackings; bomb scares and bombings; cyber attacks (computer-based); and the use of chemical, biological, nuclear and radiological weapons." It also includes "threats of terrorism," meaning a hoax is just as dangerous as the real thing since terrorists use those threats to "create fear among the public" to "try to convince citizens that their government is powerless to prevent terrorism" while attempting to "get immediate publicity for their causes."

Receiving the most attention are the "Big Three": biological, chemical, and nuclear attacks. Setting aside the fact that the GAO already dismissed the probability of these types of attacks, we'll tackle the government's advice on reacting to these situations one by one.

The ready.gov booklet informs, "Unlike an explosion, a biological attack may or may not be immediately obvious." This is true. Unless the terrorists scream out what they are doing, any sort of biological attack, to be effective, would remain secretive until symptoms began to develop among the population. As the ready.gov booklet explains, "You will probably learn of the danger through an emergency radio or TV broadcast or some other signal used in your community. Perhaps you will get a phone call or emergency response workers may come door-to-door." Really? Will the lucky person going door-to-door to inform people of biological attack perpetrated by terrorists be wearing a biohazard suit when they come a-knocking?

In FEMA's *Are You Ready?* booklet, it explains what an individual should do in a suspected biological attack a little more clearly. "The first evidence of an attack may be when you notice symptoms of the disease caused by exposure to an agent. Be suspicious of any symptoms you notice, but do not assume that any illness is a result of the attack. Use common sense and practice good hygiene." This coincides with ready.gov's caveat "At the time of a declared biological emergency, if a family member becomes sick, it is important to be suspicious. However, do not automatically assume you should go to a hospital emergency room or that any illness is the result of the biological attack." So, how will you know if you've been exposed to a deadly agent or just have a case of the sniffles? According to ready.gov's booklet, the TV will tell you all you need to know. "What you can do is watch TV, listen to the radio or check the Internet for official news including the following: Are you in the group or area authorities consider in danger? What are the signs and symptoms of the disease? Are medications or vaccines being distributed? Where? Who should get them? Where should you seek emergency medical care if you become sick?"

If you're not willing to wait for some talking-head television entity to tell you what to do or not do, FEMA gives a little more guidance. It explains, "If you become aware of an unusual and suspicious substance nearby: Move away quickly; wash with soap and water; contact authorities; listen to the media for official instructions; [and] seek medical attention if you become sick." If there is little doubt that you were indeed exposed to a biological agent, then FEMA advises the following: "Remove and bag your clothes and personal items. Follow official instructions for disposal of contaminated items. Wash yourself with soap and water and put on clean clothes. Seek medical assistance. You may be advised to stay away from others or even quarantined."

Amazingly, there is one household device you could purchase to prevent potential infection according to FEMA. It isn't plastic sheeting or duct tape. "Consider installing a High Efficiency Particulate Air (HEPA) filter in your furnace return duct. These filters remove particles in the 0.3 to 10 micron range and will filter out most biological agents that may enter your house. If you do not have a central heating or cooling system, a stand-alone portable HEPA filter can be used." Terrorism thwarted by a HEPA filter? Hard to fathom, but true.

While the duct tape/plastic sheeting protection isn't a necessity in a biological attack, it seems to be the government's preferred method of dealing with a chemical one. In fact, it is recommended to seal up an interior room, on the upper floor of your home if possible, to protect yourself in such a situation. How do you know if you are caught in the middle of a chemical attack? Ready.gov's booklet asks you to keep vigilant and, "Watch for signs of a chemical attack such as many people suffering from watery eyes, twitching, choking, having trouble breathing or losing coordination. Many sick or dead birds, fish or small animals are also cause for suspicion." Now what do you do if you're experiencing some of these symptoms for yourself? "If your eyes are watering, your skin is stinging, you are having trouble breathing or you simply think you may have been exposed to a chemical, immediately strip and wash. Look for a hose, fountain or any source of water." Try explaining that to the police if it's a false alarm.

Unfortunately, this is no joke. FEMA's booklet lays out proper decontamination procedures in a little more detail since "decontamination is needed within minutes of exposure to minimize health consequences." If you were or thought you were contaminated by some sort of chemical agent and could not get immediate professional help, this is how FEMA's booklet explains you should do it yourself:

"Remove all clothing and other items in contact with the body. Contaminated clothing normally removed over the head should be cut off to avoid contact with the eyes, nose, and mouth. Put contaminated clothing and items into a plastic bag and seal it. Decontaminate hands using soap and water. Remove eyeglasses or contact lenses. Put glasses in a pan of household bleach to decontaminate them, and then rinse and dry. Flush eyes with water. Gently wash face and hair with soap and water before thoroughly rinsing with water. Decontaminate other body areas likely to have been contaminated. Blot (do not swab or scrape) with a cloth soaked in soapy water and rinse with clear water. Change into uncontaminated clothes. Clothing stored in drawers or closets is likely to be uncontaminated. [Then] proceed to a medical facility for screening and professional treatment."

True medical attention is likely to be your only hope in surviving such an attack.

The granddaddy of all such attacks is, of course, a nuclear one. This has been generating fear in people for over 60 years and for good reason. Despite six decades of testing and planning, how prepared is the average citizen for such a scenario? According to Irwin Redlener of Columbia University's Mailman School of Public Health who was quoted in an April 2010 *USA Today* article, "There isn't a single American city, in my estimation, that has sufficient plans for a nuclear terrorist event." Though that may not sound comforting, Redlener was quick to add, "What citizens need to know [about a nuclear event] fits on a wallet-sized card."

Ready.gov's booklet is kind enough to explain what a nuclear blast is to those that may not know. "A nuclear blast is an explosion with intense light and heat, a damaging pressure wave and widespread radioactive material that can contaminate the air, water and ground surfaces for miles around. While experts may predict at this time that a nuclear attack is less likely than others, terrorism by its nature is unpredictable. If there is a flash or fireball, take cover immediately, below ground if possible, though any shield or shelter will help protect you from the immediate effects of the blast and the pressure wave. In order to limit the amount of radiation you are exposed to, think about shielding, distance and time." FEMA's booklet echoes these sentiments, stating "If an attack warning is issued: Take cover as quickly as you can, below ground if possible, and stay there until instructed to do otherwise. Listen for official information and follow instructions." If you cannot get inside shelter in time then you should the following: "Do not look at the flash or fireball—it can blind you. Take cover behind anything that might offer protection. Lie flat on the ground and cover your head. If the explosion is some distance away, it could take 30 seconds or more for the blast wave to hit. Take shelter as soon as you can, even if you are many miles from ground zero where the attack occurred—radioactive fallout can be carried by the winds for hundreds of miles. Remember the three protective factors: Distance, shielding, and time."

Distance, shielding and time. These are the government's three buzzwords for surviving a nuclear blast and have been since the 1950s. In FEMA's booklet, the reasoning why these three concepts are critical to those unfortunate enough to be caught in or near a nuclear blast is explained. The first is distance. FEMA states, "The more distance between you and the fallout particles, the better. An underground area such as a home or office building basement offers more protection than the first floor of a building. A floor near the middle of a high-rise may be better, depending on what is nearby at that level on which significant fallout particles would collect. Flat roofs collect fallout particles so the top floor is not a good choice, nor is a floor adjacent to a neighboring flat roof."

As for shielding, the idea is the more the merrier. FEMA says, "The heavier and denser the materials—thick walls, concrete, bricks, books and earth—between you and the fallout particles, the better." Of course, there should be a caveat attached to that sentiment. Say you get significant warning of an impending nuclear blast and you race into a civic fallout shelter, built as many were in the 1950s and 1960s in the basement of a city skyscraper. The nuke detonates…and collapses the building on top of the fallout shelter in which you hid. This was actually a worry of some engineers who designed and built such shelters. A high rise building with all of its reinforced steel and concrete would make excellent shielding, yet due to the increase in yield of many nuclear devices, the fact is a nuclear blast could topple many of these buildings, sealing those seeking shelter in an underground, yet fallout proof tomb. You might find yourself saved by the very thing that ultimately kills you as no one can clear the building off of the shelter prior to you and the others down there suffocating. This possibility aside, seeking shelter is better than being caught out in the open in a nuclear blast.

The last concept, time, is an interesting one. In April 2010, the Obama Administration publicly reiterated what was written in the Homeland Security Council's 2009 report *Planning Guidance for Response to a Nuclear Detonation* stating, "There will be no significant Federal response at the scene [of a nuclear detonation] for 24 hours and the full extent of Federal assets will not be available for up to 72 hours." All of the immediate response to such an incident will fall to the local level, much of which could be decimated in the nuclear explosion. Even so, the Homeland Security Council's report states as a key point that, "The most effective life-saving opportunities for response officials in the first 60 minutes following a nuclear explosion will be the decision to safely shelter or evacuate people in expected fallout areas." How that decision will be made and communicated to those affected (considering the electro-magnetic pulse from the blast may destroy all electronic equipment in the vicinity of "ground zero") in less than 60 minutes is not fully answered. And yet clearly, time is of the essence.

While little can be done for the unfortunate souls caught in the immediate area of the nuclear detonation, several thousand if not millions of people will have to deal with the resultant radioactive fallout. Time comes into play in surviving this situation, yet within FEMA's booklet different ideas exist on just how much time may be required before anyone can poke their heads back out above ground. It is first written, "Fallout radiation loses its intensity fairly rapidly. In time, you will be able to leave the fallout shelter. Radioactive fallout poses the greatest threat to people during the first two weeks, by which time it has declined to about 1 percent of its initial radiation level." Reiterated further in the booklet is that "during periods of increased threat [of a nuclear blast] increase your disaster supplies to be adequate for up to two weeks." Then FEMA changes its tune. After a nuclear blast, it is written, "Decay rates of the radioactive fallout are the same for any size nuclear device. However, the amount of fallout will vary based on the size of the device and its proximity to the ground. Therefore, it might be necessary for those in the areas with highest radiation levels to shelter for up to a month." So, would it be two weeks, or a month? Many factors will come into play to truly determine this. But maybe it wouldn't be even that long. Maybe it would be just a few days. It adds, "The heaviest fallout would be limited to the area at or downwind from the explosion, and 80 percent of the fallout would occur during the first 24 hours. People in most of the areas that would be affected could be allowed to come out of shelter within a few days and, if necessary, evacuate to unaffected areas." Judging from these varied estimates, one should tend to err on the side of caution, and keep out of harm's way as long as possible.

If all of this information is news to you, you're not alone. While disaster preparedness is every individual's own responsibility, the federal government does only so much towards providing the public with this valuable information. Even what it accomplishes is an uphill battle. Both ready.gov and its associates in the DHS sponsored Citizen Corps have a staff of under 15 people. The Citizen Corps budget is just $15 million annually. That small amount coupled with the miniscule staff that accompanies it can only go so far in attempting to prepare 300 million people for every sort of possible emergency. It doesn't help that part of that money is spent on unusual advertising campaigns, ranging from odd billboards featuring giant red arrows stating "You are here" superimposed over a map asking "Do you know where your family is?" to television ads that are unintentionally humorous as opposed to informative. All of this is supposed to direct people to ready.gov and its related information, but if Americans don't follow through and do so, who's at fault for not being prepared to face an emergency?

What doesn't help is the thought process most Americans have regarding the subject of disaster preparedness. How often do disasters actually happen? Why should I prepare for something that may never come? Why waste the time and the money? What's the point? While these remain personal questions for everyone to contemplate, they are nonetheless important to consider. Not because a major disaster is lurking around the corner, but because it's highly doubtful the government can and will save you should you be unfortunate enough to be smack dab in the middle of one.

Ready.gov's booklet leaves the reader with one simple piece of advice: "In all cases, remain calm." Your level of peace likely would depend on your proximity to the disaster at hand, yet even if you were caught at ground zero, remaining calm, or as calm as humanly possible, would help in any such situation. Panic is the enemy. It is also the point and reason behind most terrorist attacks. But a person armed with a little foresight, some preparedness, and the knowledge of what to do and when to do it in any disaster situation is likely to fare better than the panicking fools around them. While one can only prepare so much for being caught out in the open during a disaster, there are many things one can do to prepare for the same situation within one's own home. Do you need to build a bomb shelter? Not necessarily. Should you stockpile some canned goods and a few bottles of water, just in case? That probably wouldn't be a bad idea, but it is up to each individual to decide. Just remember to heed the government's warning: they will not be there to help you immediately after a disaster or in an emergency situation. If you're foolish enough not to take that to heart, you only have yourself to blame.

CONTINUITY OF GOVERNMENT

"Government must survive if its people are to survive"
- actor Glenn Ford narrating the 1957 CBS produced civil defense film
"A Day Called X"

A black Cadillac limousine speeds away from Washington, DC. It leaves the known comfort of the Beltway, disappearing into the sprawling Virginia countryside. Inside, surrounded by his Secret Service agents, apprehensively sits the President of the United States. Looking out the back window, he no longer can see any of the landmarks that boldly dot the nation's capital. Instead, trailing behind his car is a train of similar black, unmarked vehicles filled with his top advisors. The convoy's destination? An undisclosed location.

Was that the government's reaction after the 9/11 attacks to protect its most valued members? Yes, albeit with Vice President Dick Cheney rather than President George Bush speeding to a secret destination. More specifically, that was the exact tactic used by the federal government to spirit President Dwight D. Eisenhower out of Washington, DC during Operation Alert 1955, the federal government's first ever Continuity of Government exercise.

Continuity of Government (COG) is a simple concept with a myriad of entangled results. The idea is rather basic: during any emergency—be it a natural disaster, terrorist attack, or even nuclear war—have a plan in place which will allow for the government to continue operating as completely as possible. A major portion of this planning revolves around protecting the nation's top leaders. The thought is that if they are protected during time of emergency, it would allow for the chain of command to remain in place. This would then lead to the proper response, saving both the country and those of us living within it.

Unfortunately, while that seems straightforward enough, in reality it is utterly complex. The logistics themselves can be mind boggling. Perhaps more importantly, such planning brings up fundamental questions that were never even considered by the Founding Fathers, thus often leading to plans and laws that skirt around the Constitution. At the same time, the Founding Fathers never had to deal with the very real possibility of the entire federal government being eliminated in a nuclear blast. Since the 1950s when that threat first reared its ugly head, the concept of Continuity of Government has never been too far from the government's mind.

The problem lies in discovering what exactly these plans consist of. Since COG plans involve protecting our nation's most high, the government isn't very forthcoming in letting everyone know what they have in mind when the proverbial shit hits the fan. In fact, COG plans are some of the most top secret documents the government has on file. That makes sense. If you and I could learn where the president will be hiding when the bombs are falling, it only follows that our enemies would know that information as well, rendering those plans moot. So, what follows from this point onward is what is known and what can be assumed (or at least guessed) about the government's COG operations. That means much of this information is likely already obsolete. But that doesn't mean it's irrelevant. Knowing this history gives one a keen eye to the future, and you might want to have a good idea of these plans, just in case.

Operation Alert

The concept of Continuity of Government was officially born on April 17, 1952. President Harry Truman's Executive Order 10346 titled "Preparation by Federal Agencies for Civil Defense Emergency Plans" used the term for the first time, stating in part, "Each Federal department and agency shall prepare plans for maintaining the continuity of its essential functions at the seat of Government and elsewhere during the existence of a civil-defense emergency." That was suddenly a national necessity due to the advancement of the Soviets' nuclear weapons program. No longer was America the world's sole nuclear power. Its number one enemy now became its assumed equal, especially once the Soviets detonated their first hydrogen bomb in August 1953. Since we had the weaponry to reach all corners of the USSR, the U.S. government realized it was highly probable the Russians could do the same. For the first time in the nation's history, there was a chance, albeit a remote chance, an attack by a foreign power could effectively decapitate the nation's leadership. No president. No vice-president. No Congress. No federal government. All possible with just a single, well-timed and placed bomb.

Witnessing the Soviets rise to a nuclear power, the federal government decided it was high time to reinvest in its survival planning. But in fact, the government really never had such a plan in place to begin with. In early 1954, Eisenhower's National Security Council presented him with what was called a "mobilization" plan. In short, it was a way to evacuate the capital if the need arose. This wasn't very detailed or organized; it was more of an outline accompanied by a checklist. Much of it was lifted from British plans dating to World War II for when the Nazis bombed London. Eisenhower's reaction was straightforward: test it and see if it works. This was not something the government had ever done before. They weren't even sure what they were testing. Who should it cover? How big should it be? Where should they go? What should they do once they get there?

Following Eisenhower's orders, the federal government in 1954 tested its evacuation and relocation plans in what was the first "Operation Alert" exercise. That first test of Truman's Continuity of Government ideas was extremely low-tech. In April 1958, Innis D. Harris the Deputy Assistant Director for Plans and Readiness for the Office of Defense Mobilization addressed the Industrial College of the Armed Forces in a speech titled "Lessons Learned from Operation Alert 1955-57." In that presentation, Harris detailed the first Operation Alert exercise as, "A few high-level officials, assuming several hours warning of a hypothetical attack, left Washington with a checklist of possible actions. They assembled in a cave. Water was dripping from the ceiling and oozing from the walls. This was the setting for our first exercise." How did it go from there? Harris elaborated, "The exercise lasted only a few hours, but a great deal was learned, believe it or not. The participants needed information on the attack situation to determine what policies were actually necessary. They didn't have it. They needed assistance in the preparation of documents to reflect policy decisions. They didn't have it. They needed to communicate policy directives to the departments and agencies concerned. They couldn't do it. They needed to know that the agencies had a capability to carry out the policy directives if they could issue them. They had no way of knowing." Undeterred by that foolhardy exercise, the government gave it another whirl in 1955. This time, there was full participation by many of the federal government's top officials, including President Eisenhower who was escorted from Washington in the manner described at the beginning of this chapter. Eisenhower's undisclosed location wasn't a cave. The president was taken to a military-style tent in the woods, some 300 miles outside of the nation's capital. Posted there were signs reading, "This is a classified location. Disclosure of the location, plans or facilities of this site to unauthorized persons is prohibited." Keeping this secret were nearly 6,000 federal employees, including 21 department and agency heads reporting directly to Eisenhower.

The federal government wasn't alone in this exercise though. Operation Alert was tested nationwide, and in many "target" cities residents were required to take cover for fifteen minutes during the drill. In some areas, this was more than mandatory. New York State passed a law in which failure to comply with the Operation Alert order could result in a $500 fine as well as a year in jail. A group of nearly 30 anti-war protestors in New York City openly ignored the law and were arrested during the drill. Their sentences were later suspended.

From a folding chair in his tent at the "secret retreat" (as the press dubbed it), the president addressed the nation. Eisenhower said, "We are here to determine whether or not the government is prepared in time of emergency to continue the function of government so that there will be no interruption in the business that must be carried out." During the second day of the scheduled three day exercise (which was meant to simulate a 30-day crisis period), Eisenhower was heard to remark the operation involved "more complications than I ever believed possible." That sense of being overwhelmed was perhaps why during that second day Eisenhower announced to his Interim Assembly of 21 department and agency heads he was declaring martial law in the nation. No one expected that. No one had seemingly even considered it an option. But upon the order, Eisenhower dismissed his Interim Assembly and sent them back to their respective departments' relocation areas. As Harris explained to the Industrial College of the Armed Forces, "The decision caused no end of consternation to both civilian and military agencies. Everyone was speculating as to what it meant. Would the civilian agencies or the military make the allocations of resources, do the rationing and so forth and so on? The lawyers were running for the books to draft an appropriate proclamation, looking back to see what Abraham Lincoln did."

Needless to say, Operation Alert 1955 wasn't a success. Nor was it a complete failure. Despite the oddity of President Eisenhower's declaration, the exercise revealed what was possible, what was in need of change, and what didn't work. The concept of relocation, even in mass numbers, proved promising given enough warning time. In Operation Green Light conducted in September 1955, the city of Portland, OR and its population of just over 400,000 completely evacuated its downtown area in just 34 minutes. The problem was in finding the proper place to which to relocate. During a simulated evacuation of St. Louis at that same time, it was realized most of the people evacuating would have relocated to an area where the heaviest nuclear fallout would have fallen. Overall, it was determined more preparation on every level and in every aspect was necessary if the government planned on actually functioning during a massive emergency.

Operation Alert 1956 attempted to outdo its predecessor. Harris explained, "The scope included mobilization, civil defense, and military activities—a three way exercise—at the national, State, and local levels. The exercise lasted seven days with 10,000 federal employees participating. Operations included the full gamut of activities, some 21 in all, including air defense warning, civil defense actions, activation of relocation sites, performance of essential functions, military support for civil authority, damage assessment, allocation of surviving resources, implementation of wartime controls [rationing], and regional coordination. The magnitude of the attack and the gravity of the situation with which we would try to deal was stepped up about 30 percent over that of 1955." While that exercise seemed to be more of a success, it still revealed flaws. Harris reported that in the simulated nuclear attack, one of the relocation headquarters of a branch of the military was wiped out and two civilian agencies' relocation sites would have received heavy fallout. Another point of contention was communications between the varied players. Communication lines were often found to be overwhelmed. When communications could get through, often the messages were too verbose or unnecessarily classified, especially considering the likelihood of the chain of command being disabled during such situations. Having been given a year to make plans and develop various scenarios, Operation Alert 1956 was a step in the proper direction for ensuring a continuity of government.

The following year's exercise ramped up the nation's preparations even more. This time, some 13,000 federal employees were involved along with approximately 500,000 more participants ranging from the military down to local government officials. Operation Alert 1957 also marked a first in American history: President Eisenhower, during his evacuation drill, became the first president to ever travel in a helicopter while in office. While the exercises seemed to show that the federal government, having now worked on these plans for nearly four years, was ready—but not completely prepared—to operate successfully in a post-nuclear attack environment, on the local level, the situation remained dire.

"Many things—most things actually—have to be carried out at the local level," Harris pointed out. "Greater emphasis must be placed on planning and action at the local level. To avoid placing unwarranted reliance on the regional and central machinery of the Federal Government, efforts must be made to utilize to the maximum local governmental authority, services, and resources, together with State controls, leadership, and persuasion." Operation Alert 1957 revealed that many localities weren't properly prepared to either do their part or to help their citizenry. Some of those areas told the federal government flat out that they didn't believe recovery after a nuclear attack was even possible; hence why prepare to survive it? That sentiment wasn't just relegated to local government officials. There were several likeminded individuals at the federal level who felt the same way about COG exercises, considering them to be rather pointless. For those at the local level who did want to do their part in this national effort, it still wasn't easy to comply. They simply didn't have the tools or resources available to them to conduct such survival operations. While the government attempted to mitigate the problem by providing fallout shelters stocked with provisions, ultimately the government's decision regarding its population was much like it is today: you best prepare yourself to survive nuclear war because the federal government is going to saving itself first, and come to your aid sometime down the line.

When John F. Kennedy took over the reins in the White House, Operation Alert continued to be a yearly nationwide event. Kennedy oversaw his first Operation Alert on April 28, 1961. During that exercise, New York City mayor Robert F. Wagner made a public broadcast from the New York Operation Alert headquarters in Times Square (perhaps not the safest of places to be in an actual emergency). His portion of that radio broadcast, carried via the CONELRAD network, stated:

"Fellow citizens, civil defense air raid warning sirens have just sounded the three minute warbling 'take cover' signal, initiating the public participation phase of the nationwide civil defense training exercise 'Operation Alert 1961.' Merely clearing the streets of pedestrians and the stoppage of traffic is not the purpose of these test exercises. It is intended that the public learn the sounds and the meaning of the civil defense air raid warning sirens and to react intelligently when they are sounded in a public participation test by going to shelter in basements or inner corridors of structures away from windows. In time of actual emergency, this action may very well mean survival. Shelter, any form of shelter, is better than leaving oneself exposed to destructive elements. Persons in sheltered areas on the perimeter of a damaged area can survive. Those in actual fallout shelters have an even better chance of survival. Civil defense is wholly a non-military program. Its purpose is to ensure knowledgeable, organized, and orderly mutual emergency helpfulness in all areas of human needs. We cannot afford to be unprepared in the event of a crippling disaster to administer to our fellow being in need of medical care, to provide food, water, emergency housing and other necessities to preserve life, including guidance and leadership in avoiding injury and death from radioactive fallout and other forms of disastrous contamination."

Notice the very pre-political correctness era message hidden within Wagner's speech. There was no talk of nuclear detonation. No talk of war. In fact, there was barely a mention of radioactive fallout. Instead it was referred to simply as a "crippling disaster." The exercise was to "ensure knowledgeable, organized, and orderly mutual emergency helpfulness in all areas of human needs." Wagner used a very peaceful, "remain calm" approach. Yet the population was well aware of what they were truly preparing for and knew that if this was the real deal with the nukes were on their way, the notion of organized and orderly would be thrown out the window. Practicing was one thing, but there was no substitute for the actual event. The government recognized that as well which was why they decided to stop panicking their own population with these yearly forced participation exercises.

Presidential Emergency Action Documents

While the Operation Alert series died out, by no means did it mean the death of COG planning. It was just ramping up. With the Cold War at its hottest point during the Kennedy administration, COG was on the forefront of the government's collective mind. Just two days prior to JFK issuing those 10 executive orders granting broad power to various agency heads during times of "national emergency" as discussed earlier, Kennedy's National Security Advisor McGeorge Bundy issued a command of his own. On February 14, 1962, Bundy wrote National Security Action Memorandum 127 which was stamped Top Secret. Its subject was "Emergency Planning for Continuity of Government" and was addressed to the Director of the Office of Emergency Planning, the Secretary of Defense, and the Director of the Bureau of the Budget. The memo was also cc'd to the Secretary of State, the Attorney General, the Secretary of the Interior, the Secretary of Commerce, and the Administrator of the Housing and Home Finance Agency.

National Security Action Memorandum 127 was rather short and sweet. It read, in part:

"It is requested that the Director of the Office of Emergency Planning establish a high level committee, under his chairmanship, with other members representing the Department of Defense and the Bureau of the Budget, to re-examine Federal policy with respect to emergency plans and continuity of government in the event of nuclear attack on the United States. The Committee should be prepared to report to the President by June 1, 1962...The Committee's study should include an examination of the present relocation plans for Federal personnel, including the procedures for selecting the necessary emergency personnel, the physical relocation sites and their communications, and the evacuation plans for moving personnel to the relocation centers. In addition, the study should examine the relations between the proposed improvements in the National Military Command and Control system and the plans for continuity of other U.S. Government agencies, with particular emphasis on the plans for insuring the survival of the Presidency....In making its study, the Committee should review present National Security Council Actions, and the existing package of standby Executive Orders and directives which constitute the emergency actions program for the White House."

Bundy gave his newly formed committee until June 1, 1962 to submit its COG report to President Kennedy. As the subsequent National Security Action Memorandum 166 points out, they missed their deadline date by 10 days. In this previously secret memo, Kennedy responded to the recommendations of the committee which were officially submitted on June 11. Kennedy wrote in his response, "I agree that the change in concept of emergency planning set forth in that report—from the present plan of evacuation to distant sites to an examination of the possibilities of dispersion within the Washington metropolitan area and delegation to field offices—is appropriate to the developing military technology. As the report states, this change requires corresponding changes in other elements of emergency planning, including the assignment of responsibilities for emergency functions within the government and the organization of communications. Accordingly, I endorse the substance of the report's conclusion." What was interesting about JFK's response was that the committee seemed to suggest that the use of relocation sites was no longer feasible due to the changing "military technology." That meant the committee believed that due to the speed with which the enemy's nuclear missiles could reach the U.S., there wouldn't be enough time from a surprise attack launch detection for anyone to evacuate to the relocation areas prior to the bombs' detonations. If those were indeed the committee's findings, ultimately they were ignored because it was during that same period of time that the federal government was building its most elaborate relocation sites known to exist (more on that in the next chapter).

In returning to Bundy's original National Security Action Memorandum 127, an item he casually mentions—"the existing package of standby Executive Orders and directives"—is something that should not be overlooked. Reportedly, today there are approximately 22 "standby" executive orders that have already been written and ready to sign into being once the proper emergency occurs. These are stashed away collecting dust somewhere in the White House. These unsigned, top secret executive orders are part of the set of Presidential Emergency Action Documents (PEADs) known as Federal Emergency Plan D.

It is unknown what today's PEADs within Plan D will actually allow. These are incredibly classified documents. Even so, some of the mystery surrounding PEADs was revealed via the FBI through the Freedom of Information Act. Yet prior to discussing what is in these documents, consider for a moment just how "Top Secret" they once were. In a series of FBI memorandums from 1958 and 1959, it was revealed that there were originally just eight PEADs. These were accompanied by a corresponding list of code words that would be regularly updated. The FBI was to receive a copy of both the PEADs and the code word list initially in 1958. It was written in one FBI memorandum, "Due to the strict security requirements regarding the documents and code word list, they should not be transmitted to Quantico [which was the FBI's emergency relocation site] together in the same vehicle and upon arrival at Quantico, they should be maintained in separate cabinets in the confidential file room." The code word list was not to be accessed until "receipt of message to effect President has signed certain documents signified by code words." Someone within the federal government missed that message and accidentally opened the code word list. The code words list was deemed "compromised" and had to be rewritten while all of the originals were destroyed. A new list was created and specially delivered to each agency as appropriate. But that was just the beginning.

There were strict rules as to the care and placement of both the PEADs and the code word list. For one, the documents were to be "stored in safe-type containers or otherwise store in accordance with the provisions of Executive Order 10501." Such a safe was to have its combination changed every six months. This was information kept on a truly "need-to-know" basis. "Each agency shall keep a master headquarters record of all individuals with the agency who are aware of the presence and location of documents." To ensure these and the other directions that came attached to the PEADs and code word list were followed, an inspection was to occur. The first took place during Operation Alert 1959. In the case of the FBI, three men—two from the Office of Civil and Defense Mobilization and a member of the White House Staff—traveled to Quantico, Virginia on August 24, 1959. "They physically inspected the Presidential Emergency Action Documents, counting the pages in each document, and they inspected the corresponding code word list. They advised these documents are maintained in an excellent manner and they had no comments, suggestions, or criticism concerning the maintenance of them."

Why all the fuss? Determine that for yourself as you read the titles and, where available, the description of some of these now known Presidential Emergency Action Documents.

Dated from June 1958:

- Document A1-7 "Proclamation for Control of Enemy Aliens" – The signing of this would allow "for apprehension and detention of those dangerous alien enemies presently included in our Security Index" and "otherwise control of all alien enemies."
- Document A1-8 "A Proclamation Suspending the Privilege of the Writ of Habeas Corpus and Authorizing the Apprehension and Detention of Certain Persons, the Search of Persons and Premises, and the Seizure of Property" – This was discussed in the previous chapter.

- Document A1-53 "A Proclamation Proclaiming the Existence of an Unlimited National Emergency and a Civil Defense Emergency" – "This document recognizes that an unprovoked armed attack has been launched against the United States by foreign military forces and that as a result thereof proclaims the existence of an unlimited national emergency."

- Document A1-57 "An Executive Order Authorizing Additional Departments and Agencies of the Executive Branch to Classify Information and Material Pursuant to Executive Order 10501 of 11-5-53" – To be done in the interest of "national security."

- Document A1-59 "An Executive Order Suspending Publication of the Federal Register and Establishing an Alternate System for Filing and Publishing Executive Agency Documents"

- Document E-2 "An Executive Order Providing for the Utilization of the Personnel, Materials, Facilities, and Services of Federal Agencies During the Civil Defense Emergency" – The Federal Civil Defense Administrator was allowed to direct other agencies' personnel, materials, et.al. for civil defense purposes as long as it didn't interfere with the continuity of those agencies prescribed functions essential to national security.

Dated September 1958:

- Document A1-42 Revision 7/58 "Proclamation Regarding the Establishment of Military Areas and Other Emergency Measures" – In essence, this establishes martial law. However, it presumes "the U.S. has been subjected to armed attack which has caused millions of deaths and injuries and the destruction or paralysis of many state and local governments and other essential functions." Should that transpire, this document—once signed—grants the Secretary of Defense the power to basically maintain public order using federal troops. There were apparently restrictions on the Secretary of Defense, including not interfering with "any functioning civilian courts," but for the most part, he would be given free reign.

- Document A1-69 "Proclamation Providing for Continuity of Local Civil Governments, Military Assistance to Civil Governments, and Other Emergency Measures" – This, too, assumes "an unprovoked armed attack has been launched against the U.S. by foreign military forces" but it adds that "the territory of this country is being invaded by persons seeking to destroy the Government by force and violence." Should that come to pass, then this would "confer upon the Director of the Office of Civil and Defense Mobilization (OCDM) the right to assume and exercise all necessary Government functions vital to the maintenance of law and order in those areas in which the civil government of a state or political subdivision thereof is unable or unwilling to perform such functions." Of course, this also "provides that control of local civil government would be returned to local authorities at the earliest practicable date."

- Document A1-70 "Proclamation Providing for the Establishment of Military Areas" – "This document would complement A1-69…should [it] be utilized."

From February 1959:

- Document A1-28 Revised 5/58 – The title of this is unknown, but its contents were revealed. After "an unprovoked attack," the Secretary of State was "to designate those enemy countries whose official representatives should be controlled." This included enemy members of the United Nations as well as "diplomatic, consular, and official personnel."

From January 1961:

- Document A1-16 "Providing for Civil Defense Measures and Mobilization of the Nation's Resources" – This was to supersede Document E-2.
- Document A1-48 – Title unknown, but the description read, "A proclamation convening Congress at the Congressional Relocation Site upon an 'extraordinary occasion' when Congress is not in session, or when Congress is in recess, or because the session has been disrupted by an armed attack or other disaster."
- Document A1-98 – Title unknown, but the description read, "A proclamation foreclosing anyone's departing or entering of U.S. territories and waters unless bearing valid passports or permits or unless exempted under rules and regulations issued by the Secretary of State and/or Attorney General."
- Document A1-99 – Title unknown, but the description read, "A proclamation foreclosing anyone's departing or entering U.S. territories and waters under its jurisdiction until determined to be consistent with National interests."

From November 1961:

Though not specific PEADs, a document (or set of documents) titled "Executive Powers Available by Virtue of a Declaration of War or National Emergency" was reviewed by the Office of Legal Counsel. In the ensuing memorandum, it read, "The legislation covers a wide range of subjects, including Presidential authority to control the movement of aliens in and out of the United States; provisions relating to Armed Forces, the Reserves and National Guard; regulations over transactions in foreign exchange and over communications; suspension of provisions covering Government contracts; provisions relating to security and the protection of defense information; and law governing merchant shipping and use of vessels."

On March 21, 1968, President Lyndon Johnson approved a new set of PEADs submitted to him by a committee. These were actually included in Federal Emergency Plan D as Annex A. Annex

B provided for the "establishment of the Office of Defense Resources (ODR) which will mobilize the Nation's resources." The rewritten and updated Presidential Emergency Action Documents were also given a new numbering system, simplifying it to PEAD 1, 2, 3, 4, etc. It is likely that not much changed content-wise in the rewritten PEADs; however, it is here where the trail of details grows cold. What could be discerned were the following:

- PEAD 2 – "deals with the Congressional Relocation Site and is the primary responsibility of the Federal Preparedness Agency."
- PEAD 5 – "concerns the detention of all natives, citizens, denizens, or subjects of the hostile nation or government."
- PEAD 8 – "authorizes the Secretary of State to initiate measures for the protection, surveillance, and control of certain foreign diplomatic, consular, and other official personnel."
- PEAD 9 – "authorizes the Secretary of State to take over property of enemy governments."
- PEAD 11 – "concerns the classes of persons who would be permitted to enter or leave the United States."
- PEAD 15 – "a proclamation imposing restraints and regulations on alien enemies."
- PEAD 16 – "an Executive Order…authorizes the Secretary of State to institute measures for the protection, surveillance, control, and repatriation of certain foreign diplomatic, consular, and other official personnel and members of their families."
- PEAD 17 – "authorizes the Secretary of State to seize property"
- PEAD 18 – "a proclamation delegating to the Attorney General the authority to prescribe more stringent

documentary requirements for citizens and aliens entering or leaving the United States."

- PEAD 20 – "an Executive Order directing the Secretary of Defense to restore and maintain law and order when it has broken down."
- PEAD 21 – "an Executive Order providing for a temporary suspension of the privilege of the Writ of Habeas Corpus."

That is where the FBI file on PEADs ends. The last entry pertaining to these documents is dated from 1976. While it is highly likely these are still waiting for the proper emergency to be signed into action, it's certain that these PEADs have been rewritten and updated with the changing world.

There is another set of prewritten documents set aside and ready to go for Congress in a mass emergency setting. These are (and I swear I'm not making this title up) the "Documents for Contingency (Other Than a Plan D Situation) Which Justify Application of Emergency Measures on a National Scale." Some of these "Other than Plan D" documents are pre-written bills for Congress to pass, one of which is a declaration of war. Supposedly contained within the president's package of PEADs is a similar proclamation of the "existence of a state of war," just in case Congress isn't in existence to make the official declaration.

Reagan Revitalizes

Reagan entered the White House in 1981 seemingly ready and raring to go toe-to-toe with the Russians. He made it clear that they were the enemy; and the enemy had their finger on the trigger eager to annihilate the U.S. on a moment's notice. This might not have been the exact truth of the situation, however. By the end of Reagan's second term, Mr. Gorbachev had heeded Reagan's call to "tear down these walls" and a new era of *glasnost* had seemingly enveloped the once hard-lined communist nation. Nonetheless, by putting the fear of the Russians back into the hearts and minds of the American population, Reagan ramped up COG preparations within the halls of government.

Right from the get-go, Reagan had Continuity of Government on his mind. On March 16, 1982, Reagan issued National Security Decision Directive (NSDD) 26 which laid out the official United States Civil Defense Policy. It read in part: "It is the policy of the United States to enhance the deterrence of strategic nuclear war through a strong and balanced program of strategic forces, including effective capabilities for strategic defense. Civil Defense, along with an effective Continuity of Government program, emergency mobilization, and secure and reconstitutable telecommunications systems, is an essential ingredient of our nuclear deterrent forces. It is a matter of national priority that the US have a Civil Defense program which provides for the survival of the US population."

Obviously in a nuclear war not everyone would survive. So the question remained, just how much of the U.S. population was Reagan planning on saving? The answer could be found within NSDD 26. It stated, "The US Civil Defense program will: ...Provide for survival of a substantial portion of the US population in the event of nuclear attack preceded by strategic warning and for continuity of government, should deterrence and escalation control fail." How many U.S. citizens exactly constituted a "substantial portion" remains unknown. Interestingly, in Reagan's NSDD 23, which was published a month earlier on February 3, 1982 and also had Civil Defense as its theme; the exact same passage regarding the survival of the U.S. population was written. However, two words—"substantial portion"—have been redacted, and are still considered classified to this day.

In order to save a substantial portion of the U.S. population, someone had to have a plan of action. Luckily, in NSDD 26 Reagan laid one out for everyone to follow. Under the heading "Implementation," it read: "Population Protection. By the end of 1989, the development of plans and deployment of supporting operational systems will be completed. Primary reliance will be placed upon relocating the population of US metropolitan and other potential high-risk areas to surrounding areas of lower risk during a period of international crisis, taking advantage of extensive US transportation resources."

That philosophy was interesting for three reasons. One, in the aforementioned NSDD 23 written about five weeks before NSDD 26, the exact same plan was described regarding mass evacuations, only with the beginning caveat of "By the end of 1987…." In other words, sometime in that five week time span, someone in Reagan's office realized the task would take an extra two years to work out, never mind the threat of war was supposedly looming *now*. It was also convenient that by the end of 1989, Reagan (if re-elected) would have been out of office. If the date remained 1987, Reagan might have still been around to see that his plan had failed. The second point regarding Reagan's plan of action was that it wasn't a new idea. Massive evacuations of major metropolitan areas had been considered and practiced dating back to the Operation Alert exercises. Granted in the 20+ years since Operation Alert most of those plans needed an overhaul, but the fact remained the groundwork for those plans had already been laid. However, and this perhaps is the most important of these three points, *no one in the civilian circles ever bothered to attempt to actually test Reagan's master evacuation plan.*

Of course, which agency did Reagan put in charge of those untested relocation efforts? According to NSDD 26, "The Federal Emergency Management Agency will have overall operational supervision of this program."

While Reagan's inner circle sweated over those civil defense-minded evacuation plans, the public was blissfully unaware of them. FEMA never attempted to reinstitute Operation Alert or anything on par with it. Which means had the U.S. and the U.S.S.R. actually launched their nukes; the massive evacuation of the major U.S. cities would have likely been a monstrous disaster in and of itself. All of the evacuation information—and the government did have emergency pamphlets ready to distribute along with evacuation routes and relocation sites pre-planned—would have been foreign to the intended recipients. Without any sort of a dry run, few average Americans would've known what to do, where to go, and what to expect. So whether Reagan kept the date as 1987 or pushed it back to 1989 (or even 2009 for that matter), his plan was set up to fail since no one ever tried it to see if it would work.

That was on the civilian side of the coin. On the other side lay the government's own evacuation and relocation planning. This was checked, rechecked, and tested on numerous occasions.

The problem for anyone interested in researching these COG plans is that Continuity of Government planning is a Top Secret endeavor. This is not an exaggeration. Even today these operations are given the highest security and run on a literal need-to-know basis. While some information has leaked out over the years, the true inner workings of these operations are still largely unknown. And for good reason. Much of what Reagan's administration developed remains the current operational model for COG, at least in terms of the evacuation and securing of the upper echelon of the federal government. For COG to work as intended, these plans must remain secret.

Even so, some of this classified information has been identified. In the book *Code Names*, author William M. Arkin related the titles of some of the presidential Continuity of Government exercises run during the 1980s and early 1990s. Remember a few facts while reading through this list. One, it likely is not comprehensive. Two, it spans a little over 10 years worth of time, most likely from Reagan's start in office through President Bush Sr.'s exit from the White House. Three, all of these programs were run in a top secret fashion. And four, none of them were concerned with saving regular civilians, just the upper echelon of the federal government—and that doesn't necessarily include the Congress. Having stated that, note just how many variations of this project there were. These titles included such code names as Crown Shelter, Flash Burn, Nine Lives, Pine Ridge, Sage Brush, Ski Jump, the entire Snow series (Snow Fall, Snow Storm, and Snow Time among the list), the Log series (including Log Horn and Log Tree), Southern Pine, Surf Board, Swarmer, and Timber Line.

Oddly enough, one of those exercises—Nine Lives—was scheduled to take place on what wound up being the day after President Reagan was shot. As far as could be determined, the Nine Lives exercises never actually took place. Instead, a very real situation occurred mirroring a COG exercise as Vice President Bush and Secretary of State Alexander Haig fought over who should be in control of the White House during the aftermath of the assassination attempt. Vice President Bush rightly won, while Haig was later pushed right out of the administration and from his role in the State Department. Your author attempted to pry more information from the federal government regarding these exercises via the Freedom of Information Act, but was told either such files do not exist, could not be located, or were still classified and would not be released.

Project 908

Author James Mann, who was a Washington correspondent for the *Los Angeles Times* and later became a senior writer-in-residence for the Center of Strategic and International Studies (CSIS) in Washington, DC, was able to dig out some background information on these 1980s era COG exercises. In his book *Rise of the Vulcans: The History of Bush's War Cabinet*, Mann related some of the nitty-gritty involved. Perhaps the reason why Mann was able to acquire this information was due to the fact that the CSIS devised some of those COG exercises to study the functioning of the War Powers Act.

Mann described the genesis of Reagan's COG program thusly: "Ronald Reagan established the continuity-of-government program with a secret executive order. According to Robert McFarlane, who served for a time as Reagan's National Security Adviser, the President himself made the final decision about who would head each of the three teams. Within Reagan's National Security Council the 'action officer' for the secret program was Oliver North, later the central figure in the Iran-contra scandal. Vice President George H.W. Bush was given the authority to supervise some of these efforts, which were run by a new government agency with a bland name: the National Program Office. It had its own building in the Washington area, run by a two-star general, and a secret budget adding up to hundreds of millions of dollars a year. Much of this money was spent on advanced communications equipment that would enable the teams to have secure conversations with U.S. military commanders."

The Reagan administration's COG plan of action was quite straightforward though it possessed the cryptic name "Project 908." When an attack was either considered eminent or actually underway, three separate teams would be evacuated from Washington and sent to undisclosed locations spread around the United States. These teams, given color coded designation names, were each headed by a cabinet member and were to assume control of the nation should the actual, seated and elected government be eliminated. These teams included a "replacement" president, a White House chief of staff, and representatives from the State Department, Department of Defense, and even the CIA among others. The reason three teams were deployed was in case the Russians learned of the location of one and destroyed it, the second (and if need be, third) team would assume command. The idea the Russians could find these hiding places wasn't farfetched; the U.S. had already identified all of the Soviets' "fixed leadership" shelters which could reportedly hold upwards of 100,000 top Russians officials. As Mann wrote, "The idea was to practice running the entire federal government with a skeletal crew during a nuclear war."

Having a cabinet member as part of these relocation teams was vital. Should the actual president and vice president have been killed, the line of succession to the presidency includes every cabinet member based upon when their office was first established. As Mann pointed out, "The Reagan Administration's primary goal was to set up a chain of command that could respond to the urgent minute-by-minute demands of a nuclear war, when there might be no time to swear in a new President under the regular process of succession, and when a new President would not have the time to appoint a new staff." A cabinet member, whether sworn in as the new president or not, would lend some legitimacy to the surviving government's actions. For it was already determined that should Congress have been destroyed, or at least its membership unable to constitute the required quorum to operate, the government would continue to operate without them. Constitutional? No. And no one within Reagan's inner circle even attempted to get such an action legalized, nor did they seem to develop any sort of plan in which to ensure the survival of congressional members. Congress, it seemed, was expendable. Considering the horrific circumstances that would have surrounded such an extra-constitutional situation, *someone* would have had to respond and act in the name of the people of the United States. Given the circumstances, a cabinet member might have been the best option available.

While that was the guiding principle for saving the presidency, the other governmental agencies had a similar, yet slightly different method of preserving their officials. Once again, three teams were involved, albeit with different lots in life. The "A" team would remain at the given agency's headquarters until "unable to function" (meaning, more likely than not, killed). The "B" team would vacate to the High Point Special Facility better known as Mount Weather. Since it was quite probable that the underground facility at Mount Weather was known to America's enemies and would be a high-priority target in a nuclear war, the "C" team was to deploy to an alternate location and assume control of operations if the A and B teams were rendered inoperable. Members of those teams were given special privileges, including passwords and ID cards which allowed them unrestricted movement in times of national emergency (and today, this includes specially encoded cell phones).

Most COG exercises were conducted during congressional breaks. Participation was not mandatory; however, those who were available to participate often did. When a drill took place, those involved would be whisked away to secure locations—sometimes in convoys of nuclear hardened vehicles—while their family would remain in the dark as to the actual whereabouts of their loved ones. Even the routes the participants took to get to those hideouts were elaborate, as the government did their best to disguise their location from the Soviets' spy mechanisms. Often times, participants wouldn't know where they were once they had arrived at the secure location; the windows in their delivery vehicles were blacked out. The drills themselves would last for up to two weeks, though most participants were only directly involved in play-acting for a few days. During that time those participating weren't staying in five-star hotels with room service. They lived as if nuclear war had taken place. High level government officials were crammed into dank military-like bunkers which were quite austere and lacked any amenities. The "survivors" ate the military MREs (meals ready to eat) and slept in bunks. Their only contact with the outside world was in sending and receiving reports on how the "war" was going.

Among the list of people who participated in these COG exercises are two familiar names. Future Vice President Dick Cheney and two-time Secretary of Defense Donald Rumsfeld willingly had their lives interrupted for the drills. During Reagan's administration, Cheney was a congressman from Wyoming while Rumsfeld had left the politics of Washington behind for a job in the private sector. Yet the two were often called upon to act as part of Reagan's makeshift, underground government. According to author Andrew Cockburn in his book *Rumsfeld: His Rise, Fall, and Catastrophic Legacy*, Rumsfeld acted as president in the 1989 COG exercise, relishing the role. Yet neither of these governmental heavyweights was directly involved with developing the COG plans and operations; they were simply two of its many actors so chosen because of their background in national security matters. Remarkably, that training coupled with the knowledge developed by the pair during those exercises was put to actual use during 9/11. In fact, had things played out slightly different on that infamous date, what Cheney and Rumsfeld knew could have potentially saved the federal government.

NSDD 47

In returning to the confines of 1982, mid-July of that year saw Reagan issue NSDD 47 entitled "Emergency Mobilization Preparedness." This document was prepared by the Emergency Mobilization Preparedness Board. The preamble of the 12 page directive read: "A fundamental obligation of government is to provide for the security of the Nation and to protect its people, values, and its social, economic, and political structures. Inherent in that obligation is the requirement to have an emergency mobilization preparedness program which will provide an effective capability to meet defense and essential civilian needs during national security emergencies and major domestic emergencies. This directive aims not to commit the Federal Government to a particular course of action, but rather to assure that a range of options are available in time of grave national emergency." That statement was somewhat comical considering the government really had just one plan, albeit one that was two pronged: evacuate as many of themselves as possible while taking command and control of every other feasible aspect of the nation. There was little flexibility in that.

The "Principles for Emergency Mobilization Preparedness Programs" as written in NSDD 47 continued with the charade. It stated: "The general principles apply to all emergency programs, while the division between national security and domestic emergency principles emphasizes that the respective and appropriate response for each category may differ." As in, the federal government may practice COG exercises until they are blue in the face while evacuation plans for the rest of us will sit on the shelf collecting dust until the day the bombs drop. That was a bit of a difference. NSDD 47 continued: "Taken together, however, these principles define a common ground upon which mobilization programs can be developed and used at the discretion of the President to prevent avoidable emergencies, to combat and reduce the effects of those that are unavoidable, and to mitigate the effects of those that do occur." In the context of this National Security

Decision Directive, however, Reagan's mobilization planning wasn't really discussing events like hurricanes and other such natural disasters. That was just given lip service. The focus was firmly on nuclear war. That should have been considered an "avoidable emergency," but many within Reagan's staff looked upon it as just the opposite, otherwise they wouldn't have even bothered preparing.

While it would be another six years before Reagan would issue Executive Order 12656 which rewrote Nixon's national emergency preparedness plans, Reagan already began to set the groundwork for that document here in NSDD 47. Some of the "General Principles" laid out in NSDD 47 sounded akin to the bizarre freedoms first granted by President Kennedy in the event of a national emergency. For example, one of the "Principles for National Security Emergencies" read, "Resource management and economic stabilization programs should include standby plans and procedures for governmental intervention, as necessary, into the market place to ensure the enhancement of supply and the allocation of resources to military and essential civilian needs. These mechanisms should provide for both gradual and abrupt replacement of market forces by governmental regulations." But that's nothing compared to some of the overriding "General Principles" written in NSDD 47. Those included: "Plans and procedures should be designed to retain maximum flexibility for the President and other senior officials in the implementation of emergency actions both above and below the threshold of declared national emergencies and wars. Plans should avoid rigid 'either-or' choices that limit Presidential options….Preparedness measures that involve the waiving or modification of socioeconomic regulations that delay emergency response should receive priority attention….Preparedness measures that are, or may be, impeded by legal constraints should be identified as a priority task." Note that NSDD 47 was clearly stating that there were "emergency actions" already planned that were "above…the threshold of declared national emergencies and wars" and that some "preparedness measures" were "impeded by legal constraints." In other words, laws and perhaps the Constitution itself would be thrown out given the right set of circumstances. The government didn't need to follow those things *all* the time, did it? It would be okay to call "time out" on some of those points, given the proper set of circumstances, right?

It would depend on if the end justified the means. Continuity of Government programs and operations sometimes go by another name, Enduring Constitutional Government. NSDD 47 stated, "These [mobilization] programs...will contribute to...preservation of constitutional government..." as do many other COG related documents, even when all signs seem to be pointing in the opposite direction. Setting aside any conspiracy theories you choose to believe, preserving our constitutional form of government is supposed to be the primary point to all Continuity of Government programs. Some severe national emergency like a nuclear war may knock out our government (or at least disable it) to the point where if we're going to respond, we're going to have to be able to set aside some of the notions of how our government normally functions. The hope would be that if such an extra-constitutional event did occur, the government would revert to adhering to the Constitution as soon as possible. Of course, that's the exact point where the conspiracies rightfully lie. Would we go back? Could we go back? Would those who gain power outside of the Constitution give it up or would we be facing a coup situation?

The hope, at least as laid out in NSDD 47, would be that the national mobilization plan would interfere with any such situation from occurring in the first place. In terms of the government's operations, the mobilization program was to do four main things: "Ensure continuous performance of essential government functions; provide timely and effective transition to emergency government operations; provide a mechanism for the reconstitution of the operations of government following a nuclear attack, as required; and ensure that government officials at all levels are capable of responding predictably and effectively to emergency conditions." If the mobilization plan worked as advertised, then the constitutional government should continue to function no matter the situation at hand. Given an emergency, the government was supposed to be able to switch gears or even operate with a limited staff all the while continuing with the form of government we expect.

Whether that would have actually been the case was another question entirely.

Reagan didn't just create these programs and then forget they existed. Reportedly, by the end of his first term, the administration was spending $1 billion a year on various COG projects. In all matters civil defense related, Reagan stuck to his guns, realizing the seriousness and importance of what was being planned. His administration bridged the civil defense gap from the beginning of the Cold War to today. Much more was developed during this era than is discussed here. Though already covered were FEMA's involvement during the Reagan years (including exercises like REX-84), Reagan's EO 12656, the above mentioned NSDDs, and the COG exercises uncovered by authors Arkin, Cockburn and Mann, there are still reams of information the government possesses in relation to Reagan-era COG exercises and planning that are considered classified and have not been released to the general public. Just under the NSDD heading alone exist such untouchable documents as: NSDD 55 – Enduring National Leadership, NSDD 61 – Contingency Planning…(the rest of the *title* is even classified for this one), NSDD 95 - Crisis Information and Management System, NSDD 231 - Crisis Management Policies and Procedures, and NSDD 237 - Director, Presidential Contingency Programs as well as another 6 or more NSDDs in which the material including the title is completely classified.

Moving more towards the present, that sort of control over information doesn't get much looser.

Bush to Bush

Serving as vice president under Reagan, George H. W. Bush had a direct hand in many of the COG programs run during

Reagan's tenure. Not only did Bush participate in those plans and exercises; he often directly oversaw them. So, it was of little surprise that when Bush himself became president, Reagan passed the COG baton to a willing recipient. That made the officials charged with maintaining COG operations quite happy as they would not have to spend time trying to explain the complexities of the issue to a newbie.

Bush wasted little time in continuing Reagan's COG plans. In the official "National Security Strategy of the United States," issued in March of 1990 there was still talk of nuclear war. The focus here was mainly on deterrence which "remains the cornerstone of U.S. national security." Even so, it was written that "Regardless of improved U.S.-Soviet relations and potential arms control agreements, the Soviets' physical ability to initiate strategic nuclear warfare against the United States will persist and a crisis or political change in the Soviet Union could occur faster than we could rebuild neglected strategic forces." Hence, COG planning was still a necessary aspect of national security (though the notion that America's strategic forces could be "neglected" seems laughable). "Another basic element of deterrence is the security of our command and control, enhancing the certainty of retaliation. In addition, we maintain programs to ensure the continuity of constitutional government—another way of convincing a potential attacker that any attempted 'decapitating' strike against our political and military leadership will fail." The enemy's rationale must have been assumed to be, "If we can't kill America's top brass right off the bat, then why bother attacking?" If it wasn't, then no matter the COG plan enacted, it wouldn't have been much of a deterrent. Instead, it would have merely been an escape plan. Of course, that also assumed the enemy realized we even had such a COG program to begin with (despite its top secret status) and that they hadn't learned where our leadership would be hiding if and when such a war began.

Civil defense was also not forgotten in Bush's administration. It would be hard to fight a war if (1) everyone in the nation was either dead or dying or (2) an all-out nuclear attack weakened the will of the people to even consider fighting back. So, though saving civilians was a secondary concern, it was still worth discussing. While there seemed to be next to nothing in the way of actual, active participation by the general population in civil defense activities, National Security Directive (NSD) 66 issued on March 16, 1992 once again laid out the nation's civil defense plan. Much like Bush's idea of COG in the national security strategy, "Civil defense can contribute to deterrence by denying an enemy any confidence that he could prevent a concerted national response to attack."

Upon reading the section labeled "Implementation" in NSD 66, it makes one wonder if Bush or the rest of the government really believed the validity of that notion. Because despite talking a good game, none of these civil defense measures seemed to ever be implemented. This section of NSD 66 read:

"The [civil defense] program…will include: (1) Population protection capabilities, with the Federal Government providing guidance and assistance to enable State and local governments to effectively support the population in all catastrophic emergencies.

"(2) State and local government crisis management capabilities to effectively support the population in all catastrophic emergencies.

"(3) Information to promote a clear understanding by the public of the civil defense program, all threats which may affect their localities and actions they should take to minimize their effects.

"(4) Information to assist U.S. business and industry in taking measures to protect their work forces and physical assets in all catastrophic emergencies and encouragement of the private sector to make maximum use of private sector capabilities.

"(5) Voluntary participation by citizens and institutions in community civil defense activities and emphasis on citizen protective actions.

"(6) Plans for sustaining survivors, for restoration of critical life support capabilities, and to establish a basis for recovery.

"(7) Definition of and an assessment of the base capability necessary to respond to emergencies that do not provide warning, and the development of those base capabilities which are common to all catastrophic emergencies and unique to attack.

"(8) Plans for a civil defense surge from the base capability to the total required capability in a national security crisis involving the threat of attack. These plans should assume advance warning, adequate time to conduct the surge, and the required base capability from which to surge. Total required capability is that operational capability necessary to protect the population and vital infrastructure through preparedness measures common to all catastrophic emergencies and unique to attack emergencies."

Was any of this ever begun? It doesn't appear so. Part of the problem may have been that no one really knew what they were supposed to be preparing for. By 1992, the threat of nuclear war with the Soviets had dropped from the nation's collective radar. America's only threat appeared to come from smaller, "rogue" nations that weren't nuclear powers by any stretch of the imagination. Despite that, FEMA's oft-confused mandate continued to flip-flop from civil defense to natural disaster emergencies. The government during Reagan's and Bush's tenure pointed FEMA in a very civil defense orientation. Yet what was more important to America's citizens? Civil defense preparations for a war that appeared to be nowhere near beginning, or other disaster-related preparedness? Clearly, after the disaster (both natural and man-made) that was Hurricane Andrew in 1992, America's population knew in which direction they preferred FEMA to head—and that wasn't civil defense.

That didn't mean the government left COG planning completely in the rearview mirror. Bush issued NSD 37 in early 1990, followed by NSD 69 in mid-1992. Both still-secret documents were in regards to "Enduring Constitutional Government," the other name for COG. Bush also updated Reagan's NSDD 306 in his own NSD 37 which involved the

"National Coordination of Emergency Relocation Sites." There was also a National Security Review (NSR 20) published by Bush under the title "Review of Policy and Programs Concerning Continuity of Government," but that document, too, remains classified.

By the time the Clinton era was ushered into the White House, the Soviets and their communist allies were almost considered to be our allies. The looming menace of nuclear annihilation that dominated the early 1980s had completely dissipated. According to author Cockburn, though the COG exercises continued during Clinton's administration with a budget that had plummeted down to approximately $200 million a year, these nuclear war games were often overseen strictly by Republicans, most of whom were leftovers from the Reagan and Bush years. During Clinton's first term it appeared as if COG and its related programs were barely considered by the administration. It wasn't until late October 1998, deep into Clinton's second term, that a major COG document emanated from the White House. This was Presidential Decision Directive (PDD) 67 which is believed to be titled "Enduring Constitutional Government and Continuity of Government Operations." No one seems to know for sure as PDD 67 remains classified and no White House Factsheet exists to summarize its contents. All that is known about PDD 67 is that it replaced Bush's previously issued NSD 69 (which also remains classified). NSD 69 had itself replaced a previous Bush era NSD—the classified NSD 37—and Reagan's still classified NSDD 55 titled "Enduring National Leadership."

"Comity"

The only publicly known document from George W. Bush's administration that dealt with Continuity of Government is the National Security Presidential Directive (NSPD) 51. This was subtitled as Homeland Security Presidential Directive (HSPD) 20, but it is most commonly referred to by the previous delineation. Published on May 9, 2007, nearly six years after the 9/11 attacks, it revoked Clinton's still classified PDD 67. While one would like to think that NSPD 51 with its ability to be read showed a new spirit of openness in the federal government, don't be fooled. There are several annexes to NSPD 51 which, according to the document itself, "are classified and shall be accorded appropriate handling, consistent with applicable Executive Orders." It is likely within those classified annexes lies the true nature of Bush's COG plan…and many of the conspiracy theories associated with it.

Even with that being the case, NSPD 51 was fairly forthright. It stated its purpose right at the start:

"This directive establishes a comprehensive national policy on the continuity of Federal Government structures and operations and a single National Continuity Coordinator responsible for coordinating the development and implementation of Federal continuity policies. This policy establishes 'National Essential Functions,' prescribes continuity requirements for all executive departments and agencies, and provides guidance for State, local, territorial, and tribal governments, and private sector organizations in order to ensure a comprehensive and integrated national continuity program that will enhance the credibility of our national security posture and enable a more rapid and effective response to and recovery from a national emergency."

NSPD 51 also went so far as to give actual definitions of not just Continuity of Government and Continuity of Operations (COOP, which one can think of as COG's little brother), but Enduring Constitutional Government and more. It defined these ideas as follows:

"'Continuity of Government,' or 'COG,' means a coordinated effort within the Federal Government's executive branch to ensure that National Essential Functions continue to be performed during a Catastrophic Emergency;

"'Continuity of Operations,' or 'COOP,' means an effort within individual executive departments and agencies to ensure that Primary Mission-Essential Functions continue to be performed during a wide range of emergencies, including localized acts of nature, accidents, and technological or attack-related emergencies;

"'Enduring Constitutional Government,' or 'ECG,' means a cooperative effort among the executive, legislative, and judicial branches of the Federal Government, coordinated by the President, as a matter of comity with respect to the legislative and judicial branches and with proper respect for the constitutional separation of powers among the branches, to preserve the constitutional framework under which the Nation is governed and the capability of all three branches of government to execute constitutional responsibilities and provide for orderly succession, appropriate transition of leadership, and interoperability and support of the National Essential Functions during a catastrophic emergency;…

"'National Essential Functions,' or 'NEFs,' means that subset of Government Functions that are necessary to lead and sustain the Nation during a catastrophic emergency and that, therefore, must be supported through COOP and COG capabilities;

"'Primary Mission Essential Functions,' or 'PMEFs,' means those Government Functions that must be performed in order to support or implement the performance of NEFs before, during, and in the aftermath of an emergency."

Hidden within those definitions was one of the biggest question marks/conspiracy theories that crop up in discussing NSPD 51. Within the definition of Enduring Constitutional Government is the passage, "…a cooperative effort among the executive, legislative, and judicial branches of the Federal Government, coordinated by the President, as a matter of comity with respect to the legislative and judicial branches…." The key word here is "comity." What does it mean? By strict definition in the *Merriam-Webster Dictionary*, comity is "the informal and voluntary recognition by courts of one jurisdiction of the laws and judicial decisions of another." In more layman's terms and within the confines of NSPD 51, comity refers to the fact that both the legislative and the judicial branch will give their power over to the executive branch, namely the president, who will "coordinate."

That appears rather contradictory. On one hand, the

definition in question refers to Enduring Constitutional Government. Yet on the other, within that very definition was the idea that the president is going to assume command over everything. How is that considered constitutional?

Well, it's not. Nowhere in the Constitution was the president given the lead of the federal government. It was supposed to always be three separate, yet equal branches. Here lies the doubled edged sword of Continuity of Government. The purpose of COG as was clearly stated within NSPD 51 is, "Ensuring the continued functioning of our form of government under the Constitution, including the functioning of the three separate branches of government." Yet at that initial moment of emergency, when all general hell is breaking loose, the constitutional form of government as we know it is going to have to cease to function if it is to survive. If some enemy of the U.S. launched an all-out nuclear strike against us, the country is not going to have the time to assemble Congress to vote on a bill as to whether we go to war with this attacking enemy. Someone has to respond and do so immediately. That person is the president. That's supposedly why he was elected—to make those sorts of decisions in the name of the rest of us. Such power as the ability to respond to an attack was granted to the office via the War Powers Act. Now if some other unforeseen calamity occurs within the nation on a similar scale— such as the eruption of the mega-volcano located within Yellowstone National Park—again, America will not have time to wait to form a response. We will need one, and need it now. In order to save the country and the Constitution by which it is governed, certain laws stipulated within it may have to be broken. There will be no choice.

On the flip side, and this is where the conspiracy theories come into play, NSPD 51 allows the president to not only be the quarterback in an emergency situation, but the head coach, general manager, and team owner as well. Consider the following: Only a president can declare a national emergency. He can do so via an executive order which acts as law, even though Congress—which is given the constitutional right to make laws—has no say in the matter. Once a national emergency has been declared, a wide variety of powers (as seen in the executive orders of Kennedy, Nixon, and Reagan) which allow for the control of nearly everything from transportation to communication to even the military for implementing martial law opens up for the president to use at his discretion. If the emergency is deemed dire enough, Continuity of Government plans could be officially enacted. The government could be ordered to disperse and effectively go into hiding. Now here in NSPD 51, George W. Bush declared that in such an emergency the president (which just happened to be Bush himself at this time) would run the show and both Congress and the Supreme Court would have to bow down to his rule. All in the name of protecting the Constitution and the American way of life. That's what comity meant in this usage.

The table is completely set for a coup. The president, by his authority alone, can create a situation which gives him total control of the country with the ability to push the other two branches of the government aside, all while claiming this to be an exercise in "Enduring Constitutional Government." As was also written into NSPD 51, "The President shall lead the activities of the Federal Government for ensuring constitutional government." That is, if he's not too busy burning the Constitution while setting up his independent regime. Needless to say, the president couldn't just do that from the phone on his desk in the Oval Office. Any president attempting this sort of "legal" coup would need some backing from other members within his administration. Such an evil-minded president likely wouldn't take an incident like the declared national emergency due to the situation in Zimbabwe and turn it into a COG situation complete with the all trimmings. The fact remains, however, any such national emergency declaration sets up the dominos, and all a president would need to do is knock the first one over for those events to fall in his favor. The paperwork and subsequent laws have already been filed. All that is lacking is the proper triggering event.

Of course, the stated "Policy" of NSPD 51 seemed to ignore the conspiracy minded of us out there and instead focused on how the government was going to continue to be the shining light of the world, no matter the disaster at hand. Besides ensuring the constitutional form of government never fails, NSPD 51 stated that these COG plans would accomplish the following as well:

"Providing leadership visible to the Nation and the world and maintaining the trust and confidence of the American people;

"Defending the Constitution of the United States against all enemies, foreign and domestic, and preventing or interdicting attacks against the United States or its people, property, or interests;

"Maintaining and fostering effective relationships with foreign nations;

"Protecting against threats to the homeland and bringing to justice perpetrators of crimes or attacks against the United States or its people, property, or interests;

"Providing rapid and effective response to and recovery from the domestic consequences of an attack or other incident;

"Protecting and stabilizing the Nation's economy and ensuring public confidence in its financial systems; and

"Providing for critical Federal Government services that address the national health, safety, and welfare needs of the United States."

Many of us may like to see these sorts of initiatives coming from the White House now, without the need of a national emergency to spawn them.

The reminder of NSPD 51—at least the portion that can be read—concerned itself with various housekeeping duties. It also created a new COG-related system, the Continuity of Government Readiness Condition (COGCON). According to NSPD 51, "In order to provide a coordinated response to escalating threat levels or actual emergencies, the COGCON system establishes executive branch continuity program readiness levels, focusing on possible threats to the National Capital Region. The President will determine and issue the COGCON Level. Executive departments and agencies shall comply with the requirements and assigned responsibilities under the COGCON program. During COOP activation, executive departments and agencies shall report their readiness status to the Secretary of Homeland Security or the Secretary's designee." The idea of having a continual COGCON level (which operates like the nation's Defense Condition (DEFCON) status) as well as these other ongoing tasks and COG preparations gives one a good sense of how serious the federal government seems to be taking these programs today. The threat of terrorism has scared the nation's top leaders into a position where they consider running and hiding a good option given the current circumstances in the world.

The biggest problem with these new and improved COG plans may be that some of the people one would think "need to know;" don't. Just after NSPD 51 was released, Congressman Peter DeFazio (D-OR) asked to see what exactly was in the classified annexes of NSPD 51. DeFazio felt he had a right to read them. Not simply because he was a member of Congress, but due to the fact that he served on the congressional Homeland Security Committee which granted him the proper security clearance to read such classified materials. His request was denied. Outraged, DeFazio went on to discover that not a single member of the Homeland Security Committee was able to access the annexes, despite the fact that he and every other member of the committee had full clearance to see all COG-related information. Yet the denials came directly from the White House because of "national security."

Right or wrong, that is how top secret Continuity of Government plans are. Members of Congress cannot even access them.

Which makes one wonder, if no one in Congress knows what the plans are, how well are they going to work if called into action? How well would a secret fire evacuation plan work if no one knew the floor plan, where the exits were, or even bothered to test it?

Besides those who created the plan—in this case Bush's White House staff—no one else would know where to go or what to do. It's a system set up for failure, which harkens back to the conspiracy theories regarding COG and especially NSPD 51. If Congress doesn't know what it is supposed to do when a national emergency occurs and COG is activated, most members may likely be left by the wayside to perish while the president and his staff survives. Thus Congress will be eliminated, leaving only the president to run the country. Is this Enduring Constitutional Government; or something else entirely?

RELOCATION SITES

"Mr. President, we must not allow a mine-shaft gap!"
— George C. Scott as General "Buck" Turgidson in the motion picture
Dr. Strangelove or: How I Learned to Stop Worrying and Love the
Bomb

For the uninitiated, what follows may seem utterly fantastic. The emergency relocation sites the U.S. government has constructed over the past 60 years may sound more like James Bond-esque super villain hideouts than actual real world locales. Yet they are as physical as the room you're currently sitting in to read this book. Many are known—one you can even tour—but in all likelihood, more exist than those detailed here. These are black holes on the map, rarely revealed over time, and accessed only by those with the proper clearance. A book like this will likely be your only window to this top secret world.

Most of these governmental relocation sites (also known as alternate facilities) take the form of a bunker. People often think of bunkers as something straight out of World War II; an underground location where one waits out the latest bombing raid. In fact, it was that very idea the federal government expanded upon to create the vast array of COG locations scattered across the nation. Immediately after World War II, the Army and Navy Munitions Board began surveying various caves and caverns as locations for stashing people during future attacks (in fact, the Department of Homeland Security continues to maintain a database of over 300 caves and mines that have been determined as "suitable" for human occupation). Once the atomic age ushered in the Cold War and the ever-present threat of nuclear annihilation, the idea of hiding deeper and deeper underground seemed to hold sway over decision makers. Clearly during the Operation Alert series, when President Eisenhower sought shelter under a tent while seated on a folding chair, those in government realized more secure and better equipped locations were needed if the United States was going to fight back and survive. Some ideas tossed about at that time were rather extreme. Edward Teller, the man who created the H-bomb, proposed constructing all future public buildings underground to create shelter-like conditions from the get-go. The idea that ultimately won out was to build vast secret, underground facilities in a geographical arc around Washington, DC so that should the nukes be on their way, our beloved government officials could evacuate the city and seek a shelter that would not just sustain them, but keep them interconnected in order to coordinate a counter attack.

What is perhaps the most intriguing aspect of these relocation sites was the fact that one could be hidden virtually anywhere. You could be sitting above one right now and not realize it. Not possible? Consider the following: Today the Department of Defense alone owns approximately 29 million acres of land in the United States. That is equivalent to just over 45,000 square miles. The military's White Sands Missile Range in New Mexico itself covers 3,200 square miles. While many COG-related sites and bases of operation are nestled within the confines of military bases, there is no rule or law stating that all such sites must follow suit. It is possible, if not quite likely, that many COG sites were not built on what appears to be government owned land. The most famous site like this sat underneath a hotel.

The Greenbrier Resort is located in White Sulphur Springs, West Virginia, about 250 miles from Washington, DC. In 1959, the resort began a massive construction project during which it built a new wing onto its existing hotel structure. The project took two and a half years to complete. When the new section opened in 1962, something else became operational as well. What few hotel employees realized was that underneath the resort the U.S.

government had just constructed a top secret two-story, 112,000 square foot bunker built to house Congress in the event of a nuclear war. The site remained virtually unknown and undetected even by most members of the federal government until *Washington Post* reporter Ted Gup exposed its existence in a 1992 article. Less than three years later, the government officially decommissioned that COG facility as it was no longer a safe refuge due to Gup's investigative work. The Greenbrier now conducts tours of the stripped down bunker. Prior to that time, the site code named Casper (and later, Greek Island) stood ready to accept the members of Congress in the direst of situations for over 30 years.

The building of that massive bunker was a feat unto itself. It required over 50,000 tons of steel-reinforced concrete to construct, creating walls two feet thick buried 64 feet beneath the hotel. Amazingly, not even the construction workers discussed what they had built. While the government footed the bill for building the Greenbrier's addition (at a reported cost of $14 million) as a cover story, the creation of the underground portion set the nation back a staggering $86 million. A group of 12 members of Army Intelligence were tasked with keeping the site in a constant state of readiness. Often times, those workers posed as television repairmen to keep the hotel staff from wondering who they really were. Had an emergency caused the site to become operational, the staff would have become quite aware of those "TV repairmen" as they would have taken control of the entire hotel to secure it for the arrival of Congress.

When members of Congress arrived, they would have registered at the hotel's actual front desk prior to descending into the bunker. A 25-ton reinforced steel door hidden in the hotel's wall welcomed one inside (there were two exterior entrances to the bunker as well). The 16,000 square foot entrance hall just behind the massive blast door would have been converted into a workplace for congressional aides, but often times the hotel used this area for meetings and conventions with no one realizing they were actually inside a top secret government installation. Once inside, assuming nuclear war had begun, each person would have gone through a decontamination process including a shower and the destruction of their civilian clothing. They would have then dressed in green jumpsuits with white sneakers for the duration of their stay. Further inside, one would find the actual living space to be quite austere. There were 18 dorm rooms each of which could hold 60 occupants in double bunk beds, much like a military barracks. The more senior members of Congress were to get the lower bunks. There was a dining room decorated with fake window frames depicting pastoral nature scenes, yet the food available would have also been very military-like with a 60-day stockpile on hand. If any survivors were injured, there was a 12 bed, fully stocked hospital complete with surgical rooms and an intensive care unit. The workers at the site even monitored the prescriptions taken by all congressional members so that a fresh drug supply was constantly on hand in the bunker's clinic. There were isolation chambers (in case someone lost their mind due to the circumstances) and a pathological waste incinerator, better known as a crematorium, for those not fortunate enough to survive.

The plan was for Congress to operate out of this facility for three weeks, though supplies would have been able to keep them there much longer. The bunker held three massive water tanks, a water purification system, its own power generators, and a separate air filtration system to keep out any nuclear fallout while supplying fresh air. Exercise equipment was available to the occupants as were a cache of weapons, just in case. In order to communicate with the outside world, there was another bunker built to hold a microwave relay facility four miles from the main site. Back inside the main bunker was a functional television station so that congressmen could tell the suffering nation "all is well." Those comforting speeches could have been given in front of a false backdrop of either the Capital Building or the White House. Meanwhile, the business of Congress was not supposed to cease. The bunker held separate chambers for both houses to meet, as well as a room large enough for a joint session.

The biggest question surrounding the Greenbrier bunker was would any members of Congress actually go there if directed? Despite having the housing capacity for nearly 1,100 persons, no members of Congress were to be allowed to bring their families with them. While Congress combined equates to just 535 people, the remainder of those bunks was to be filled with congressional aides, secretaries and staff. That gave many members of Congress a moment of pause. Duty to country was one thing, but few congressmen felt they would be able to abandon their families to certain death while they survived in the government's secret bunker. Many opined that they would not go; rather they would stay with their family given the circumstances.

That may be one of the biggest holes in the entire COG program. Yes, the government can indeed keep such a massive construction site as its bunker under the Greenbrier secret, and yes, it can also maintain that secrecy for over 30 years, but if it can't convince the people it was meant to save to go there, then the whole project was rather moot. A 1978 Government Accounting Office report backed that sentiment. It found that at least 20 percent of those tasked with COG duties would not report to their designated sites, mostly due to the inability to bring their families along. The same report also revealed that only 56 percent of respondents even knew what their emergencies duties were supposed to be. That revelation indicates another potential drawback to these massive COG projects as witnessed in the case of Congressman DeFazio and his inability to read any of the secret annexes to Bush's COG documents. If no one knew what they were supposed to do in an emergency situation, all of these vast plans would fall apart. Amazingly, when the government faced an actual situation when COG plans needed to be operational, the decades' worth of preparedness it had spent billions of dollars on failed.

Welcome to September 11, 2001.

9/11

Without a doubt, there are many theories surrounding the

events that occurred on what's simply become known as "9/11." Some of those seem so extreme as to be absurd, while others often appear to make more sense than what's considered to be the government's official version of what happened that day. If one pushes all of those notions aside—both the logical and the crazy—the events of 9/11 reveal for the first time how Continuity of Government programs operate in a real-time situation. For at no other time in America's history have these plans actually been called into service.

In sticking closely with the timeline of events in the official version of 9/11, some of the government's secret bases of operation as well as its relocation sites were revealed by the actions of the principal players involved. 9/11 also showed how the government plans on protecting its key officials outside of the normal role taken by the Secret Service. But perhaps more worrisome than anything, 9/11 betrayed the years of COG planning and billions of dollars in exercises and war games meant to smooth out the entire process. In a very real sense, while several Continuity of Government procedures were implemented that day, many of them failed because most of the officials tasked with specific duties didn't know what they were supposed to do in the emergency environment created on 9/11.

As the events of that infamous morning unfolded, one place in particular played a key role as the nation's ultimate overseer. That was NORAD—the North American Aerospace Defense Command headquartered at Peterson Air Force Base in Colorado. Interestingly, NORAD is a joint U.S.-Canadian operation. It tracks not just every flight in North America, but monitors over 8,000 objects in orbit around the Earth, most of which are recognized as "space junk." It also oversees the satellites that make up the Global Positioning System (GPS). NORAD's primary mission, however, is to act as the nation's early warning system for enemy attack, especially nuclear missiles. NORAD claims it can determine whether a missile is hostile or not in under two minutes. One of the most interesting aspects of NORAD and what it is best known for is its operations center located underneath Cheyenne Mountain just outside of Colorado Springs. This underground site technically isn't NORAD; it is the Cheyenne Mountain Operations Center (CMOC). The site became famous for its depiction in the film *WarGames*. In actuality, the interior of the CMOC is much less exciting than its Hollywood counterpart—there is no main control room containing massive screens that depict incoming missiles—but it is no less interesting.

Built between 1961 and 1965 at a cost of $695 million, the site became operational on April 20, 1966. Carved out of the solid granite of the mountain and located about 1,750 feet beneath its peak, it was designed to withstand a nuclear attack. Entrance to the actual site is gained through a mile long tunnel which is nearly 25 feet in height and 30 feet wide and at the end of which is a stop light. The CMOC covers approximately four and a half acres of the mountain's interior with 15 buildings nestled inside, 11 of which are three stories in height. All of these buildings sit atop over 1,300 massive metal springs which would act as shock absorbers in a nuclear blast (the springs allow up to one foot of vertical movement). This is an aspect of the CMOC that many don't quite grasp until seen first-hand (which one could do in the past when visitors were allowed to tour the installation). The "rooms" at CMOC do not possess rock walls. The buildings inside CMOC are just that—separate metal bunker-like buildings that sit inside the hollowed-out tunnels dug by mining machines that created the site. In fact, the buildings do not even touch the walls. They merely float atop those huge, 1,000 pound springs. The site can be sealed off from the outside world by a 30-ton blast door which closes in under a minute. Amazingly, despite these safety measures, by the late 1960s many believed the CMOC would not survive a direct hit from a Russian missile.

While neither NORAD nor the CMOC were Continuity of Government sites, the underground portion of Cheyenne Mountain does possess many similar capabilities. The site could maintain approximately 800 people for 30 days, albeit with no sleeping quarters. It does, however, possess its own water supply as well as six power generators complete with battery backup. The site is also hardened against electro-magnetic pulses (EMPs) which are created in a nuclear detonation and can destroy electronic equipment. Its breathing air can be filtered for chemical, biological and nuclear contaminants, yet the Cheyenne Mountain complex has no heating or air conditioning system as it is warmed and cooled by the mountain itself. In 2006, the site's main directive was altered and it now serves as both NORAD's and NORTHCOM's Alternate Command Center.

When the second plane crashed into the World Trade Center, most everyone realized something wicked was afoot. At that very moment, President George W. Bush was in a Florida classroom reading a book with a group of schoolchildren. Despite the fact that his itinerary for that day was publicly known in advance, thus making him a possible target for knowledgeable terrorists, the Secret Service took nearly 20 minutes before removing Bush from the school. This was perhaps the first failure of Continuity of Government that day. Bush even took the time to make his first statement regarding the planes striking the Twin Towers in the school's library, stating in part, "Terrorism against our nation will not stand." His removal from the school should have been instantaneous.

Though the Secret Service may have delayed in acting, there is one emergency item always as the president's beck and call—the "Football." The Football is officially known as the President's Emergency Satchel. It is a black leather-bound metal briefcase with a combination lock containing the United States' nuclear response capabilities. Weighing in at a hefty 45 pounds, it has always been at the president's side since Eisenhower's presidency. There are five main items held within the Football: a procedure manual for the Emergency Alert System (in order to inform the nation of the pending nuclear Armageddon), a list of the president's emergency facilities, a "black book" detailing both our enemies' potential nuclear attack patterns and capabilities as well as a list of our own responses (options ranging from a single strategic missile to all-out bombardment), a secure phone with which to communicate to such facilities as Offutt Air Force Base, and the president's secret identification codes. The identification codes are not the actual missile launch codes as is often depicted, but codes that would identify the person ordering an attack as the president. Somewhat frighteningly, when President Reagan was nearly assassinated, the FBI discovered a card in his wallet with those same codes printed on it.

Once Bush did exit the school with the Football in tow, he was escorted into the backseat of "The Beast," the armored presidential Cadillac limousine. The Beast possesses ballistic armor as thick as a phone book, making the vehicle blast proof. It also has self-sealing fuel tanks as well as virtually puncture-proof tires which will continue to roll even if somehow deflated. If need be, there is a self-contained supply of oxygen available inside the limousine. The Beast is taken overseas on a special C-130 military cargo plane to ensure the president is protected no matter where he may travel.

After leaving the comfort of The Beast, Bush boarded Air Force One, the presidential VC25 jet which is actually a militarized Boeing 747. There are two Air Force Ones both of which are identical in makeup (actually any plane carrying the president has the designated call sign of Air Force One). Every flight of this plane is considered a military mission. The plane itself, while seemingly cozy to its passengers, is souped up both inside and out. Compared to the average Boeing 747, Air Force One possesses 16,000 more pounds of thrust, has a top speed of 630 miles per hour, carries 1,000 more gallons of fuel, and can remain in flight for 14 hours. At 230 feet, the plane is actually longer than the White House. Once airborne on 9/11, Air Force One was flanked by military fighters which escorted the presidential plane in a zig-zag pattern at high altitudes across the country. Despite that protection, Air Force One possesses its own secret aerial defense mechanisms and is shielded from electro-magnetic pulses.

From the sound proof conference room inside Air Force

One, Bush was able to communicate with Vice President Dick Cheney. However, at some point during 9/11, President Bush's secure cell phone ceased to function. He continued to lead America from Air Force One using a staffer's unsecure cell phone. This wasn't the only break down in communications that day. The federal government appeared to become unhinged. Bush's National Security Advisor Condoleezza Rice told the History Channel program *9/11 State of Emergency* that, "Despite all of the sophisticated hierarchy, the sophisticated command and control, the sophisticated equipment that we had, at that moment, much of it didn't function very well. And instead, people did whatever they could to communicate messages and frankly then we had to make it up." Much Continuity of Government planning, it seemed, had gone for naught.

That morning Vice President Dick Cheney had been at work in the White House when Secret Service officers physically removed him from his office (something the Secret Service did *not* do with President Bush). Cheney was taken to the bunker located 100 feet beneath the White House's East Wing known as the Presidential Emergency Operations Center (PEOC). Likely built during Eisenhower's administration, the bunker is reportedly quite large. According to author Richard Sauder Ph.D. in his book *Underground Bases and Tunnels*, a source of his claimed to have been inside the bunker and stated that it went down at least 17 levels. Whether that is true or not, I cannot say for the bunker isn't exactly on the White House tour. What is known is that the White House (which goes by the code name 18 Acres) had been structurally reinforced during World War II in case of a bombing raid. Also, members of a Special Forces unit based at Olmsted Air Force Base in Middletown, Pennsylvania known as Outpost Mission have been trained to extract the president from the PEOC should a nuclear bomb ever level Washington, DC. Even so, Condoleezza Rice stated in *9/11 State of Emergency* that, "We didn't think the bunker at the White House was safe at that point [during 9/11]." Rice also revealed the room inside the PEOC was so crowded, the oxygen levels dropped. When that occurred, the Secret Service stepped in and dictated who could remain inside the bunker and who wasn't essential to national security.

During the conversations between Bush, Cheney and Rice, Bush had stated his intent to return directly to Washington. Cheney and Rice became alarmed at the suggestion. Recalling his days as a participant in the Reagan-era COG exercises, Cheney knew that having both the president and vice president in the same location during an attack of unknown origin and scope was a recipe for disaster. Apparently, Bush was ignorant of such ideology. Clearly, the president wasn't aware of COG protocol. Cheney emphatically told Bush to stay clear of the city for the time being, directing him to fly anywhere but there. Bush listened to his VP's advice.

Instead of heading to Washington, Air Force One was directed towards Barksdale Air Force Base in Shreveport, Louisiana. This base was chosen because in an odd bit of coincidence on 9/11, Barksdale was conducting a "nuclear exercise" and base security was already at its highest level. The choice didn't go undebated. There are supposedly 75 or more Presidential Emergency Facilities spread across the nation (a list of those is contained in the president's Football). Author Edward Zuckerman wrote in *The Day After World War III* that at least nine of those facilities were within a 25 minute helicopter ride of Washington, DC. Exactly where those are located and what they contain remains top secret. Yet one such facility, having long since been abandoned, existed in Palm Beach, Florida. It was built for President Kennedy and his family on Peanut Island, just across the bay from the Kennedy's winter residence. According to official government documents, the bunker was built by 10 men in a week's time. Consisting of just one 800 square foot room buried on military-owned land, the facility was akin to a backyard bomb shelter that Kennedy had advised much of the nation to build during the Cold War.

During his brief stay in Louisiana, Bush made another public statement regarding the on-going events while it was confirmed his wife and children were taken to a safe and "undisclosed" location. It was perhaps at this time the Central Locator System was activated. This system, designed by FEMA during the Reagan years, constantly tracks the location of the president and each of his 17 successors to the office. The purpose is two-fold. One is to ensure that not all of those people are in the same place at the same time. Should that occur and a well-placed bomb or an attack take place, there may be no surviving successor to the office of the president. The other reason the system exists is to be able to not just locate, but to contact, and if needed, evacuate the individual as fast as possible in a given emergency, such as the one on 9/11. While it is rumored, though not confirmed, that modern presidents and fellow executive officers have a microchip complete with a GPS locator physically implanted into them to aid in that endeavor; the Central Locator System was not always as technically advanced as it may be today. Previously, it acted more as a reporting system informing its operators whether the individual in question was simply in Washington or not. That effort could be ramped up as threat levels increased to pinpoint the person in question as being in specific building or in a certain mode of transportation.

That might have come in handy considering that at a very key juncture on the morning of 9/11; Secretary of Defense Donald Rumsfeld could not be found. By his own admission, Rumsfeld was in the Pentagon and aware of the two planes crashing into the World Trade Center when he began his scheduled briefing with CIA officials. When the third plane smashed into the Pentagon, Rumsfeld abandoned his post. Being Secretary of Defense and thus the number two man in the National Command Authority behind the president, what Rumsfeld should have done even prior to taking that meeting with the CIA was to enter the National Military Command Center (NMCC) just down the hall from his office. Then he would have known about the third plane as it approached Washington instead of learning about it due to the explosion caused upon its impact into the building in which he sat. The NMCC is an ultra-high tech center staffed by upwards of 200 people 24 hours a day. It is designed to be the hub for every major national crisis, including hijacked airliners. In fact, since June 2001, the Department of Defense—the agency Rumsfeld headed—operated under new guidelines that specifically stated the Secretary of Defense was to be in command of every potential hijack situation. Yet when Rumsfeld appeared before the 9/11 Commissioner in 2004 he stated, "A civilian aircraft [hijacking] was a law enforcement matter to be handled by law enforcement authorities and aviation authorities." That was, without a doubt, a lie.

Where was the nation's number two man in terms of all things military during what Captain Charles Leidig, who was temporarily in charge of the NMCC during Rumsfeld's absence, deemed "an air attack on North America?" Rumsfeld was on the Pentagon's lawn. Much like befuddled Midwesterners who go outside to look for the tornado when the sirens sound instead of immediately seeking shelter, Rumsfeld was outside the Pentagon surveying the damage done. He was even caught on film assisting an injured victim into an ambulance. Upon arriving at the Pentagon soon after the plane had struck it, acting Chairman of the Joint Chiefs of Staff General Richard Myers could not believe Rumsfeld's location was unknown. When finally convinced to return inside, Rumsfeld still did not enter the NMCC. Instead he walked to his office and spoke with President Bush. While no one knows what the two spoke about, when finished, Rumsfeld again ignored the pleas to do his assigned duty and join the frantic staff in the NMCC.

Instead, Rumsfeld moved further down the Pentagon's halls and entered the Executive Support Center (ESC). That may not have been as absurd of a maneuver as it first appeared. The ESC is a series of conference rooms secured against electronic eavesdropping devices. It is within the ESC the Pentagon's top brass are to go to coordinate military operations during a national emergency. After a brief and secret meeting there, Rumsfeld finally assumed his proper post inside the NMCC. Once he gained an understanding of the situation, Rumsfeld spoke with Cheney ensconced deep under the White House. He then learned that Cheney, well outside his authority as vice president, had been effectively doing Rumsfeld's job and commanding the U.S. military response to the ongoing situation.

Meanwhile the man who was supposed to be the supreme overseer for the nation's military response, the president, finally found himself at a proper location from which to work. After Air Force One left Barksdale, Bush landed at Offutt Air Force Base in Bellevue, Nebraska. Why Offutt? This base is home to STRATCOM or the U.S. Strategic Command Center, previously known as Strategic Air Command (SAC). Selected by General Curtis Lemay to be the home of SAC in 1948 due to its central location within the United States, what is today known as STRATCOM has the command and control of the entire U.S. nuclear arsenal. Operating in a constant state of readiness, supposedly this is the only site from which the president could personally override any nuclear launch order. Located at STRATCOM is a two-story, underground command post that is about 14,000 square feet in size, nuclear hardened, and protected from electro-magnetic pulses. It is the highest of high tech, including a high powered computer and video conferencing system that can instantly connect with the president, vice president, etc. on a moment's notice. STRATCOM also is in constant contact with over 200 military facilities and nuclear missile silos located around the world. It was here that Bush waited out the remainder of 9/11.

Perhaps another reason Bush was taken to Offutt was because STRATCOM is the home base of the aircraft known as "Looking Glass." This was SAC's command plane during the Cold War. Originally launched on February 3, 1961, this aircraft remained constantly airborne until July 24, 1990. When one plane landed, another immediately launched. The eight hour flights usually circled the Midwest, often between Minneapolis and Kansas City. Onboard was either an Air Force General or Navy Admiral alongside an 11 or 12 person staff. Two armed guards escorted the nuclear launch authentication codes onboard each flight and secured them in the aircraft's safe. Should a nuke take out SAC, Looking Glass could assume all of the base's duties. Today, Looking Glass remains on constant ground alert. It is a militarized 747, or more specifically, a Boeing E-4B which has been specially shielded from electro-magnetic pulses and radiation. From this plane the president could command the nation's nuclear forces. The aircraft can stay aloft continuously for only 72 hours; not because of the inability to refuel it in fight, but due to the fact that the oil in the plane's engines would likely break down and need replacement. It has also been wondered if in the event of a nuclear war the fallout associated with the explosions wouldn't clog the aircraft's engines, rendering it inoperable.

There is another similarly modified Boeing E-4B based at Andrews Air Force Base in Maryland, just outside Washington, DC. This is "Night Watch," or more colloquially, "the doomsday plane." Officially it is the National Airborne Operations Center (NAOC) which was once known by the moniker the National Emergency Airborne Command Post (NEACP). The modus operandi of the NOAC is similar to that of Looking Glass, yet due to its location at Andrews (which is also the home of Air Force One) the NAOC is more likely to be the plane carrying the president in the event of a nuclear war. In fact, the NAOC is basically a Continuity of Government relocation site in the sky (there was also at one time during the 1960s a National Emergency Command Post Afloat, located somewhere off the East Coast of the United States). While the aircraft holds a private presidential suite decorated in gold, the NAOC can carry upwards of 90 people. Inside the plane are a conference room, a communications station, and a miniature "war room" which can hold a battle staff of 15 people. The NAOC possesses the capability to communicate directly with the Navy's fleet of nuclear submarines thanks to a five mile-long low frequency antenna trailing from the aircraft which is just one of the 67 antennae and satellite dishes built into the aircraft. Meant to be part of an array of planes in the air during a nuclear attack, to this day the NAOC stands in a constant state of readiness, able to be airborne in 15 minutes.

According to the research of author Dr. David Ray Griffin in his book *The 9/11 Mystery Plane and the Vanishing of America*, the NOAC or a similar E-4B was in fact airborne over Washington, DC on 9/11. Griffin has photos, including video taken from CNN, showing an E-4B in flight. While these photos verify the plane flying at a low altitude near both the White House and the Pentagon during the morning of 9/11, Griffin has not determined who was on that flight, where it was headed, or why it was even airborne. Despite that, the flight's origin has been pinpointed to Andrews Air Force Base. What is even more surprising is the further Griffin has dug into the mystery surrounding the flight; the more he has come to the conclusion that there very well may have been two E-4Bs flying in the skies above Washington that day. The purposes of those 9/11 NOAC operations remain shrouded in mystery.

Evac

Once the "all clear" had been given, Bush did eventually return to Washington, arriving at the White House sometime around 7 pm. Well before then, the White House, the Executive Office Building, the State Department, the Treasury Department, and Congress had all been evacuated. That didn't mean they were evacuated under strict COG or even COOP protocol. On the History Channel program *The President's Book of Secrets,* Anita McBride, the Chief of Staff for Laura Bush, stated of the evacuation of White House, "At that point then we gathered the staff to evacuate and we just told them to run. Run out of the complex as fast as you can." Over forty years of COG preparations led to this command when disaster struck: RUN FOR YOUR LIVES!

The one thing Secretary of Defense Donald Rumsfeld seemed to get right on 9/11 was in ordering his immediate successor Deputy Secretary of Defense Paul Wolfowitz to vacate Washington. Cheney did likewise. He ordered House Speaker Dennis Hastert, Agriculture Secretary Ann Veneman, Interior

Secretary Gale Norton, and a host of other unnamed government dignitaries out of the city. Apparently, only Rumsfeld and Cheney realized the potential ramifications for the government if more of Washington had been destroyed that day, thanks to their involvement in the Reagan-era COG exercises. The reminder of those high ranking members of government appeared oblivious to the fact that the United States government had for decades planned how to effectively evacuate officials in a situation exactly like that in which they found themselves. Without being told to leave town, apparently none would have. Some were even reportedly opposed to the idea.

Where did Wolfowitz and the others go? Most sources indicate their final destination was the High Point Special Facility, better known as Mount Weather. The site has been owned by the government since the 1890s when it was originally acquired by the National Weather Bureau. It was on this mountaintop that the bureau built an observatory and launched hundreds of weather balloons and kites for upper atmosphere research, hence the name. Mount Weather was designed and built based on the needs noted from the Operation Alert exercises. Today, this is the queen mother of all COG facilities. Located approximately 50 miles from Washington in Berryville, Virginia, Mount Weather is home to FEMA's National Emergency Coordinating Center and it is from here that FEMA tracks the president and his successors via the Central Locator System. Six other major disaster operation centers are also headquartered here including the National Processing Service Center, the Satellite Teleregistration Center, the Disaster Finance Office, the Disaster Information Systems Clearinghouse, the Disaster Personnel Operations Division, and the Agency Logistics Center. Above ground there are a dozen buildings employing approximately 900 workers, but buried beneath those buildings in the Blue Ridge Mountains is where the true COG facility resides.

Construction on the underground portion of the site began in 1954 by the Bureau of Mines and was completed four years later by the Army Corps of Engineers at a cost in today's money of over $1 billion. A 34-ton, 10 foot by 20 foot blast door protects the entrance to the underground areas which by all accounts are enormous. Some have called it an underground city. Hewn from the solid rock of the mountain are at least 20 office-size buildings, some of which are three stories tall. Much like the COG site under the Greenbrier Resort, Mount Weather contains living quarters, dining and recreation areas, a hospital, reservoirs of drinking water (some reports have stated that this is actually an underground lake fed by a mountain spring), a power plant, a radio and television broadcast station, a sewage treatment facility, and a crematorium. Some unconfirmed reports claim that a mass transit system exists to transport people among those various underground locales. While it holds a month's worth of supplies and sleeping quarters for up to 2,000 people, there are separate and private areas quartered off for the president, his cabinet, and the Supreme Court. A doctor is assigned to Mount Weather, and those people designed to relocate there are recommended to specifically visit that doctor to ensure the proper medications are stocked in the site's hospital.

Prior to 9/11, the Special Facility was only fully operational as a COG outpost once. That was on November 9, 1965 due to a huge power blackout that affected most of the Northeastern portion of the United States. Researchers believe Mount Weather was placed on "full alert" on several other occasions including during the Cuban Missile Crisis, when JFK was assassinated, during the riots of 1967-68, and when President Nixon resigned from office in 1974.

During the Cold War, Mount Weather controlled the nation's Bomb Alarm System to authenticate any potential nuclear detonation within the country. By 1966, there were 56,715 radiological monitoring stations scattered across the nation which were tied together within that system. Despite that mission, Mount Weather remained secret from the public for quite some time. It wasn't until TWA Flight 514 crashed into the mountain on December 1, 1974 killing all 92 people aboard that the site became public knowledge, though it wasn't "officially" acknowledged until a congressional inquiry in 1975. The accident occurred just one and a half miles from Mount Weather's entrance and actually severed its main underground phone line. According to a *New York Times* article, the Emergency Broadcast System was briefly interrupted while various news and telephone company teletype machines began transmitting nonsensical, garbled information due to the severed line. Mount Weather security forces ordered the crash site secured and when rescue workers arrived at the scene, they were shocked to find numerous cars parked in the middle of nowhere. A government spokesman didn't help the situation when he refused to divulge any information about Mount Weather including who worked there, what kind of work was performed at the site, and how long the government had been using the location.

The secrecy and security around Mount Weather continues to this day. Not just due to it stated mission, but because the site very well may be the home of America's "shadow government." It is known that teams of employees from each of the major government departments including Treasury, State, Commerce and Labor are stationed at Mount Weather on a rotating basis. This work is overseen by senior substitutes who are often addressed as "Mr. or Mrs. Secretary." The belief is those people lurking beneath Mount Weather would become our federal government if the true federal government was destroyed. Even so, the everyday workers at the Special Facility don't appear to be as secretive as their underground counterparts. For starters, there is a federally funded bus service for many of Mount Weather's above-ground workers with routes running from area communities to the Special Facility. Those people need to be on call 24 hours a day, seven days a week and live within one hour of the site. They all possess top secret clearance.

Mount Weather was also thought by many to be the "undisclosed location" Vice President Dick Cheney was taken to once President Bush returned to Washington on 9/11. That may be true; however, it has also been suggested Cheney was taken to several different relocation sites during his missing time in office. That was all but confirmed by Cheney's successor, Vice President Joe Biden. In early 2009, Biden made the gaffe of revealing one previously unknown secret relocation site—the one meant to protect his own life. At a dinner for Beltway insiders, Biden told diners about the existence of a bunker beneath the old U.S. Naval Observatory which has been the home of the vice president since 1974. He was given a tour of the site by an officer who revealed that the bunker was where Cheney and many of his aides were kept during their post-9/11 lock-down. That made sense. If there was a massive bunker beneath where the president lived, logic would almost dictate a similar structure hidden under the vice president's residence as well. While the *Washington Post* reported on December 8, 2002, that neighbors surrounding the US Naval Observatory were complaining of loud underground blasts and construction work at the site, no one knew the bunker's existence as fact until Biden let it slip.

COG relocation sites were not always meant to be top secret installations. In the 1957 CBS-sponsored civil defense production *A Day Called X*, the film not only detailed how the city of Portland, OR would react should the people there learn a Russian attack was eminent, but it revealed inner workings of the city's COG site. CBS's production crew filmed inside Portland's COG bunker with the actual members of the city's government taking their expected command posts. The film explained that Portland's COG site was about six miles outside of the city, contained a cafeteria stocked to maintain 300 people for one week's time, and that backup files of the city's records were stored there on microfilm. There was nothing sinister about this site's existence. It was simply a matter of fact.

Considering the film claimed Portland was determined to be "one of 99" Russian target cities, there are likely 98 similar COG sites scattered across the nation, not far from most major urban areas (Chicago had such a station at Soldier Field where the NFL's Bears play). Having gone unused, most of these are long forgotten relics of a by-gone era. Yet there are several known COG sites in existence that were built relatively recently. One was constructed in Oakville Grade, CA, replacing two previously known COG locations in both Benicia and Ukiah, CA. Two others exist in Maryland near the cities of Boonsboro and Hagerstown. The Pennsylvania town of Mercersburg also contains an underground COG bunker, as do the West Virginian cities of Martinsburg and Harper's Ferry (at the former site of Storer College). The U.S. Army operates an underground relocation site in Warrentown, VA. The Navy even possesses one in Kaneohe, Hawaii. Recently revealed on the History Channel program *Lost Worlds* was a bunker beneath the Lorton Correctional Complex located just 20 miles outside Washington, DC. Here was built an operations center for the emergency services chiefs of DC's civil defense response teams. This site operated virtually unknown to those working in the prison above for nearly 40 years. When shut down in 2001 (coincidentally just prior to 9/11), the site was outright abandoned, leaving behind maps and materials including coffee cups sitting atop desks. If so inclined, one could even purchase such a site. A former underground Strategic Air Command base in Amherst, MA was put up for sale in 1992. For a reported $250,000, you could own a three story, 44,000 square foot, nuclear blast-hardened bunker.

The Department of Homeland Security maintains many of these sites today through FEMA. FEMA's Federal Regional Center in Maynard, MA houses a two-story underground facility nicknamed "the mushroom factory" which is fallout protected, EMP hardened, and capable of withstanding a nuclear blast should the epicenter be more than two miles away. There is a similar facility attached to at least three other of FEMA's regional headquarters (Bothell, WA; Denton, TX; and Thomasville, GA) if not all nine. FEMA's largest Federal Regional Center in Olney, Maryland also oversees the Alternate National Warning Facility. This is the back-up site for Mount Weather and home to FEMA's main radio communications center. Reports have it that the location could contain up to 10, maybe even 20 levels below ground. It is the only known Federal Regional Center capable of housing government officials in times of emergency.

Buried beneath Raven Rock Mountain near Blue Ridge Summit, Pennsylvania is the Alternate National Military Command Center which goes by the moniker of "Site R." In essence, it houses the back-up Pentagon. It was originally conceived in 1948 with construction beginning in 1951. Completed in 1953, this massive base possesses five, three-story tall buildings with upwards of 750,000 square feet of floor space. Like many of the previously discussed COG sites, Site R holds food, water and supplies for upwards of 3,000 people, though only about 500 people work there on a normal basis. Amenities at Site R include a barbershop, convenience store, exercise facility and a chapel. Site R sits approximately six miles north of Camp David, the presidential retreat situated on the Pennsylvania-Maryland border which was deemed in the late 1950s to be the relocation site for the White House. Though unconfirmed, it is believed that an underground tunnel connects the two.

Treated like part of the federal government though in actuality a separate, private institution, the Federal Reserve had its own COG-like site buried beneath Mount Pony in Culpepper, Virginia. Operational since 1969, the Mount Pony site contained nearly 140,000 square feet of nuclear hardened workspace. There were seven massive and specially protected computers housed there which monitored and stored all of America's electronic funds. The site could maintain over 500 people for a month, yet there were only enough bunks for approximately 200. The biggest claim to fame of Mount Pony was the fact that the Federal Reserve stored several billion dollars in currency inside a 24,000 square foot vault at the location, including massive amounts of $2 bills should currency supplies have needed to be restocked in a post-nuclear war environment. In 1997, the Federal Reserve Board handed the site off to the Library of Congress which began using the vault for storage of motion pictures, recordings and other collections. Today, the Federal Reserve has an individual relocation site for each of its 12 branches. None of those locations are known.

In mentioning the Library of Congress, it is interesting to note that plans exist to protect many of the nation's treasures in the event of a disaster or attack. The Library of Congress possesses a "Top Treasures Inventory" which includes such works as the Gutenberg Bible and the Gettysburg Address that will be the first collected and removed from the premises. The National Archives earmarked a group of "Freedom Documents" meant to be saved at all costs. Crates have already been prepared to hold and store many of the masterpieces contained in the National Gallery's collection. Most of those priceless works were to be sent to Mount Weather in times of emergency, where the artistic works were to decorate the bunker's walls. While both the Declaration of Independence and the Constitution have their own 55-ton nuclear hardened vault, if a nuke wiped out Washington, it may be years before anyone could retrieve them. Luckily, tucked behind Mount Rushmore sits an unfinished Hall of Records where 16 porcelain tablets engraved with the Declaration of Independence, the Constitution, the Bill of Rights, and the Gettysburg Address were buried in a titanium time capsule in 1998.

Also stashed away by the United States government is anywhere between $3-$5 billion worth of goods in the Defense National Stockpile Center. As part of this program, there are 11 guarded warehouses across the nation in Scotia, NY; Binghamton, NY; Somerville, NJ; Curtis Bay, MD; Point Pleasant, WV; Warren, OH; New Haven, IN.; Hammond, IN.; Baton Rouge, LA; Clearfield, UT; and Stockton, CA. Another 66 unguarded locations exist not just in the U.S., but around the world. These depots hold over 80 different strategic and critical materials considered essential for military and industrial needs that would be allocated to both in a national emergency. This includes such materials as beryllium, copper, chromium, cobalt, industrial diamonds, germanium, iodine, lead, maganese, platinum, rubber, silver, tantalum, titanium, tungsten and natural quartz. While the government began to stockpile certain strategic raw materials sometime during World

War I, they didn't get serious about it until after World War II. Today, resource stockpiling is controlled by the Department of Defense's Defense Logistics Agency (DLA) which often sells off parts of the national stockpile at a profit. In 1998, the 275 member staff of the DLA oversaw the sale of more than $460 million worth of these goods.

The federal government has many other underground locations beyond those already mentioned. The Social Security Department has records stashed away in an old limestone mine in Pennsylvania. The Los Alamos National Laboratory in New Mexico has several underground components to it. The Department of Energy built the massive, yet still unused depository for the nation's spent nuclear fuel rods under Yucca Mountain in Nevada. The Federal Bureau of Investigation revealed in 2010 the existence of a "secret file room" where it kept its most sensitive (and at times, damning) files in upwards of 79 file cabinets, including some directly related to COG and the evacuation of key officials, portions which were revealed in the previous chapter. The list could go on down to the state and local COG facilities in existence, but again, all of these are known.

The question is: what exists out there that remains secret?

At this point, one runs into massive speculation, some of which can border on the absurd. Even those with only a cursory knowledge about the subject of UFOs have heard of Area 51, the government's "secret" base in the middle of the Nevada desert. While there is no doubt the base exists, some have claimed there is a massive underground component to it. In fact, rumors abound of what have been labeled as DUMBs—Deep Underground Military Bases. Whether any of these actually exist is conjecture. Yet stories of underground bases and tunnels surround the American Southwest, including reported sites at Sunspot, NM; Corona, NM; Taos Pueblo, NM; Albuquerque, NM; the Santa Catalina Mountains in AZ; Grand Mesa, CO; Needles, CA; both Edwards AFB and Norton AFB in CA; Blue Diamond, NV; Tonopah, NV; and Papoose Lake, NV. One of best stories surrounding the subject involves a supposed DUMB in Dulce, NM. There, as the story goes, at some time in the 1980s U.S. government officials were working in league with extra-terrestrials when a fight broke out between the two factions. During the battle, the space aliens took over the lowest levels of the base. Eventually, cooler heads prevailed though there were causalities on both sides.

Some theories even go to the point of stating that there is an expansive series of underground tunnels crisscrossing the American Southwest, complete with high speed trains connecting some of these known and unknown underground constructions. While it seems incredibly farfetched, in the late 1970s President Carter proposed a $33 billion plan that would have built a similar construct for the nation's MX nuclear missiles. In the plan, for each of the 200 missiles the U.S. possessed, 23 silos were to be constructed and scattered about the Great Basin Desert in Nevada and Utah. Each of these 4,600 silos was to be spread out over a mile apart and connected by an underground train. That would have allowed one missile to appear at 23 different sites, making it virtually impossible for the Russians to target the entire complex. Apparently the technology existed to build it; only budgetary constraints (and a few complaints from local ranchers) stopped the plan from moving forward.

Perhaps even more outlandish is the notion that some of these underground bases may not be under the earth, but under water. One may scoff, but since 1967 the U.S. Navy has controlled the Atlantic Undersea Test and Evaluation Center (AUTEC) in the Bahamas. The base sits on "the tongue of the ocean," a basin that is 110 nautical miles long, 20 nautical miles wide, and reaches depths of over 6,000 feet. The Navy maintains three test ranges here, including one for hydrospace trajectory. Adding to this idea, there are highly specialized U.S. Naval units known as Underwater Construction Teams (UCT) and an underwater engineering program known as the Naval Facilities Engineering Service Center. Author Richard Sauder, PhD wrote in his book *Underwater and Underground Bases* that the technology to build such undersea bases has existed since the mid-1960s. In one particular government document he uncovered regarding a potential US Navy project, the plans called for building an underwater base complete with a domed observation post, a nuclear power generator, locks for allowing submarines to come and go, and housing for extended stays beneath the ocean.

Without a doubt, the government has either built or is currently constructing more of these underground relocation sites. Where? Right under your feet perhaps. No one really knows. Since the bunker beneath the Greenbrier Resort was uncovered and decommissioned, there has to be another place to which Congress can evacuate. Add to that the fact that NORAD, Site R, and Mount Weather are all known entities; it's probable that a modern nuclear war would involve the destruction of each and every one of those target-worthy sites. Therefore, alternate sites to the alternate sites would be necessary. While one could debate how many billions of dollars should be spent on the construction of these sites that have historically gone unused, the bigger question remains of what happens when those government officials whose lives are to be spared in the confines of those COG sites don't make it there in time? Who's going to be running the show?

ORDER OF SUCCESSION

"A Republic, if you can keep it."
--Benjamin Franklin

William Henry Harrison, the ninth President of the United States, died in office on April 4, 1841. It was the first time a seated president had ever vacated the position, and it caused an instant constitutional crisis. The writers of the Constitution had not seriously considered the question of succession to the presidency. In fact, the role of vice president wasn't included until very late in the Constitutional Convention (the first two major drafts of the Constitution made no mention of a vice president). What ultimately was written about presidential succession was included in Article II: "In Case of the Removal of the President from Office, or of his Death, Resignation or Inability to discharge the Powers and Duties of the said Office, the Same shall devolve on the Vice President, and the Congress may by Law provide for the Case of Removal, Death, Resignation or Inability, both of the President and Vice President, declaring what Officer shall then act as President, and such Officer shall act accordingly until the Disability be removed, or a President shall be elected."

When Harrison died, Vice President John Tyler stepped into Harrison's role. That sparked the debate of whether Tyler was supposed to assume the presidency, or if the Constitution stipulated that he was just to *act* as president until a new one could be elected. Tyler settled the argument himself. Seeing his opportunity amid the confusion, Tyler took the presidential oath of office on his own accord. Despite this bold act, no one complained. Congress retroactively approved Tyler's decision by willingly referring to him as president, yet it never officially sanctioned his taking of the oath. Amazingly, while Tyler's ascent from vice president to president became the standard line of succession, such an action wasn't ever officially constitutional until the 25th Amendment was ratified in 1967.

Previous to the passage of the 25th Amendment, there had been both talk and action concerning the line of succession to the presidency. In 1792, the Succession Act determined that the President Pro Tempore of the Senate and the Speaker of the House (in that order) were to succeed to the office if both the position of president and vice president were vacant. Oddly enough, there were several times in American history that the Office of the Vice President was indeed vacant. On 18 different occasions, the United States found itself without a vice president. Often, these were not short stints. James Madison was without a vice president for his last three years in office. Tyler, once assuming the office after Harrison's death, never had a vice president. Millard Fillmore, Andrew Johnson (both after Lincoln's assassination and upon his re-election), Chester A. Arthur, and Theodore Roosevelt (for his first term) also never possessed a vice president during their respective presidencies. The last significant absence of a vice president occurred when Lyndon Johnson assumed the presidency after the assassination of John F. Kennedy. Johnson ran the government for two years without an immediate successor.

It was the assassination of James Garfield in 1881 that led to the second major revision in presidential succession. While Chester A. Arthur stepped into Garfield's role without debate, there was a period of time immediately upon Arthur's swearing in when internal strife within Congress caused there to be no President Pro Tempore of the Senate or a Speaker of the House. Since there was no sort of vice presidential re-election to fill Arthur's vacated role and both houses of Congress lacked an official leader, there was no one in place to assume Arthur's new role as president if he, too, should have perished. The Succession Act of 1886 remedied that. While the act increased the number of successors in line to the presidency, its main purpose was to insure that whichever political party controlled the executive office maintained that position of power in the event of the president's death. It did this by dropping the President Pro Tempore and the Speaker of the House down the succession ladder. In their place was to be the president's cabinet which often was strictly comprised of members of the president's own political party. The new line of succession based on cabinet officers was determined by the chronological order in which each department were created. Originally, this included five officers—Secretary of State, Secretary of the Treasury, Secretary of War (now Defense), Attorney General, and Secretary of the Interior—after which would have followed the President Pro Tempore of the Senate and the Speaker of the House.

This served as the status-quo until Vice President Harry Truman assumed the office of the president after the death of Franklin D. Roosevelt in 1945. Truman requested Congress change the order of succession, arguing that it was more appropriate for an elected official (such as the Speaker of the House) to potentially serve as president over a cabinet officer that had merely been appointed. Congress agreed, though not without again debating whether the president's successor should be from the same political party or not (as the Speaker of the House may or may not have been). In 1947, Congress passed the Presidential Succession Act which again placed the Speaker of the House and the President Pro Tempore of the Senate above the line of cabinet officers in the order of succession. The act also flip-flopped the position of the President Pro Tempore and the Speaker of the House, making the Speaker number three in line, ahead of the President Pro Tempore.

When Lyndon Johnson took over the presidential reins from JFK in 1963, he did so without a vice president. There had never been a line of succession for that office. Amidst the Cold War, many believed this was a dangerous gap in the chain of command, despite the ever-growing list of presidential successors (the number of cabinet posts continued to accumulate, increasing the number of successors to 12 at that point in history). Out of that fear evolved the 25th Amendment, which remains the current guideline for presidential succession. In the amendment, it was made clear—for the first time—the vice president would assume the duties of the president if the president died, resigned or was removed from office. It also set forth that the vice president would also assume the role if the president was incapacitated and temporarily could not serve. If the vice president was officially inaugurated as president, the 25th Amendment allowed him to nominate his successor as vice president. That nomination would then have to be approved by a simple majority of both houses of Congress. This has happened twice in the nation's history: in 1973, when Vice President Spiro Agnew resigned from office and was replaced with Gerald Ford, and in 1974, when President Nixon also resigned and was replaced by Ford, who in turn nominated Nelson A. Rockefeller to his former post (this was also the first time and only time a non-elected person served as president).

Today, with the creation of the Department of Homeland Security, there are 18 people in line to succeed the president. In order, they are:

- Vice President
- Speaker of the House
- President Pro Tempore of the Senate
- Secretary of State
- Secretary of the Treasury
- Secretary of Defense
- Attorney General
- Secretary of the Interior
- Secretary of Agriculture
- Secretary of Commerce
- Secretary of Labor
- Secretary of Health and Human Services
- Secretary of Housing and Urban Development
- Secretary of Transportation

- Secretary of Energy
- Secretary of Education
- Secretary of Veterans Affairs
- Secretary of Homeland Security

Occasionally the people occupying these posts do not possess the constitutional requirements to actually serve as president. Some have not been natural born citizens, were not at least 35-years old, or (depending on when they were needed) had not been confirmed by the Senate, thus only "acting" Secretaries, not the actual "official" Secretary. If such a person was next in line and was required to serve, that person would be skipped. Luckily, the United States has never had to reach beyond the vice president to find a successor to the presidency. If we had, the nation might have run into serious trouble.

Questions of Succession

The 1947 Presidential Succession Act created the potential for two interconnected problems to arise for the leadership of the nation in times of national emergency. If, for example, nuclear war occurred and much of the command structure of the federal government was killed, it could be that one of the lower echelon members of the succession list would assume the presidency. If the Secretary of the Interior was the highest ranking member of the president's cabinet to be found alive, he would by law (Article I, Section 6 of the Constitution) have to resign his office at the Department of the Interior prior to assuming command of the nation. When Congress was able to reconvene, they would likely name a new President Pro Tempore of the Senate. At that point, the person made President Pro Tempore could resign his Senate seat, supplant the Secretary of the Interior, and instantly rise to the rank of the President of the United States. This is due to the wording of the 1947 Succession Act. It stated that any person acting as president could be replaced at any time by a "qualified and prior-entitled individual." In other words, the highest living person in the line of succession was entitled to fulfill the role of the president until a new president was officially elected. Because of this, the above scenario could be further complicated if a week later, the House of Representatives elected a new Speaker of the House. The new Speaker could quickly resign and take similar actions, declaring himself president while ousting the President Pro Tempore. Meanwhile, since both the Secretary of the Interior and the President Pro Tempore of the Senate had to resign their previous posts to assume the presidency, once the Speaker took charge, they would both find themselves lacking a title.

Such a scenario could even be further complicated. In the chaotic aftermath of a nuclear attack, perhaps those presumed to be dead weren't. What if the newly elected Speaker of the House, now acting as president, found the original Speaker of the House alive and well inside the rubble of Mount Weather? Would the original Speaker be able to legally supplant the latter Speaker as president? Would the "illegal" president's orders and decisions still be considered lawful? Or what if in the initial nuclear attack it was only known that the president and vice president were killed while the other members of Congress and the president's cabinet were scattered to the winds in the hurried evacuation process? If communication lines were severed, despite all of the previous COG planning (which 9/11 proved had been largely forgotten), who would know who was in charge? Whose orders should be followed? And who was overstepping their legal limits? Could someone acting as president, simply assuming their rightful command, make decisions that the actual, legally acting president would not? Continuity of Government planning was designed to prevent these sorts of complications, but in reality, they may just exasperate them.

Another question of who is in charge arises every four years during the time of presidential transition. When a newly elected president supplants the old, there is a period of time when an unforeseen death or well-timed attack could throw the nation for a loop. For example, in 1872 Horace Greeley was the presidential nominee for the Democratic and Liberal Republican Parties. He died about three weeks after the election. Though Greeley was soundly beaten by Ulysses S. Grant in the election, he did win 66 electoral votes. Since Greeley couldn't serve as president, 63 of those electors voted for other candidates while three stood by their man and voted for Greeley (those three votes were later ruled invalid by Congress). If Greeley had won, no one is sure what would have transpired. Today, if a similar situation occurred in which a victorious candidate died prior to inauguration day, the 20th Amendment makes it clear that the vice president-elect would become the president-elect and be sworn into office, whereupon his first act would likely be to nominate a new vice president.

In the modern age of terrorism, a new question with a similar aim has arisen. What would happen if an attack occurred on inauguration day itself? What if a large bomb (a nuclear one, even) blew up at the very moment the president-elect was sworn in? Who would be in charge then? If the former president survived, would he be allowed to continue running the show? Even if he had been a two-term president, thus exceeding the constitutional laws? And what if neither president survived, would the former president's line of succession be enacted? Since the new president could not have yet selected a cabinet, would a surviving member of the former president's cabinet be allowed to step into the presidential role? And if so, for how long? Could that unelected individual legally serve the entire four year term as president?

Remarkably, there are no specific answers to any of these questions. There are guesses and assumptions, but no concrete definitives to fill in these blanks. In April 2008, the Congressional Research Service published a report titled *2008-2009 Presidential Transition: National Security Considerations and Options*. The report stated the fears of a terrorist attack at that critical juncture in the exchange of power in the national government, yet it fell back on relying on COG and COOP procedures to alleviate those concerns. While the report highlighted the fact that in a presidential transition over 7,000 federal government jobs change hands, there was no mention made of what would happen if all—or even most—key government leaders were killed at that time. Perhaps no one can actually answer that question.

The only safety net the country seems to possess lies in the role of the "designated survivor." This is a person, often a member of the president's cabinet, intentionally left off the guest list of many official functions. The idea is to always keep one member of the president's line of succession away from the rest, in case of a "decapitation strike" against the nation's top officials. In this way, there should always be one constitutionally allowable presidential replacement alive no matter the circumstances. The designated survivor program has been an on-going since the 1950s. Often at least one key member in the line of succession does not attend the president's State of the Union address, any presidential address to a joint session of Congress, or the presidential inauguration—just in case. It is never the same person or the same cabinet position every time. For example, for the 2008 State of the Union address, the Secretary of the Interior Dirk Kempthorne was the odd man out. For the 2009 presidential inauguration, Secretary of Defense Robert Gates did not attend. During these official occasions, the designated survivor is taken under guard to an undisclosed and often physically distant location. If the worst of the worst were to occur, that person would be in charge of the country.

Everyone Else

The idea behind Continuity of Government is to preserve "Enduring Constitutional Government." It seems odd then that the line of succession for the president is rather clear and forthright, yet gaping holes exist for filling massive vacancies in both Congress and the Supreme Court.

Should some sort of attack or disaster wipe out most of Congress, the Senate would be the easiest to replace. The 17th Amendment states, "When vacancies happen in the representation of any state in the Senate, the executive authority of such state shall issue writs of election to fill such vacancies; provided, that the legislature of any state may empower the executive thereof to make temporary appointments until the people fill the vacancies by election as the legislature may direct." Nearly every state in the country allows its governor to appoint a temporary Senator to fill a vacated Senate seat. In time, a statewide general election is then held to elect a permanent replacement. If Washington, DC was annihilated while the rest of the country remained relatively intact, the Senate could be instantly restocked with Senators.

The same cannot be said of the House of Representatives. If and when vacancies occur here, the only currently allowable way for that congressional seat to be filled is through a special election. Representatives cannot be hand-selected by a governor as Senators can. Herein lays the problem. If some sort of attack or disaster eliminated most of the House of Representatives, it could be months before those seats were re-filled. Finding candidates, holding elections, and determining the results take time. The best estimates conclude that the fastest any such election could be held would be within four months, yet that doesn't account for the confusion and disorder associated with whatever disaster caused the elections to be needed in the first place, nor does such an estimate consider having to conduct such elections on a nationwide level.

Could a constitutional government conduct any business without a functioning Congress for four months? It is an important question to contemplate due to the fact that in order for Congress to legally function, a quorum is required. As stated in Article I, Section 5 of the Constitution: "...a Majority of each [House] shall constitute a Quorum to do Business, but a smaller Number may adjourn from day to day, and may be authorized to compel the Attendance of absent Members, in such Manner, and under such Penalties as each House may provide." In other words, without a majority of its complete membership, Congress can either adjourn for the day or compel its absent members to appear (which is hard to do if they are dead). Yet only Congress can declare war. Only Congress can appropriate money. Only Congress can make laws. All of which would likely be needed in a true national emergency. Without a quorum, none of that could transpire. Into that legislative void only may the president dare step, and then the notion of a constitutional form of government would die.

The definition of "quorum," however, has often been debated. In the strictest sense, it was to mean a majority of elected officials. This would be 51 of the 100 Senators, or for the House, 218 of the 435 Representatives. Today the Senate claims a quorum exists when a "majority of the Senators duly chosen and sworn" are in attendance. For the House of Representatives a quorum is considered to be gathered when a majority of its members who are "chosen, sworn, *and living*, whose membership has not been terminated by resignation or by action of the House" are on the floor.

This poses two potential problems. If a quorum was only comprised of those members alive after some sort of disaster, perhaps the House would discover that only a handful of its representatives survived. Technically, it could still conduct business with just 1% of its membership alive, even though a vast portion of the nation went unrepresented. On top of that, should there be only perhaps nine functional representatives, it would require just five votes for some manner of business to pass the House. Such a lawful act of the House could be the naming the next Speaker, who could then, if given the right set of circumstances, step into the vacated role of the president on a mere five votes cast. The second "what if" scenario that could derail Congress would be if a majority of either House was poisoned or somehow incapacitated, yet not killed. Legally, Congress could not function if a majority of its members were incapacitated (another term that has also never been truly defined by Congress). Meaning a virulent strain of the flu could effectively knock Congress out of commission for a period of time. Currently, there is no mechanism in place for either the Senate or the House of Representatives to temporarily fill seats vacated under such conditions.

To answer these and other Continuity of Government-related questions, the Continuity of Government Commission was formed in 2003. Oddly, it was not an official federal government undertaking. The Continuity of Government Commission was a joint venture of the American Enterprise Institute and the Brookings Institution, though it was chaired by many former federal government officials. Two of its major concerns were what has been discussed above, namely the need to be able to rapidly fill vacated representatives' seats as well as what to do in the case of the massive incapacitation of Congress. Since the Commission released its May 2003 report, *Preserving Our Institutions: The First Report of the Continuity of Government Commission*, a few proposed constitutional amendments have been attempted to speed up the replacement of empty seats in the House of Representatives, whether due to death or mere incapacitation. Most of those involved allowing governors to temporarily fill these seats as they do with Senators. Yet none of these proposed amendments have gotten very far within Congress, despite the fact that it is these very people who should be most concerned and aware of the lack of procedures available in desperate times. It's not surprising though. Between 1945 and 1962 alone, more than 30 similar amendments were attempted. Three even passed in the Senate. Yet despite the constant Cold War threat of nuclear war that inspired this legislative action, no such amendment flourished, even though in 1954 the committee reviewing one potential amendment wrote, "It would be the height of folly to leave a constitutional gap of this nature in a representative government such as ours."

The judiciary branch of the federal government, better known as the Supreme Court, is often the last group to be thought of in terms of Continuity of Government. However, the events of 9/11 made those responsible for planning rethink their efforts due to an unusual quirk. On the very morning of September 11, 2001, the Supreme Court was holding the Judicial Conference of the United States. Gathered under one roof in Washington, DC were all nine Supreme Court justices, the chief justices of the all 13 U.S. circuit courts, the chief judges of the appeals courts, and other prominent judges from various district courts—basically the entire leadership of the nation's federal judiciary system. Had the plane that crashed into the Pentagon instead hit here, the Judiciary Branch of the government could have been wiped out completely.

During that meeting on 9/11, security personnel approached Chief Justice William Rehnquist three or four times and whispered in his ear. No one else was spoken to. The judges gathered there then heard a distant thud—the sound of the plane hitting the Pentagon—still no one informed the conference what was occurring outside. According to some reports, at that time another security official approached the chief justice, spoke privately with him, and again without informing anyone else, the officer escorted Rehnquist from the building. Once outside, Rehnquist was shuttled to an undisclosed location (most likely Mount Weather). Meanwhile, the other Supreme Court justices and judges assembled there were left to fend for themselves. Security informed them of an evacuation and promptly cleared the building. Many of the judges were seen wandering the streets of DC, not sure what to do or where to go.

Supposedly there is an official, top secret COG plan covering the Supreme Court. Why it was not put into effect on 9/11, no one will say. Had the Supreme Court suffered a catastrophic loss on 9/11, it would be fairly easy for the nation to reassemble it in short order. In fact, the loss of the Supreme Court wouldn't really affect the immediate operations of the federal government at all. If all of the Supreme Court justices were killed, the vacancies could be refilled by the normal processes used for finding a single replacement (though considering a Supreme Court justice's appointment is for life, many would be up in arms over one president being able to nominate all nine judges). In the event of a partial loss within the court, it is stipulated that only a quorum of six justices is required to hear a case. If there were fewer than that allotment alive, any case due to be heard by the court would have its lower court ruling automatically affirmed. Thanks to the All Writs Act, all of the other district and circuit courts across the nation are allowed to issue writs. Because of this, the judiciary branch has been effectively spread out across the nation. Any sort of decapitation strike against it would do little harm.

The only potential nightmare scenario that could occur is under a situation like that of a nuclear war in which not only was the Supreme Court destroyed, but the Senate as well. By the Constitution, it is the Senate that confirms any presidential appointment to the Supreme Court. If the Senate could not convene its quorum, the president could determine that the Senate's inability to form equated to its adjournment. Then the president could make his own temporary appointments to the court. Worse yet, a Congressional Research Service report stated that another option available to the president, if he lacked an operational Senate and did not want to appoint a temporary Supreme Court, could be for the president to declare martial law and put the court's authority into military tribunals, enforcing federal law completely through the military. If it ever comes down to that; however, it's highly probable that we'd all be in a bit of a pickle.

The Shadow Government

There have always been rumors and rumblings that a "shadow government" existed within the United States, stashed away inside some underground installation, waiting for the right catastrophe from which to emerge and assume command of the nation. This secret government consisted of unelected officials who were assigned to fulfill specific roles upon the true government's destruction. When presented with such a story, most people would laugh and write it off as pure paranoia. Unfortunately, the joke's on them. The shadow government is very real.

Francie Grace, writing for CBSNews.com, detailed the existence of the shadow government in a series of articles for the website. As she wrote on March 1, 2002, "A 'shadow government' consisting of 75 or more senior officials has been living and working secretly outside Washington since Sept. 11 in case the nation's capital is crippled by a terrorist attack." The *Washington Post* also wrote about the shadow government and its general modus operandi. On 9/11, high ranking officials representing most major government departments including the White House were sent to work in undisclosed locations scattered around Washington, DC. A majority were confined to Mount Weather. Many of these government workers remained secluded and secure until late October when rotations were begun to relieve the sequestered officials. As Grace wrote, "Officials who are activated for the duty live and work underground 24 hours a day, away from their families….The shadow government has sent home most of the first wave of deployed personnel, replacing them most commonly at 90-day intervals."

This was not considered to be an actual activation of COG plans, but rather the implementation of Continuity of Operations (COOP). Either way, it was taken as being a vital government mission. President Bush commented on it stating, "I have an obligation as the president and my administration has an obligation to the American people to put measures in place that should somebody be successful in attacking Washington there is an ongoing government. That is one reason why the vice president was going to undisclosed locations. This is serious business. And we take it seriously."

The amazing part was no one outside of the White House appeared to know this was taking place. Many congressmen were not aware the shadow government existed, and if they did, few realized it was fully operational in the months (maybe years) immediately after 9/11. According to the *Washington Post*, Senate Majority Leader Thomas Daschle (D-SD) didn't know about it. House Minority Leader Richard Gephardt (D-MO) was in the dark as well. Even the President Pro Tempore of the Senate at the time, Robert Byrd (D-WV), was unaware—and he was the fourth person in line to succeed the president.

Besides the top-secret-to-the-point-of-ridiculousness nature of COG operations, another reason those three top ranking members of Congress may have been unaware of the shadow government was because they were all Democrats. While it would seem odd party affiliation would play a role in who was escorted to Mount Weather and who wasn't, that very well may have been the case with the Republican representative Bush in office. The last major round of COG exercises were conducted during the combined Reagan-Bush administration, both of which were Republican controlled. When the Democrat Clinton was elected president, COG exercises continued, but these were mainly overseen by Republicans. As Andrew Cockburn detailed in the book *Rumsfeld*, "In earlier times the specialists selected to run the 'shadow government' had been drawn from across the political spectrum, Democrats and Republicans alike. But now, down in the bunkers, Rumsfeld [a Republican] found himself in politically congenial company, the players' roster being filled almost exclusively with Republican hawks." Cockburn went on to quote a former Pentagon official with knowledge of those exercises who stated, "You could say this was a secret government-in-waiting. The Clinton administration was extraordinarily inattentive, [they had] no idea what was going on." On 9/11, perhaps the once again Republican controlled White House was out to save the government by protecting their party members first and foremost.

While the Democrats, the Supreme Court, and other governmental heavyweights were on their own to survive 9/11 and any other acts of terrorism that may have followed, regular civilians joined the ranks of those protected within Mount Weather. Who were those people? They were perhaps the members of the true shadow government, the National Defense Executive Reserve.

Shortly after John F. Kennedy became president in 1961, his National Security Advisor McGeorge Bundy received a pair of memos from former President Dwight Eisenhower's Presidential Assistant Frederick Dutton. In the memos, Dutton revealed something that no one outside of Eisenhower's very inner circle knew. In 1958, Eisenhower had sent out 10 letters to private citizens informing them of their future job running the federal government should the actual government be destroyed in World War III. The existence of what's now known as the "Eisenhower Ten" would have remained a forgotten fact if not for the work of Steven Aftergood of the Federation of American Scientists and the writers of the great civil defense-era website Conelrad.com.

The Eisenhower Ten were truly what's thought of as the shadow government. Ten non-elected men, some true captains of industry, who were to be in control of the nation should the worst of the worst come to pass. Eisenhower hand-selected each of the men personally, conferring with no one else on the matter, and sent out just 10 letters. None of the men chosen refused the call to duty (though one did later resign his post). In the 50 years following their selection, none of the Ten ever revealed their secret role within the government. What surprised JFK's National Security Advisor Bundy more than the existence of the Ten was the fact that there was no termination date on the appointments. Theoretically, those 10 men could have remained part of the shadow government until their death.

The 10 men selected by Eisenhower to run the nation and their assigned positions in the shadow government were:

- John Edgar Warren, Senior Vice-President of the First National City Bank of New York - Head of the Emergency Energy and Minerals Agency
- Frank Stanton, President of CBS – Head of the Emergency Communications Agency
- Frank Pace, Jr., President of General Dynamics Corporation – Head of the Emergency Transportation Agency (Pace resigned this post in 1959)
- Dr. George Pierce Baker, Faculty Member of the Harvard Graduate School of Business – Head of the Emergency Transportation Agency (Pace's replacement)
- Aksel Nielsen, President of Title Guaranty Company of Denver, CO – Head of the Emergency Housing Agency
- James P. Mitchell, Eisenhower's Secretary of Labor – Head of the Emergency Manpower Agency
- William McChesney Martin, Jr., Chairman of the Board of Governors of the Federal Reserve System – Head of Emergency Stabilization Agency

- Theodore F. Koop, Vice-President of CBS – Head of the Emergency Censorship Agency
- Harold Boeschenstein, President of Owens-Corning Fiberglass Corporation – Head of Emergency Production Agency
- Ezra Taft Benson, Eisenhower's Secretary of Agriculture – Head of Emergency Food Agency

Apparently there were determined to be only nine crucial jobs in a post-nuclear war environment (and one was still censorship). None of the job openings included a president or Congress or Supreme Court. Perhaps they would have survived thanks to COG planning. Perhaps not. Either way, these vital positions within the future U.S. government were given the highest priority, yet induction into that strictly classified collection of leaders was presented in a simple form-like letter that was just one page in length. Each read much like this version sent to CBS President Frank Stanton on March 6, 1958:

"Dear Mr. Stanton:

"It is always possible that the United States might need suddenly to mobilize resources for a maximum national effort. Although it is my devout hope that this will never happen, the national interest requires that against that possibility we achieve and maintain a high state of readiness.

"I am delighted to know of your willingness to serve as Administrator of the Emergency Communications Agency in the event that a national emergency would compel its formation, and, accordingly, I hereby appoint you such Administrator effective upon activation of the agency. As Administrator, you will, in the performance of your duties, be subject to the direction, control and coordination of the Director of the Office of Emergency Resources, and you will receive such compensation as the President may hereafter specify. Your tenure as Administrator-designate or as Administrator shall be at the pleasure of the President.

"In the event of an emergency, as soon as you have assured yourself, by any means at your disposal, that an Emergency

Communications Agency has been activated, you shall immediately assume active direction of that agency and its function. This letter will constitute your authority.

"I have requested the Director of the Office of Defense Mobilization to communicate with you regarding any planning activities in connection with the creation of and activation of an Emergency Communications Agency.

"Until such time as an Emergency Communications Agency may be created, I am certain that you will treat your designation as Administrator as classified information and that you will impress upon any staff you select to assist you that their designations are to be treated similarly as classified information.

"You have my deep appreciation of your acceptance of this vitally important assignment.

"Sincerely,

"Dwight D. Eisenhower"

As this letter shows, even in a post-nuclear war environment, there was to be bureaucracy. The unnamed Director of the Office of Emergency Resources was to oversee the nine positions created secretly by Eisenhower. It would perhaps only be that Director who knew that the Eisenhower Ten even existed and the roles they were to fill. In the event of that Director's untimely death, the Eisenhower Ten were told "this letter will constitute your authority." Try explaining that to an angry post-apocalyptic mob.

After Dutton's revelation of the program to Bundy, did the Eisenhower Ten immediately lose their prime positions within the secret government? It's not really known. According to an article written about the Eisenhower Ten on conelrad.com, "What is known...is that the *New York Times* reported in its October 27, 1961 edition that on October 26th Director of Emergency Planning Frank B. Ellis disclosed on NBC's *The Today Show* that President Kennedy had a list of men who would assume administrative power ("in such areas as transportation, the mobilization of necessary foods, the re-establishment of communications and all of the other very critical aspects that are necessary to place into working order following an emergency") should an atomic attack or other calamity kill senior Government officials. Ellis declined to name the individuals saying only that 'they are known.' His only elaboration was that the designees would periodically 'make a complete study of their operation.'"

Given more time to consider the notion begun by Eisenhower, JFK and his administration must have thought the idea to be a good one. In Executive Order 11051 issued on September 27, 1962, Kennedy wrote in Section 305: "Executive Reserve. The Director, under authority of, and in accordance with the provisions of, Executive Order No. 10660 of February 15, 1956, shall develop policies and plans for the provision of an Executive Reserve of personnel capable of filling executive positions in the Government in time of emergency."

Two years later, JFK's successor Lyndon Johnson issued Executive Order 11179 titled "Providing for the National Defense Executive Reserve." It began: "There shall be in the Executive Branch of the Government a National Defense Executive Reserve composed of persons selected from various segments of the civilian economy and from government for training for employment in executive positions in the Federal Government in the event of the occurrence of an emergency that requires such employment." The head of the National Defense Executive Reserve (NDER) was to receive nominations from each of the secretaries of the various government departments and agencies for membership into the NDER. Those individuals, once approved by the NDER's Director, could serve as a member for "a period not to exceed three years." The duties of a NDER member would be limited to "receiving training for mobilization assignments under the Reserve program" and would not include "acting or advising on any matter pending before any department or agency" prior to their becoming active in a national emergency situation.

The control of the NDER was turned over to FEMA upon the agency's creation in 1979. Less than four years later, in February 1983, the United States General Accounting Office conducted an overview of the NDER. At that time, the GAO found:

"The Federal Emergency Management Agency (FEMA) has placed renewed emphasis on revitalizing the program. However, until recently, it did not make any significant progress toward this goal. During 1982, FEMA (1) updated regulations covering NDER activities, (2) issued new member identification cards, and (3) began work on a training plan. But we also found that: participation in the program by Federal agencies and overall membership remain low; recruiting efforts vary among agencies; most NDER units do not conduct regular training; most members do not have specific job assignments; the program is minimally funded; and FEMA's central data base on program membership is inaccurate and incomplete."

The GAO's report further explained the state of the government's NDER program. "FEMA records show there are 15 NDER units, consisting of 13 units distributed among 8 civil agencies and 2 units within DOD. However, only five units are now fully operational....Two units have only recently been formed and several others seem to be improving, but much more recruiting, planning, and training is required to make them operational." The departments with NDER units were the Department of Commerce, the Department of Defense, the Department of Energy, the Department of Housing and Urban Development, the Department of the Interior, the Department of Labor, and FEMA. As the GAO pointed out, "Since program participation is voluntary, some agencies with important emergency responsibilities do not maintain NDER units. As examples, FEMA officials mentioned the Departments of State, Agriculture, Health and Human Services, Education, and Justice; the Office of the Secretary of Defense; and the intelligence community. FEMA also lacks the authority to direct agency NDER program actions."

Even among the 15 operational NDER units, the GAO found that most went lacking basic requirements. Only three of the 15 units conducted regular annual training. Seven units had identified NDER reporting locations. Only four had detailed specific job assignments. On top of that, "FEMA's data base also has many missing data elements. Three areas of vital information—reservists' locations, individual members' skills, and current membership status—are frequently incomplete." Also missing in many cases were NDER members' phone numbers, addresses, social security numbers, and security clearance. Even with all of that seeming mismanagement against the program, the GAO stated, "FEMA is generally aware of these problems and has begun actions to address some of them." FEMA's stated goal at the time was to have a membership of some 10,000 NDER members and a "greater participation by agencies" over the next several years.

Despite its failings, the NDER lived on. In President Clinton's Executive Order 12919 issued on June 3, 1994 titled "National Defense Industrial Resources Preparedness," the necessity of the NDER was reaffirmed. Besides restating what the NDER was, EO 12919 explained how an NDER unit would be activated: "The head of a department or agency may activate an NDER unit, in whole or in part, upon the written determination that an emergency affecting the national security or defense preparedness of the United States exists and that the activation of the unit is necessary to carry out the emergency program functions of the department or agency. At least 72 hours prior to activating the NDER unit, the head of the department or agency shall notify, in writing, the Assistant to the President for National Security Affairs of the impending activation and provide a copy of the determination required...."

In March 2007, the Department of Defense issued a formal "Instruction" regarding the NDER. The document stated, "The Secretary of Defense is authorized to exercise the President's authority to employ civilian personnel...when activating all or part of its NDER unit." Unlike those agencies singled out in the GAO's 1983 report, the DOD was certain its NDER division was well prepared to serve as part of the shadow government. "Ensure that, within funding limitations, the appropriate annual training is conducted for each NDER unit. This training shall include general orientations and provision of up-to-date information on the actions planned in the event of mobilization and on the associated responsibilities of NDER members. NDER members shall participate in mobilization exercises to the maximum extent feasible. NDER training policies shall be based on guidance provided by FEMA and the USD(P&R)." Even so, NDER members were to know their place once activated. "When policy matters are involved, NDER appointees are limited to advising appropriate full-time salaried Federal Government officials who are responsible for making policy decisions."

Does any of this sound fun to you? If so, then you have a chance of joining this version of the shadow government for yourself. While your position wouldn't be on par with the Eisenhower Ten nor would it make you privy to any real COG exercises and facilities, virtually anyone can join the National Defense Executive Reserve. If you feel you have the right stuff to join a NDER unit, all one needs to do is complete FEMA Form 85-3, the National Defense Executive Reserve Personal Qualifications Statement. It is akin to a normal job application. FEMA would then review the application to ensure the candidate meets NDER standards and isn't already serving within the federal government. If one passes through that process, FEMA very well may assign the applicant to a position within an agency's NDER unit best suited for his or her particular talents. There are several areas of expertise they are looking for, including manufacturing, auto repair, biology, mining, finance, city planning, retail trade, health care, and of course, emergency services.

CONCLUSION

Perhaps what all of this comes down to is a question not yet asked within these pages. When push comes to shove and some sort of Continuity of Government plan is enacted due to a true national emergency, do you really want your government to be saved?

This is a very valid question to ask. If there were another world war, one in which nuclear weapons were used, would the average citizen sheltered in his makeshift bunker really feel comforted knowing that the president and other members of the federal government were protected thanks to the vast network of secret underground bases scattered across the country? In the immediate aftermath, when a number of known and unknown executive orders were enacted giving the government total control of where people work, how they travel, what ration of food and energy they were allowed to consume, etc., would the nation really band together to combat whatever enemy attacked (assuming we didn't attack them first)? And if the surviving citizens didn't want to follow those exotic government demands that failed to fit within the confines of America's constitutional form of government, would armed U.S. soldiers force them to capitulate under martial law?

Such a scenario is truly possible. You've read it for yourself. It can be labeled a conspiracy theory only because "in theory" this could occur. Would it? No one can honestly say. Conditions as extreme as the ones likely needed to cause those dominos to fall have yet to transpire. This doesn't mean they could not or will not in the future. The fact that the paper trail examined here is very real and does allow for the government to take such actions should cause every citizen to pause (and this doesn't include what is still considered classified and top secret).

Most of the government's response would be done "for our own protection." Yet it is not the common citizens who begin wars; it is their "representative" government. If the nation were to be plunged into a war its citizens did not want, the result of which caused a scenario as described above, the question remains would we really want our government to be saved at all costs? The idea put forth in executive orders like those Kennedy passed in 1962 seemed to indicate that the nation of the United States of America was an idea over and above the people. This is why civil liberties could and likely would be stripped away to ensure the survival of the country. Yet it is the people that make the nation. It is the people that elect the government. But no one asked the people if they wanted their government protected no matter the circumstance. It was something only assumed...by those in government.

When did the notion come about that those elected by the people suddenly transcended those that granted them their status within government in the first place? No common citizen believes his elected officials' lives are more valuable than his own, yet Continuity of Government procedures now make that a stark reality. "They" will be protected so "we" can be helped. Later. When, exactly, they cannot say. But they warn us to prepare to fend for ourselves in every emergency situation imaginable because they don't intend on coming to our immediate rescue.

Of course, the average citizen shouldn't expect the government to do so. It was never possible to begin with, no matter the logistics. After over 30 years of seeing an agency like FEMA ensconced within the federal government and its inability to effectively respond to those in need when disaster strikes, the populace should've gotten the message: you are on your own.

What is most maddening of all is though major disasters occur on a yearly basis and affect every corner of the nation, most government funding earmarked for disaster relief is funneled instead to terrorism prevention and response. Which of these incidents occurs most often? Which has injured and killed more people? Which is most likely to happen in both the immediate and long-term future? The answer is not terrorism, but Mother Nature in all her fury. Why can't the government comprehend this simple idea?

The federal government's intentions are not evil. These government documents and laws are not really intended to cause a complete upheaval of the Constitution when a national emergency again strikes. They are simply plans—maybe overwrought and over thought plans—intended to combat every disaster scenario that could possibly occur. The problem with plans is that they often work much better on paper than in action. On paper, FEMA works. Continuity of Government works. Continuity of Operations works. But in action…?

It doesn't help that despite efforts to practice and train for various disasters, most government workers don't know what they are supposed to do when an emergency arises. This is a problem not just confined to the lower echelon; it appears rampant from the very top through to the bottom as the events of 9/11 displayed. Perhaps it is the bureaucracy that gets in the way of it all operating as it should. Perhaps it is the size, the sheer magnitude of the bloated federal government, which gums up the works. It is rare to see any government endeavor work as intended without both of these factors coming into play. Why should emergency planning—something that is rarely tapped to become operational—work as intended, too?

The worst realization from this comes in knowing that much of the work done by the various civil defense and emergency-minded agencies of the past and present was solid, well-reasoned planning. The problem became that much of it was lost in the shuffle. FEMA developed literally thousands of reports detailing the survivability of a nuclear war. It continues to research and issue similar information booklets yearly. But where is that information? How does the average citizen obtain it? Where does one go to request it? Therein lays the issue. The pathways for this information to get to the general public are entangled, confused, or outright missing. If a person isn't informed of the website ready.gov sponsored by FEMA, will he ever learn the valuable, lifesaving techniques offered there? In this instance, ignorance isn't bliss. Couldn't maybe a small fraction of that anti-terrorism budget be shifted to further public awareness? Might not a few more commercials or billboards help?

When disaster does strike you and your own—and it will someday—preparedness and planning will be your best friends. As will the willingness to help others in your community who are in need of it. Any emergency's first responders are always local entities be they fire and rescue, police, or even the National Guard. These are the people you should support and perhaps even volunteer to help. They will be the ones right there with you as the river rises, or the earth quakes, or the bombs drop. Not the federal government. Oh, they will make an appearance…sooner or later…once they emerge from their hiding places…having saved themselves first.

SOURCES

Government documents & sources

1947 National Security Act

Defense Mobilization Order 1

Department of Defense Civil Disturbance Plan 55-2

Department of Defense Implementation Plan for Pandemic Influenza

Department of Defense Instruction Number 1100.06 regarding the National Defense Executive Reserve

Department of Health and Human Services Pandemic Influenza Plan

Department of Homeland Security booklet: *Preparing Makes Sense. Get Ready Now.*

Executive Order Number: 1, 6102, 6433A, 6889A, 9066, 10340, 10346, 10952, 10995, 10997, 10998, 10999, 11000, 11001, 11002, 11003, 11004, 11005, 11051, 11087, 11088, 11089, 11090, 11091, 11092, 11093, 11094, 11095, 11365, 11490, 11179, 11519, 11921, 12127, 12139, 12170, 12211, 12444, 12470, 12513, 12532, 12543, 12635, 12656, 12657, 12658, 12722, 12723, 12724, 12725, 12727, 12728, 12730, 12733, 12734, 12735, 12738, 12742, 12775, 12804, 12808, 12865, 12868, 12919, 12923, 12924, 12930, 12934, 12938, 12947, 12957, 12978, 13047, 13067, 13074, 13088, 13129, 13159, 13194, 13219, 13222, 13224, 13228, 13235, 13286, 13288, 13295, 13303, 13321, 13338, 13348, 13375, 13396, 13405, 13413, 13441, 13448, 13456, 13460, 13464, 13466, 13469

Federal Emergency Management Agency booklet: *Are You Ready? An In-Depth Guide to Citizen Preparedness.*

Federal Emergency Management Agency booklet: *Basic Guidance for Public Information Officers.*

Federal Preparedness Circular 65

Joint Publication 3-26, *Counterterrorism*, November 13, 2009

Lawrence Kapp and Don J. Jansen for the Congressional Research Service, *The Role of the Department of Defense During a Flu Pandemic*, June 4, 2009.

National Security Strategy of the United States, March 1990

National Advisory Commission on Civil Disorders

The National Response Framework, 2008 edition

National Security Action Memorandum Number: 127, 166

National Security Decision Directive Number: 23, 26, 47, 174

National Security Directive 66

National Security Presidential Directive 51

Thomas H. Neale for the Congressional Research Service, *Presidential Succession: Perspectives, Contemporary Analysis, and 110th Congress Proposed Legislation*, October 3, 2008.

Planning Guidance for Response to a Nuclear Detonation, First Edition, January 16, 2009.

North American Plan for Avian and Pandemic Influenza

Office of Civil and Defense Mobilization Annual Report 1959

Personal and Family Survival: Civil Defense Adult Education Course Student Manual, Office of Civil Defense SM-3-11-A, November 1966

The Presidential Libraries of Ronald Reagan, George H.W. Bush, and Bill Clinton

Presidential Proclamation Number: 2039, 2352, 2487, 2525, 2526, 2527, 2914, 3972, 4074, 6427, 6867, 7461, 7462, 7463

Harold C. Relyea for the Congressional Research Service, *Continuity of Government: Current Federal Arrangements and the Future*, August 5, 2005.

Harold C. Relyea for the Congressional Research Service, *The Executive Office of the President: A Historical Overview*, March 17, 2008.

Harold C. Relyea for the Congressional Research Service, *National Emergency Powers*, September 18, 2001.

Harold C. Relyea for the Congressional Research Service, *Terrorist Attacks and National Emergency Declarations*, April 10, 2002.

Robert T. Stafford Disaster Relief and Emergency Assistance Act

John Rollins for the Congressional Research Service, *2008-2009 Presidential Transition: National Security Considerations and Options*, April 21, 2008.

U.N. Security Resolution Number 661

U.S. Army Field Manual FM 3-19.15

U.S. Code: Title 10, Title 14, Title 18, Title 42, Title 50

U.S. General Accountability Office memo B-167790 regarding National Defense Executive Reserve Program, February 28, 1983

U.S. Government Accountability Office Report: *Combating Terrorism: Observations on the Threat of Chemical and Biological Terrorism*

U.S. Government Accountability Office Report: *Global War on Terrorism: Reported Obligations for the Department of Defense*

U.S. Government Accountability Office Report: *Homeland Security: DHS Risk-Based Methodology is Reasonable, but Current Version's Measure of Vulnerability is Limited*

U.S. Government Accountability Office Report: *Risk Management: Strengthening the Use of   Risk Management Principles in Homeland Security*

U.S. Government Websites: pandemicflu.gov, ready.gov, fema.gov, uscode.house.gov, archives.gov, dhs.gov

U.S. National Academy of Sciences Report: *Severe Space Weather Events - Understanding Societal and Economic Impacts*

U.S. Senate Report 93-549: Report of the Special Committee on the Termination of the National Emergency

United States Information Agency (USIA) official fact sheet

Non-government sources:

Books

William Arkin, *Code Names: Deciphering US Military Plans, Programs, and Operations in the 9/11 World* (Steerforth Press: Hanover NH, 2005).

Andrew Cockburn, *Rumsfeld: His Rise, Fall, and Catastrophic Legacy* (Scribner Publications: New York, 2007).

Mark H. Gaffney, *The 9/11 Mystery Plane and the Vanishing of America* (Trine Day: Walterville OR, 2008).

Harry Helms, *Inside the Shadow Government: National Emergencies and the Cult of Secrecy* (Feral House: Los Angeles, 2003).

Harry Helms, *Top Secret Tourism* (Feral House: Port Townsend WA, 2007).

James Mann, *Rise of the Vulcans: The History of Bush's War Cabinet* (Viking: New York, 2004).

Peter Phillips and Andrew Roth, ed., *Censored 2009* (Seven Stories Press: New York, 2008).

Richard Sauder, PhD., *Underground Bases and Tunnels: What is the Government Trying to Hide?* (Adventures Unlimited Press: Kempton

IL, 1995).

Richard Sauder, PhD., *Underwater and Underground Bases* (Adventures Unlimited Press: Kempton IL, 2001).

Stephen I. Schwartz, *Atomic Audit: The Costs and Consequences of U.S. Nuclear Weapons Since 1940* (Brookings Institute Press: Washington, DC, 1998).

Nick Turse, *The Complex: How the Military Invades Our Every Day Lives* (Metropolitan Books: New York, 2008).

Edward Zuckerman, *The Day After World War III* (The Viking Press: New York, 1982).

Websites

Civildefensemuseum.org

Conelrad.com

Continuity of Government Commission & continuityofgovernment.org

Disastercenter.com

Fas.org (The Federation of American Scientists – especially the work of Steven Aftergood and his publication Secrecy News)

Globalsecurity.org

Semp.us (Suburban Emergency Management Project)

Governmentattic.org

Presidency.ucsb.edu (the University of California – Santa Barbara American Presidency Project)

Articles, TV Programs, & Other

Bryan Bender, "FBI gives a glimpse of its most secret layer," *Boston Globe*, March 29, 2010.

Lynn Brezosky, "US citizens to be checked in event of a storm," *San Antonio Express-News*, May 15, 2008.

CBS Production *The Day Called X*, originally aired December 8, 1957.

Matt Cover, "ACLU Official says it is not realistic to screen air passengers against the full terrorist watchlist," *CNSnews.com*, January 12, 2010. www.cnsnews.com/news/article/59587

Senator Russ Feingold, "Government in secret: The Yoo memo is just one example of Bush's hidden laws," *Los Angeles Times*, May 8, 2009.

Francie Grace, "The Shadow Government," *CBSnews.com*, March 1, 2002.

Francie Grace, "'Shadow Government' News to Congress," *CBSnews.com*, March 2, 2002.

Ted Gup, "Grab That Leonardo!," *Time*, August 10, 1992.

History Channel program *Secret Access: Air Force One*

History Channel program *Lost Worlds: Secret U.S. Bunkers*

History Channel program *9/11 State of Emergency*

History Channel program *The President's Book of Secrets*

Innis D. Harris, *Lessons Learned from Operation Alert 1955-57.* Transcription of speech given on April 30, 1958 and as published by Industrial College of the Armed Forces, Washington, DC.

Mark Hosenball, "A Loophole in the Rules," *Newsweek*, February 2, 2009.

Christopher Ketcham, "The Last Roundup," *Radar*, May/June 2008.

Charles Lane, "After Sept. 11m Judiciary Rethinks the Unthinkable," *Washington Post*, April 12, 2002.

Eric V. Larson and John E. Peters, *Preparing the U.S. Army for Homeland Security: Concepts, Issues, and Options.* RAND Corporation, 2001.

Donald G. McNeil Jr., "Swine Flu Death Toll at 10,000 Since April," *nytimes.com*, December 10, 2009. http://www.nytimes.com/2009/12/11/health/11flu.html?_r=2

Frank Morales, "Bush Moves Toward Martial Law," projectcensored.org, October 25, 2006. http://www.projectcensored.org/top-stories/articles/2-bush-moves-toward-martial-law/

Frank Morales, "U.S. Military Civil Disturbance Planning: The War at Home," *cryptome.org*, August 5, 2000. http://cryptome.org/garden-plot.htm

William J. Olson and Alan Woll, "Executive Orders and National Emergencies: How Presidents Have Come to 'Run the Country' by Usurping Legislative Power," *Policy Analysis* number 358, October 28, 1999.

Jonathan Passantino, "Biden Reveals Location of Secret VP Bunker," *foxnews.com*, May 17, 2009.

RAND Corporation Report, *3rd Annual Report to the President and the Congress of the Advisory Panel to Assess Domestic Response Capabilities for Terrorism Involving Weapons of Mass Destruction*, December 15, 2001.

Steven Sternberg, "Nuclear blast victims would have to wait," *USA Today*, April 14, 2010.

David Wood, "Codes for Armageddon: A new president to hold nuclear launch 'football'," *Baltimore Sun*, November 30, 2008.

ABOUT THE AUTHOR

Brian Tuohy writes the books he wants to read, but no one else will write. He is the author of *The Fix Is In: The Showbiz Manipulations of the NFL, MLB, NBA, NHL and NASCAR* which details how the professional sports leagues manipulate their own games for TV ratings and profit. Since the book's publication in 2010, he has become America's leading expert on game fixing in sports. A follow-up book, *Larceny Games: Sports Gambling, Game Fixing and the FBI*, is due to be released in 2013. *Disaster Government* was researched and written because it can't always be about sports.

For more information, visit:
TheFixIsIn.net
DisasterGovernment.com
LarcenyGames.com

Made in the USA
San Bernardino, CA
14 February 2013